MENTOR YOUTH NOW

A GUIDEBOOK FOR

TRANSFORMING YOUNG LIVES

by

JILL GURR

www.mentoryouthnow.com

Cover Design: Nick Bell, NC Bell Design: www.ncbell.com
Copyright © 2011 – Jill Gurr - All rights reserved
First Edition
Library of Congress – TXu 1-242-358
ISBN # 978-1466376274
ISBN: 1466376279
Printed in the United States of America

DEDICATION

This book was written for the millions of troubled children around the world; those who have fallen through the cracks of the system. If we all reached out to mentor these "forgotten children," and to provide love and guidance to *all* of our youth, then we could really help to transform their lives, and our world.

I'd also like to dedicate *Mentor Youth Now* to my beloved nephew Devan Lee Gurr, who continually teaches me how to listen and communicate better, drive slower and appreciate life even more.

TABLE OF CONTENTS

ACKNOWLEDGEMENTS

First and foremost, I owe both of my parents, Rusty and Larry Gurr, more gratitude than words could ever express for all of the love, mentoring, opportunities and support that they provided to me.

I feel indebted as well to my other beloved mentors who guided me throughout my life: Sophie Berger, Shirley Gurr, Murielle Nechamkin and Shirley Ulmer.

I've also learned a lot from my sister Michéle Lee Gurr. I treasure her, as well as my nephew Devan.

Mentor Youth Now could not have been written without the many volunteers who have dedicated their time and energy to help the vulnerable youth that **Create Now** serves. Their experiences and dedication have inspired and motivated me to keep going.

I'd also like to thank the kids themselves. It can be very frightening and difficult when venturing out to try something new. I truly applaud their courage for enduring the challenges that many of them have to face, and for trying their best to improve their lives.

Special thanks to Cassie Betts, Tasha Gregory, Brett Levine, Devin Morgan, Pamela Jaye Smith, Dennis Tardan and David Watkinson for their wonderful feedback. Tremendous appreciation also goes to Laura Kelly, Gerry Bryant and Mario Bernheim for their guidance about publishing, and Nick Bell for his great book cover.

I would especially like to acknowledge you, the reader, for your desire to learn how to be a good mentor, and to give back to your community by helping a child in need. Bravo for your good intentions and for embarking on this journey into the exciting world of mentoring youth!

✤ ✤ ✤

INTRODUCTION

Congratulations on taking the initiative to become a mentor! When you offer your time and guidance to disadvantaged youth, not only do you give back to your community, but you also touch someone's life in ways that you could never have imagined. In return, you'll also be impacted and reap many rewards.

I share the information in this book from personal experience, because I've mentored more than 50 at-risk and high-risk youth of all ages and witnessed some of their amazing transformations through my assistance. I've also trained hundreds of people to mentor.

When I discovered how powerful mentoring was as a tool to reach kids, I founded **Create Now,** a nonprofit organization dedicated to connecting volunteers to vulnerable youth through the arts.

Since our humble beginnings in 1996, **Create Now** has served thousands of the neediest youth in Southern California (as well as Orlando) through creative arts mentoring, education, resources and opportunities. We help to transform the lives of troubled children, as well as the volunteers who mentor them. Some of our mentors have changed their careers after experiencing the delights of bonding with children who yearn for connection with positive, supportive adults.

I'm very honored that **Create Now** has been featured on *NBC Nightly News with Brian Williams*, CNN's *Anderson Cooper 360°*, NBC-TV, Fox11 News, and ABC-TV, as well as in the *Los Angeles Times*. I am one of eight people in the country featured in an exhibition called "Everyday Heroes" at the Museum of Tolerance in Los Angeles, and I'm also included in the book "100 Making a Difference," by John Russo and Elizabeth Chambers (published in December 2012).

In 2010, I was one of the first four Americans ever selected to represent the United States in a *Global Xchange* program taking place in South Africa and Northern Ireland, which brought together 26 community leaders who serve at-risk youth in six countries. I have been giving presentations to dignitaries from all over the world through the International Visitor's Council. As a result, **Create Now** has received their prestigious "2011 Community Resource Award."

While I'm proud of all these achievements, I've only been able to accomplish anything thanks to the help of many wonderful people too numerous to name: those who have assisted me in building my organization, and the volunteers out in the field with the kids. Our mentors are the ones on the frontlines, and their issues, challenges and outcomes inspire me, just like the dozens of mentoring relationships from all around the United States that I've included throughout the book.

Many of the mentors that I've trained have expressed how they receive more satisfaction from their mentoring relationships than they get from their jobs and other things in their lives. *Everyone* benefits from mentoring, and with more of it, we can impact the world and make it a better place.

This journey started for me in 1991. I felt compelled to reach out to some needy kids in my community. It was important for me to make a difference in the world and to leave my mark.

Los Angeles is considered to be one of the wealthiest cities in the world, but it also has the highest poverty rate in the U.S. It's called the "Gang Capital of the World," with the most incarcerated youth in the nation. Right here in my own backyard, there were hundreds of thousands of youngsters who desperately needed help.

At the time, I was juggling two careers: working as a script supervisor on movies and TV shows, and also writing screenplays.

As a screenwriter, I had written sixteen original scripts. I was also hired to live in Madrid and Rome for several months to write other people's projects. Two of those screenplays were produced with name actors: an adaptation of a murder-mystery called "Rigged," which starred George Kennedy, and a PBS pilot for a series on famous people from history called "Socrates," with actor Ed Asner in the lead role. Several of my original screenplays were "optioned" by producers and a few came close to being produced.

Script supervising is a complex and highly responsible job, overseeing continuity during production (making sure that all the little details match). Films and most TV drama shows aren't shot in chronological order the way you see them on the screen, but according to locations and schedules.

I was there to make sure the actors knew their lines, and that all the different departments (wardrobe, set dressing, makeup and hair, props, etc.) were in sync according to the story. Also, I had to memorize such fine points as when an actor took a drink of water, how much was in the glass and if the window in the background was open or closed. In addition, I coordinated camera and sound rolls, took detailed notes for the editor, and made sure we had sufficient coverage (camera angles) to edit.

I worked as a script supervisor for 20 years and it was thrilling most of the time. I lived all over the world, spending months in exotic locales making movies with famous actors and directors.

Yet for all of my global adventures, it was while working on two local films that I was most impacted. One was "Menace II Society," which I highly recommend that you see, since it's a realistic portrayal of life in an L.A. ghetto. My eyes were opened to the violence and struggles that our inner-city youth experienced on the streets.

The other film was "My Family/Mi Familia," another movie that I recommend. We were shooting all night in East Los Angeles. It was a cold Tuesday at 3:00 in the morning. There were two kids hanging out with the crew: an 8-year-old boy and his 11-year-old brother.

I was surprised to see them out so late. I asked, "Don't you have school tomorrow? Where are your parents?" The eight-year-old replied, "I don't know where my mother is, and my father, he don't give a (bleep)."

I was shocked when I realized that there were thousands of kids just like these boys who urgently needed supportive adults in their lives and good role models.

For me, life was great! I was traveling, making lots of money and leading an exciting life as a script supervisor. In between jobs, I followed my passion of writing screenplays and my writing career was blossoming, but I couldn't get that 8-year-old boy's voice out of my head, knowing what was happening to him and so many other disadvantaged children.

I felt a strong need to give back to the community. I was blessed with terrific parents – Rusty and Larry Gurr – who gave me every opportunity to grow in life. They put me through college and helped out with loans so that I could travel around the world, living in Europe and Latin America for several years. I became fluent in Spanish, French and Italian, which helped my career. I wanted to pay it forward by helping youth less fortunate that I had been.

With no children of my own, I also experienced a strong urge to nurture kids that needed support, like those youth that I met on the streets of South and East Los Angeles.

I decided to share my love of screenwriting with a group of incarcerated youth. I hoped that it might give them an outlet for positive expression, and maybe a career. I had an idea for a script about two rival gang members that ended up at the same detention camp.

I called a number of detention facilities and volunteered to teach a Screenwriting workshop, but I was quickly brushed off. The staff connected me from one person to another. Hardly anyone ever returned my phone calls and if they did, their response was a polite, "No, thanks."

After a year of failed attempts to set up my Screenwriting workshop, the L.A. Riots exploded in 1992. In the aftermath, I joined a small volunteer organization to help change our community. There I met a wonderful artist, Wanda Patterson, who was dedicated to helping troubled teenage boys at *Optimist Youth Homes*, a detention facility in Eagle Rock, CA for 100 youth who had committed all kinds of crimes. Wanda helped me get through the red-tape to set up my Screenwriting workshop. Every week for three months, I had anywhere from 2 to 30 high-risk youth who participated in my class.

As my Screenwriting workshop progressed, I noticed remarkable changes. Many of these teenage boys had been totally illiterate or were reading at a third grade level. Yet, after just a few months of working together (only an hour or two a week), their reading and writing skills increased remarkably! Several boys in my workshop planned to go to college. A tough gang leader who had initially resisted my mentoring even had tattoos removed! The workshop ended on a very high note.

Delighted with the results of my program, I initiated a second Screenwriting workshop. This time, I set it up at *Pride House*, a coed detention facility that focused on delinquent teens with drug problems. At the end of our class, I had similar results: girls and boys who were illiterate began to read and write through my program. Others wanted to drop out of their gangs, continue their high school education and apply to local colleges.

I felt exhilarated knowing I had impacted these kids and I could see that they had grown enormously through my guidance. They would never be the same. *I* would never be the same.

I realized that using popular media and the arts was a great way to reach troubled youngsters, and that mentoring made a difference.

As we got to know each other, the kids shared things with me about their lives that broke my heart. Even though they had committed crimes, I felt more driven to help them because of the challenges they faced. I was able to give them solid feedback that had a positive influence, and it made me feel terrific, too.

Even after leading a somewhat glamorous life, I discovered that giving back and being of service was the most glorious feeling that I had ever experienced.

I realized that most people didn't have a clue about the plight of these thousands of forgotten children. Los Angeles County locks up 20,000 youth each year. Once they're released, 85 percent are arrested again and go right back into the prison system.

One third to half of these kids are foster youth who have been abused, neglected, abandoned and orphaned. The majority will end up permanently homeless or in jail, unless we give them support.

I met a fellow screenwriter named Erika Clarke and shared my experiences in teaching the two workshops. Suddenly, a thought popped into my head. Since I had learned a lot about navigating "the system" that controlled the lives of vulnerable L.A. youth, such as the Department of Children and Family Services (DCFS) and the Department of Probation, I knew that I could reach more kids if I trained volunteers in my technique and then matched them with vulnerable youth to teach screenwriting.

I casually mentioned this idea to Erika. Surprisingly, she contacted me the following week to tell me that her professor at the American Film Institute, writer/producer Leslie Stevens (*Return to the Blue Lagoon, The Outer Limits*) wanted to give me $5,000 to start a non-profit organization. I had no idea what a nonprofit organization was or how to build or run a charity, but I dropped everything that I was doing and **Create Now**, which was originally called *Write Now!,* was born. I worked long hours, seven days a week. For years, I received no salary at all. I was even close to being homeless a couple of times, but I wouldn't give up.

It has been well worth it! Today, **Create Now** thrives and provides arts mentoring to thousands of high-risk and at-risk youth. Through our programs, we've served more than 28,000 of the most vulnerable kids in Southern California since our inception.

Through my personal experiences and those of the mentors whom I've trained and helped, I've learned a great deal about what makes a productive mentor-mentee relationship. This book was created to share that knowledge with you. Anyone can become a great mentor by using common sense and following these techniques.

I caution you that it will take commitment and dedication on your part. You can't change a life, nor reap the benefits of success overnight. But, if you're willing to listen to your mentees, stay open-minded, dependable and trustworthy, then you'll be rewarded more than you could ever imagine.

In the chapters ahead, I'll supply you with a myriad of tips. You'll learn how to be an *amazing* mentor, no matter where you live or what you have to offer. The book is also chock full of information about mentoring organizations located around the country. The ideas and lessons presented here are applicable to *all* children. I hope they serve you, and our future generations, well.

Jill Gurr
Founder and Executive Director
Create Now

CHAPTER ONE

The Mentor

WHAT IS A MENTOR?

A mentor is a loyal advisor, a teacher or coach, sponsor, guide, confidante and role model. They are a concerned individual (other than a parent) who is an advocate for the needs of someone else — a special friend. A mentor wants to help another individual bring out their best qualities.

The person being mentored is occasionally called a "mentoree," and sometimes they're referred to as a disciple or a protégé, but mostly the term "mentee" is used.

Many people confuse tutoring with mentoring. Tutoring involves the teaching of a skill or discipline. It's not based on a personal relationship between the person doing the tutoring and the youth being tutored. In fact, it's not even necessary that the same tutor serve the same child over a period of time.

Mentoring, on the other hand, depends on the nurturing of a close, personal relationship between the mentee and the mentor. While helping with schoolwork can be a part of mentoring, it's just one aspect of the relationship.

A mentee is a novice, student, protégé or learner. They are "at-risk" for getting into trouble or "high-risk" and already in trouble. These kids can be of any race and religion. They generally come from disadvantaged homes in poor communities. All children require the support of a positive adult, but these kids are especially in need of assistance and encouragement.

Many of us have had a mentor at some point in our lives: a family member, neighbor or teacher. I've had some wonderful mentors. While I didn't come from a disadvantaged background, my father worked very hard as an electrician at two jobs and was rarely home. I adored my mother, but we were so close that I felt she couldn't always respond objectively to my needs. My older sister Michéle was busy with her friends and had little time for me.

Although I love my family very much, the frustrations that I experienced while growing up often involved my relatives. Like many children, there were times when I felt they just didn't understand me. I needed a confidante outside of home. My friends were great, but what I really craved was a mature adult who could be a sounding board.

When I was nine years old, our family doctor diagnosed me with Nephritis, a chronic kidney infection. Even though I felt perfectly fine, I was forced to stay in bed from morning to night, for months at a time. I had to be home schooled. Most of my friends were afraid to visit me because they thought I was contagious, even though my parents visited their homes to assure them that I wasn't. I felt very lonely and miserable.

We had some close family friends: the Bergers. Sophie Berger, a happily married housewife and the mother of three daughters, became my mentor. She taught me how to make all kinds of wonderful arts and crafts projects while I was bedridden. We often decorated cookies. I shared my deepest feelings with her. Sophie was non-judgmental and she gave me great advice.

When I was 13, I had a kidney biopsy and it was determined that I didn't have to be bedridden after all. I could lead a normal life. Sophie continued to mentor me and I knew that I could always count on her when I needed some assistance.

As I grew older, I developed even more mentors. My aunt, Shirley Gurr, became closer to me and we have spent a lot of time talking. She offers me a different perspective on life.

Sadly, both of my parents' have passed away, but their neighbor Murielle Nechamkin continues to give me great advice at age 87. My script supervising teacher Shirley Ulmer was a key guide in my life until her death in 2000. I often remember her wise words.

Mentors set an example for us and motivate us to try harder. They give us confidence to reach for more ambitious goals. They teach us how to make good choices.

Oprah's Angel Network donated funding to **Create Now** to support our literary arts mentoring program. Oprah dedicated two of her shows to recruiting a million mentors for our youth because she herself was inspired to succeed by her fourth-grade teacher Mrs.

Duncan. Oprah said, "She encouraged me to read and she often stayed after school to work with me, helping me to choose books."

Mentors open doors to new opportunities that normally wouldn't be available. At-risk and high-risk kids often lack this vital relationship in their lives.

Just as I benefited from having mentors, I've also enjoyed the delights of being a mentor to troubled youth.

Christine's mother died of a heroin overdose when she was five years old. Her father had sexually abused her and she was put into "the system." She was transferred from one foster family to another, living on the streets and often committing crimes.

I met her when she was 17 and locked up at a juvenile detention facility. **Create Now** put on a concert where we invited the kids in the audience to perform. Christine recited a beautiful poem that she had written about how gangs were bad.

At the end of the performance, I gave out my **Create Now** business cards to all the youth and encouraged them to contact us when they were back on the streets so they could record their songs at our small recording studio. Christine immediately wrote me a letter, telling me how much she valued our organization and wanted to be a part of it. She had a gorgeous singing voice and I helped her to record and also perform in front of hundreds of other troubled youth, as well as audiences at **Create Now** fundraising benefits.

Christine liked to call me "mom" and she blossomed through our mentoring relationship. At the same time, I also grew as I learned more about her plight in the social services system. I felt like I made *some* kind of an impact, and even if it was just a small one, it sure was a wonderful experience. Today, Christine is happily married and living in Phoenix with her husband and daughter where they record their original music.

You can inspire your mentee to continue their education. Help them to find a satisfying career and to take the initial steps to get there. A mentor's purpose is also to introduce their mentee(s) to new social experiences, and to enlighten them and broaden their horizons by sharing information that shows the best ways for them to achieve success and happiness.

I never thought that I could change someone else's life. *You* can be that special person who helps to impact the course of a child's life, if you're dedicated, persistent and use common sense.

Mentors can be of any age. Many schools and local community organizations have "buddy programs" to encourage upper-grade youth to get involved as mentors for younger students.

Christopher, a 16-year-old Stanton High School student, was a *Teen Trendsetter (www.volunteerusafund.org)* in Jacksonville, Florida. He chose to give back to his former school, Oak Hill Elementary, by recruiting seven of his schoolmates. Christopher instructed them on how to become a reading mentor to under-performing, at-risk third grade elementary school children.

Christopher said, "My friends and I worked One-on-One with eight little kids. We went there every Monday and it only took an hour. It was really fun!"

Of the eight Oak Hill mentees who were committed to the program, seven of them scored high on a reading test, while previously they had scored very low.

Intergenerational programs are also popular nationwide. Senior citizens are teamed with at-risk kids, which is helpful to both groups. The seniors are able to pass on their valuable life experiences, while the kids bring enthusiasm, curiosity and an open mind.

The Foster Grandparents program in rural Alaska serves an additional purpose. Elder Native Americans in the region are matched with the economically disadvantaged pre-school children who attend Head Start. These indigenous kids are exposed to the language and culture that's dying out in their communities.

The mentor's key role is to listen. Most kids need reliable adults with whom they can talk about their fears, dreams, and concerns. Mentors serve as sounding boards, and when asked, someone who can give trustworthy advice.

At-risk youth may not have any adults in their lives with the time, interest, or ability to listen to them. High-risk youth who live in residential institutions will rarely confide in staff members, administrators or even psychologists, for fear of punishment. Yet they might confide in you because of the trust that you've developed.

A mentor introduces a different adult voice. A youth generally regards their special friend with great respect. They're *especially* impressed that their mentor is a volunteer who has chosen them as a friend, rather than someone who is being paid to be there.

The most important thing to remember is that the trust you establish with your mentee is precious; it's the building block of your relationship.

Your role is to help them to feel more important and to develop their self-esteem and confidence. Do the very best that you can to support your mentee's needs. Commit yourself with the highest integrity and unconditional love.

TYPES OF MENTORING

There are a number of different kinds of mentoring. When making a decision about what type of mentor you want to be, the first thing you should consider is the length of time that you have available to commit. If you are too busy or have an erratic schedule, then a short-term commitment is the best.

However, if you have the time and you're dedicated to deeply impacting a youth's life, then a long-term commitment is ideal. Relationships that endure for a year or longer are most beneficial for the children, and also more rewarding for you.

Here are different types of mentoring:

1. One-on-One Mentoring

This is traditional mentoring, sometimes referred to as a "Special Friend" or "Big/Little" relationships. You are paired up with one child. Since you work directly with the youth, the relationship is close. It's absolutely essential that you don't take this involvement lightly and make sure that you maintain your commitment.

With One-on-One Mentoring, the mentor is usually matched with a mentee who shares their interests. The mentor often introduces his or her mentee to new experiences, such as hikes in

21

nature, visits to museums and fun activities like bowling. As trust increases over time, the mentee grows to love and respect their mentor as a valued friend, someone to turn to when things get tough.

If One-on-One Mentoring takes place through a school, it can be considered either tutoring or academic mentoring. Tutoring is where you give support with schoolwork, but a close relationship doesn't develop. However, if you form a bond with the youth during the time that you spend together and delve into some personal issues, than this is called Academic Mentoring. The schoolwork is the focus of the time spent together, yet a friendship develops.

An example of a well-known organization that builds these kinds of one-on-one mentoring partnerships is Big Brothers/Big Sisters (www.bbbs.org).

Mark was the Director of Human Resources at General Mills and the father of three kids. He had a tight schedule, yet he was also part of *Big Brothers/Big Sisters* of the Greater Twin Cities in Minnesota.

In spite of his busy agenda, Mark mentored his Little Brother "Ronald" for five years. In addition to helping him with schoolwork, Mark supported Ronald by attending his football games and getting together with him for other fun activities.

Mark nurtured their relationship by following Ronald as he changed schools three times. He helped the boy transition into middle school and a new peer group. Ronald made great progress in his life thanks to Mark's consistent support.

The benefits to this type of program are:

▲ You can bond deeply with one child.
▲ You can treat the mentee as special, without worrying about showing any sort of favoritism.
▲ You can see more direct changes in the youth.
▲ The child may become a lifelong friend.

The disadvantages are:

▼ There is the potential that things may not work out with this particular child for a number of reasons.

▼ You might have to change your job or residence and be unable to maintain your commitment.

▼ The child might have to move to another location.

▼ It can be difficult emotionally for you and the child to end the relationship (if it has to end).

2. Group Mentoring:

With Group Mentoring programs, one adult volunteer builds relationships with a number of young people. Meetings generally take place with focus on a particular project or an ongoing activity that brings you together. An example might be Arts Mentoring, where the group works together on a project like a mural. Sports Mentoring is where you coach the local soccer or baseball team.

Other types of Group Mentoring could be leading a Boy Scout troop or simply playing with a group of children at the recreation center in your neighborhood on a regular basis. The mentoring takes place as you develop personal relationships with the kids in your group.

Sometimes the mentor might bond with one of the kids in the group. When the project is completed and the Group Mentoring program ends, then the mentor might start a One-on-One Mentoring relationship with that special youth.

An organization that provides group mentoring is the Boys and Girls Clubs of America (www.bgca.org).

The benefits to this type of program are:

▲ You'll have an opportunity to reach a larger number of needy kids.

▲ If one child has to drop out for any reason, the mentoring program can still continue.

▲ Group dynamics can often enhance a project.

▲ You get to experience mentoring different types of youth.

The disadvantages are:

▼ You must treat every youth in the group equally.
▼ It can sometimes be harder to control larger numbers of children.
▼ The youth might battle for your attention, which can create tension and decrease the effectiveness of the project.
▼ It can take more time to organize larger numbers of children.
▼ It might be a challenge to get the quantities of materials needed for group projects.

An example of the benefit of group mentoring can be seen with Joe Petricca, the Executive Vice Dean at the *American Film Institute*. Through **Create Now**, he spent a few years mentoring a revolving group of six teenage boys who lived in a special group home for kids with mental health problems. With Joe's support, these boys wrote and produced their own short videos.

Joe said, "This experience was hugely life-affecting. It is something all of my friends, family and coworkers know about. It is a subject I still go on about at cocktail parties. I work in a business where people are stressed, preoccupied and always short on time. Yet I gave an hour to two hours a week to this volunteer effort -- less time than it seems that most people I work with commit to following some reality TV show -- and it gave me back something so huge that it is difficult to explain."

---

3. Team Mentoring:

A group of two or more adults can work together as a team to mentor a group of youth. This system can focus on specific goals, such as team building, leadership development and community service.

An example of an organization with a successful Team Mentoring model is Los Angeles Team Mentoring. They work in the schools to bring together a teacher, a college mentee and a volunteer from the community to teach a group of middle school children how to mentor other children younger than themselves (www.latm.org).

The benefits to this type of program are:

▲ If you must miss a scheduled appointment with your mentees, there are other mentors to help out.

▲ The youth can benefit from experiencing the unique skills and perspectives of different mentors during their time together.

▲ The children are taught the spirit of teamwork: sharing and helping each other to achieve goals.

▲ It is comforting to have additional support from other team members.

The disadvantages are:

▼ You won't have as much time alone to bond with your mentees.

▼ Your ideas might clash with those of another mentor.

▼ There is the potential for disorganization.

▼ There might be a lack of communication between the mentors and the mentees.

Another example of team mentoring is PATH, a nonprofit organization in Northwest Indiana that uses games and other activities to teach about the prevention of teenage pregnancy and sexually-transmitted diseases to at-risk, low-income youth who are ages 11-18.

"We work together with the kids as one team and we use interactive techniques to develop positive relationships," stated A-Team Director Michelle Lee. "The mentors on our A-Team serve as role models for the at-risk kids we reach." (www.pathblazer.org).

4. Family Mentoring

An entire family can be involved in mentoring at-risk and high-risk youth. This often brings family members closer together, while giving each individual the satisfaction of giving back to their community.

Low-income families face enormous pressure in getting food and shelter. The stress can severely disrupt family life and lead to homelessness. These families can be matched with another family of mentors who work with them over an extended period.

An example of an organization that offers Family Mentoring is Family Promise in Sutton, NJ., which matches economically vulnerable families with trained volunteer mentors who work with them, one-on-one, over an extended period to develop life skills, improve their situations, connect with community resources and nurture their children (www.familypromise.org).

The benefits to this type of program are:

▲ You assist disadvantaged family members to develop life skills.
▲ You connect them with useful community resources.
▲ The family's housing and employment situations can greatly improve.
▲ You are able to nurture and support their children.
▲ By strengthening the family, you provide a solid foundation for them to build on.
▲ You help the family transition from welfare to work.
▲ The family overcomes challenges with your aid and celebrates successes.
▲ If done as a family-to-family project, then your own family members will benefit greatly by sharing a heartwarming experience.
▲ You and your family members, particularly children, will reap the benefits of mentoring.

The disadvantages are:

▼ If there are numerous family members, it can be time-consuming.

▼ It might be expensive to pay for their essential supplies if the family can't afford to buy them.

▼ You could get mixed up in private family matters.

▼ You can't show any favoritism to family members, especially different siblings.

▼ You may be disappointed if you're unable to fulfill all of the family's needs.

A family in Minneapolis, Minnesota wanted to experience a Family-to-Family Mentoring program, but none existed in their community. It all started when their 13-year-old daughter wanted to tutor Latino children in foster care, since she was fluent in Spanish.

The girl's mother wanted her birth daughter and her adopted daughter (who was also thirteen) to participate in community service. She did some research and got approval for their family to mentor a sibling group of eight children, ages 3 to 18, through the *Ready Program For Youth*.

The two families became very close. The kids spent three to four hours a week together doing fun things and sharing the pleasures of life. As a result, the *Ready Program For Youth* made Family-to-Family Mentoring a permanent component of their program.

---

5. E-Mentoring:

By using email and Skype or similar services on the Internet, mentors can reach children all over the world. Many forms of computer-assisted learning are becoming popular, as mentees have access to computers at school, libraries and in their homes.

An example of such a program is the Four Directions: Electronic Mentoring Project sponsored at the University of Texas in Austin that provides online mentoring to disadvantaged Native American children all around the country.

The benefits to this type of program are:

▲ There's no need to travel or commute.

▲ You can be in touch when it's convenient; there's no strict schedule.
▲ You can be exposed to kids who live in different locations.
▲ Children develop their computer skills.
▲ It might be easier for some kids to talk more openly online about things they wouldn't feel comfortable sharing in person.

The disadvantages are:

▼ It could be harder to form a strong bond with someone through the Internet.
▼ Technical glitches can affect your communication.
▼ Children with poor literacy skills may have a difficult time writing.
▼ The youth might get easily distracted or bored without the physical presence of their mentors.
▼ Kids may not want to express their feelings because of concerns about confidentiality.

Adam Aberman founded the organization *Icouldbe.org*, a New York based mentoring site that asks its mentors to donate 20 minutes a week to give career advice to around 500 kids who attend overcrowded urban or underserved rural schools around the country. There's at least one Native American reservation school and a juvenile detention facility on their roster.

"The idea of *Icouldbe* is to be completely honest about professional life," says Aberman. "One of our mentors is a physical therapist and one day a mentee asked him point-blank, 'Do you like what you do?'

He replied, 'No, I don't like this job. But here are the things I do like about it.' All of our mentors are encouraged to paint a truthful picture rather than a rosy one."

Since *Icouldbe*'s ratio of high-school mentees to guidance counselors is around 400 to 1 nationally, online career mentors can give truthful advice about their work to help mentees decide what path to follow (www.icouldbe.org).

6. Peer Mentoring:

Peer Mentoring is when youth mentor other youth who are the same age or younger students. The youth mentor feels important and responsible, since he or she must serve as a role model. The mentee is excited to have another youth pay attention to them. They are more apt to listen to advice from another youth than from an adult.

Peer Mentoring is used primarily in schools. It helps new students, or those not fitting in, to acclimate. Academic studies are also greatly enhanced. The mentor learns at the same time, while developing leadership skills.

Tommy, 15, was a sophomore at Bedford High School. His friend encouraged him to participate in a Peer Mentoring program through *Bedford Youth and Family Services (BYFS)* in Bedford, MA. Their goal was to create more familiar faces for middle school students before they entered high school.

"Mentoring was pretty fun," Tommy said. "It's good to get to know some of the younger kids and help them by telling them about my experiences."

Melissa Weise, Youth Development Coordinator for *BYFS* and director of the Peer Mentoring program, said "Risky behavior in teens spikes upward between Grade 8 and Grade 9, when kids are moving from the middle school to the high school. Our Peer Mentoring program is a chance for them to find out what high school is really like from students who are already there."

Mentors are carefully selected and they undergo a six-week training process before participating in the after-school program. Once training is completed, each mentor may be assigned up to six mentees, always of the same gender.

The mentoring program has been really beneficial both for the high school mentors and the middle school mentees.

The success of the mentoring program helped earn the town a major accolade when Bedford was named one of the "100 Best Communities for Young People" by "America's Promise – The Alliance For Youth."

The benefits to this type of program are:

▲ You learn valuable communication skills.
▲ You find out about the importance of commitment.
▲ You are more sensitive to the needs, experiences and situations of other members who live in your community.
▲ You help to strengthen community ties.
▲ It feels great to know you're helping someone else.
▲ It looks good on your resume and college applications.
▲ It will reduce stereotypical ideas that you may have.
▲ You will make new friends.

The disadvantages are:

▼ You must commit to mentoring at the same time and place each week for an agreed upon period of time.
▼ You might not get along with your mentee and need to be reassigned to another youth.
▼ You must be patient, since positive changes may not be immediately apparent.
▼ You must respect and support your mentee's parents' rules and concerns for their children.
▼ You need to have enough time for yourself to also study and achieve your goals.
▼ Your friends may not be as sympathetic as you are to helping others, and they may resent that you're not as available to them while you're mentoring.
▼ Schoolmates might tease you for mentoring.

Think carefully about what your personal needs are and how you can best serve at-risk and high-risk youth before you decide which type of mentoring program is right for you. The worst thing that you can do is to commit to a mentoring relationship, only to break that commitment later.

These children have been let down by adults most of their lives. Imagine if you were in their shoes, with a hard life filled with challenges due to circumstances that were forced on you by adults. Kids don't ask to be beaten or to be sexually abused. They don't beg to be left without food or shelter. Perhaps their parents work two or three jobs just to pay all the bills and are rarely at home. They might be strung out on crack, alcohol, or locked up in prison.

Finally, someone new comes along. It's a mentor who is a positive, seemingly normal adult who could be your new friend and role model. Full of hope and excitement, you reach out to take their helping hand. Off you go, mentor and mentee spending time together and bonding. You slowly open up and start to trust your mentor. You know that he'll be there when you need him.

But suddenly it changes; perhaps he got a different job or a promotion that requires more work. Maybe she got a new boyfriend who takes up all of her free time. They suddenly stop coming around, or it could taper off by them not showing up every once in a while, until those empty days become permanent.

You feel hurt, disappointed and angry. Another person that you trusted has also let you down. Now you clam up even more when it comes to trusting others. And you probably think it's your fault. You're too stupid, ugly or boring for people to be around. Your self-esteem takes an even deeper dive. Abandonment can be devastating to any child, especially these vulnerable kids.

It's important not to make a commitment as a mentor unless you can absolutely keep it. This doesn't mean that you can't be a mentor. It just means that you have to think carefully about what *type* of mentor you want to be.

WHAT MENTORS DON'T DO

The mentor's role is *not* to replace the parent or guardian. You are there to be an additional guide to your mentee. You should always respect the wishes of her or his parent(s) or guardian(s), since their authority comes first.

Mentors are not disciplinarians. You signed on to be a friend, teacher and guide. Your job is not to demand control or force obedience from your mentees.

You are also not a social worker, psychologist or family therapist. Don't counsel your mentee with advice that you're not qualified to give. You might do more damage than good. If you think that your mentee needs support in a certain area where you lack expertise, then your job becomes finding a professional who can help.

Don't let the close relationship that you build with your mentee be misused, even if it means that you're not "cool." A mentor is not a peer. It's okay to use a hip slang word every now and then or to joke around, but you're not a kid, so don't act like one.

As a mentor, you are also not a hero or heroine who comes to his or her rescue. Your relationship with your mentee should be realistic, so that there are no false expectations or disappointments.

Your purpose is not to provide solutions to all the issues facing your mentee, but to be there as a friend and to listen and offer your opinions when requested. It's essential that you never reveal to anyone confidential information about your mentee, unless there is a life-threatening situation.

WHAT MAKES A GOOD MENTOR?

Because you don't need a diploma or certificate to mentor, there's no way to judge whether someone is cut out to be a mentor. What's important is that you care about helping a needy child or a group of kids, and that you engage in a positive relationship with your mentee(s).

> Brian from Haverhill, NH mentored Gregory, 12-years-old, because he didn't have any children of his own. "Seeing life through a kid's eyes is a great thing. It's changed my life having a kid around. It's everything I expected."
>
> His mentee Gregory remarked, "I finally have a friend that really cares. He helps me with my problems and I can talk to him whenever I need help."
>
> "I do all the things a parent would do — to be there for him when he asks the tough questions," Brian said.

The most essential trait needed to be a good mentor is dependability, which means showing up regularly as scheduled and being on time for your sessions. It's vital that you fulfill your responsibilities and not be another disappointment to these kids.

Also necessary are stability, a firm character and purpose. This includes maintaining a steady temperament and being able to tolerate frustrating situations that might come up. A good mentor reacts calmly to stressful events.

A good mentor nurtures a relationship that respects the child's dignity. Communicate on a level that your kid(s) can easily understand.

Children are very intuitive. They usually know when you're being phony and when you're sincere, so honesty is essential. However, be gentle with your communication and always use tact.

Other qualities that make a good mentor are:

* ✽ High self-esteem
* ✽ Listens well
* ✽ Provides leadership
* ✽ Respects alternate lifestyles
* ✽ Non-judgmental
* ✽ Consistent
* ✽ Adaptable to change

Lastly, it's important that you be somewhat demanding of your mentee(s). Most children like to be challenged and it inspires them to work harder. They need to know that there are opportunities and choices for them to make and that you have confidence in them to meet those challenges.

A good mentor realizes that each mentee has his or her own strengths and weaknesses. With this in mind, help your mentee(s) to set high standards. Cheer them on to reach for their goals. This includes assisting them in whatever way you can through any difficulties they may encounter along the way.

It's also crucial that you reinforce your mentees' successes. Encourage them to keep up the good work. Give them small rewards as an incentive (but not as a bribe).

BENEFITS OF MENTORING

It's an exhilarating feeling to see a child that you have mentored blossom and to know that you have positively affected someone who will remember you for the rest of his or her life.

You will really make a difference in the world, because not only do you help them, but through the domino or ripple effect, everyone your mentee knows will also be impacted.

You can also help create a change in the negative cycle of abuse that has afflicted generations of children. Many at-risk and high-risk youth are parents themselves. These teenagers can learn from you how to love and properly treat their children.

Erica worked full-time as a novelist. She was also married and the mother of three young children. Yet she took time to volunteer as a mentor for a teenage mother in the *Transitions Mentoring Program*, sponsored by the South Coastal Division, Children's Home Society of Florida (www.chsfl.org).

"I feel I need to make a difference, small or big, to leave the world better for my having been here."

Erica was matched with a single mother, Lydia, age 18 and her infant daughter in South Palm Beach County. She bolstered her mentee's self-esteem and helped her apply to college to study nursing. She shared her knowledge about childcare and development.

Lydia felt good that an outsider cared about her and gave her encouragement by telling her what a good mother she was. The young woman overcame her shyness and became confident. She was more assertive in ensuring her baby's safety and welfare, such as pursuing child support from the baby's father.

Erica's own three children were ages 5 through 12. Sometimes they kept Lydia's baby entertained while Erica and her mentee talked about issues of mutual concern or interest. Erica wanted her kids to know that volunteering is important and they should never be too busy to help someone else. They learned the benefits of reaching out and helping others less fortunate at an early age.

As you mentor, you will also grow and develop on both a personal and professional level. You will enhance your own self-esteem and confidence as you see the effects of your guidance on the kids you mentor. You will probably be very surprised at the intelligence and talent that they demonstrate. And you will have a new friendship with a terrific young person.

By working with at-risk and high-risk kids, you'll also be exposed to diverse subcultures. You'll learn about their unique traditions, languages and rules. Your deep connections with the children will influence your own life.

Many people volunteer to get credit for other purposes, like school requirements, community service and to enhance their resumes. It's very impressive that you volunteer your time to support a child in need of help.

Even more importantly, you will be contributing to society. By getting involved as a mentor to help at-risk and high-risk youth, you'll be giving back to your community in many ways that will have a lasting and positive impact.

Additional benefits that mentors have reported are that they feel:

- ❤ Happier with their careers.
- ❤ Fulfilled from volunteering in their community.
- ❤ Better about themselves for having impacted another's life.
- ❤ They have developed leadership abilities.
- ❤ Enhanced interpersonal skills.
- ❤ A deeper understanding of youth and societal problems.
- ❤ They have received admiration and respect from their peers.
- ❤ They had an opportunity to meet a challenge.
- ❤ They got along better with their own families.

Most mentors discover that after volunteering, they're more patient, open-minded and better prepared to deal with challenges than they once were.

Quinton was a professional screenwriter who became a mentor through **Create Now**. "I know what it's like to have a desire but not have the tools necessary to transform it into action. Along my path, I've encountered many people who have provided me with what I needed. Now it's time for me to do the same for others."

He mentored One-on-One with a youth we'll call "David," a 16-year-old, bright young man. David had been sexually abused as a child. Children who have been sexually abused often continue the cycle. David was incarcerated at age 16 for raping his younger sister.

Through Quinton's guidance, David was able to express himself creatively through writing and he healed his troubled past.

After the teen completed his sentence at a juvenile detention facility, Quinton got him a job in a video store and guided him to apply for college.

Then, David became a professional journalist in San Francisco. Quinton was able to fulfill his purpose of helping someone in need, just like he had been assisted as a youth.

Hundreds of thousands of people around the world volunteer their time and profit from mentoring at-risk and high-risk kids on a regular basis. Every individual experiences the innumerable benefits from mentoring in their unique way. Physically, emotionally and spiritually, mentoring touches us in the deepest parts of our soul.

These children represent our future. Through your support as a mentor, you can introduce them to a greater life, where they're a contributor instead of just another statistic. By showing at-risk and high-risk kids different alternatives and providing your friendship, you can make a big difference in your community, and the world.

CHAPTER TWO

The Mentee

WHO ARE AT-RISK AND HIGH-RISK KIDS?

Half of our youth population (17.6 million kids) is considered to be "at-risk" or "high-risk." While this terminology is often interchanged, I consider at-risk youth to be someone who is economically disadvantaged with the strong potential to get into trouble, but they're basically doing okay.

High-risk youth are kids who are already experiencing difficulties, such as these:

➡ They are a drug or alcohol abuser.
➡ They are the child of a substance abuser.
➡ They are the victim of physical, sexual, or emotional abuse.
➡ They have dropped out of school.
➡ They have become pregnant.
➡ They have committed a violent or delinquent act.
➡ They have experienced mental health problems.
➡ They have attempted suicide.
➡ They have experienced chronic failure in school.

Minority groups are generally at higher levels of poverty and relatively lower levels of education. Adding racial discrimination to the mix, youth of color are at significant risk for negative behaviors. However, kids of all ethnicities who come from the wealthiest communities in our country are also at high-risk. No child is immune from having problems.

I encourage you to read my detailed report in the Appendix of this book on *The State of America's Youth.* I've compiled extensive research on the different challenges that our kids face, including drug and alcohol addiction, teen pregnancy, physical, sexual and emotional abuse, homelessness, plus many other issues. This comprehensive account will give you a deeper understanding of exactly who are these at-risk and high-risk youth.

WHERE DO I FIND YOUTH TO MENTOR?

Considering that half of our youth population is at-risk, you don't have to search far and wide to find mentees. There are probably plenty of kids in your community who are in urgent need of a mentor.

Also, a mentee doesn't have to be a stranger. You might already have a child or youth in your life that you're mentoring without even knowing it: your neighbor, a friend's child, a favorite niece, nephew or cousin. They're still kids and they need support. You can deepen that relationship as a mentor by applying the same principles detailed in this book.

Perhaps you might find a youth to mentor through your work. However, be careful that you don't cross any professional boundaries.

Shrondrika was a 17-year-old single mother with no direction and no plans for the future. Although she wanted to complete high school, she found it too difficult to continue while adequately caring for her baby.

That's when her probation officer Catherine stepped in and urged her client to enroll in the Louisiana *National Guard Youth ChalleNGe Program*. Shondrika's mother offered to care for the baby.

Catherine said of her mentee, "She is smart, but she didn't feel that she was. She was unsure of herself and had no idea which way she wanted to go."

Shondrika and Catherine developed a very close relationship. The mentor visited her mentee at least once a month. They talked two to three times monthly, and each wrote weekly letters. "I wanted her to feel I'm there for her." Catherine said.

"I can't tell you how proud I am of this 18-year-old woman who has accomplished so much. I have seen her self-esteem and self-

---

confidence soar. She continues to mature and is showing skills in managing money. She is a very responsible, good parent. She keeps amazing me."

Catherine was able to transform her professional relationship as a probation officer into one as a mentor. She helped Shondrika see that this opportunity would not only improve her life; it was a step toward providing a secure future for her son (www.ngycp.org).

Through my work with **Create Now**, I have discovered that in most communities throughout the country, there are hundreds of thousands of kids who are in need of support. High-risk youth are dealing with different challenges. At-risk youth have the potential for problems. Mentoring both types of these youngsters can be very rewarding.

High-Risk Youth

These are the kids who are living in emergency shelters for domestic violence victims, runaways and other homeless youth. They're barely surviving on the streets or are part of the probation and foster care systems. They could be gang members, teenage parents or substance abusers.

Foster Youth

A half-million children in the United States are in foster care. These kids have been removed from their homes due to serious abuse, neglect, being orphaned or abandoned. Many of them live with foster families, which means they are not adopted, but are in temporary custody.

Research shows that most of these foster kids are shuttled into multiple placements, often living in 15-20 different homes before they turn eighteen. Being plucked from their birth families traumatizes them enough, but then they suffer again and again because they're bounced around to different foster families, detention facilities and group homes, just like unwanted baggage.

Each year, around 30,000 foster youth in the U.S. "age out of the system." In California, foster youth are "emancipated," or set free to fend for themselves when they turn 18. Most of them lack basic social and life skills because they don't have any family or upbringing. One in three foster youth (33%) do not graduate from high school or earn a GED. Three out of four girls and one of three boys end up surviving on food stamps.[1] Most foster kids don't have a clue about how to get a job, save their money or fend for themselves.

There are hundreds, if not thousands, of foster care agencies that place these children with families, and most of them crave mentors for their clients.

There are probably foster group homes right in your community. They are tucked away in residential neighborhoods all over the country. Some group homes are large campuses with schools on the premises that accommodate around 100 children. Others are regular houses with usually six boys or six girls living with staff who rotate in shifts around-the-clock.

Smaller group homes generally house teenage foster youth, since younger children tend to be placed with foster families or extended family members, like aunts, uncles and grandparents.

No matter what the age of a foster child, these kids truly need a mentor in their life.

Katherine, a 20-year-old foster youth, lived in a group home in Chicago with her 3-year-old daughter. She dropped out of school at age 15. She attended National-Louis University, thanks to a unique alternative educational program called *Jobs For Youth/Chicago, Inc.*, one of the 15 small alternative community schools of the *Youth Skills Development and Training Program (YSDTP)* (www.jfychicago.org).

This caring educational environment helped Katherine to reconnect with her dreams. She wanted to work with adolescents and young adults and also had political ambitions. She planned to major in political science and eventually run for office.

She commented, "Through *Jobs For Youth/Chicago, Inc.*, I received a lot of support on every level, including mentally and socially, that helped build my self esteem. It's hard being a ward of

---

[1] CNN News, October 2011

[2] U. S. General Accounting Office, Foster Care; Effectiveness of Independent Living

the state. This program helped me put all my problems aside, get my priorities straight and work hard."

Each student is assigned a full-time, paid school-based mentor. These professionals work One-on-One with students and provide coordination with DCFS caseworkers and service providers. The mentors carry cell phones and if the kids aren't in school, they are immediately notified.

Mentors also provide graduation and transition services, and coordinate community-based resources. Mentors remove obstacles to students graduating and navigate them toward college and vocational training.

Katherine said, "My mentor took me to a play and a nice restaurant, things that kids who aren't fortunate never get to do. Many of our outside activities have an educational component. They have opened up my whole horizon of the world. For example, we went to the State Capitol in Springfield and I actually got to sit in the House of Representatives."

Different research shows that many foster kids stay in the system for the rest of their lives, depending on welfare to survive or ending up in prison. One study reports that from 12 percent to 36 percent of foster youth transitioning out of the system experience homelessness.[2] Other studies estimate that around 60 percent of foster youth become permanently homeless or incarcerated.

Foster kids desperately need mentors who can provide them with continual love, guidance and support, especially to help them assimilate into society.

To find foster youth to mentor, you can call foster agencies in your community. They are the ones that place foster children with families. You can also contact your local government agency that represents foster youth.

---

[2] U. S. General Accounting Office, Foster Care; Effectiveness of Independent Living (GAO/HEHS-00-13) 4 (Nov. 1999).

In Los Angeles, this is called the Department of Children and Family Services. (http://dcfs.co.la.ca.us). In Mississippi, it's the Division of Family and Children's Services (www.mdhs.state.ms.us),

You can also research on the Internet to locate group homes for foster youth in your neighborhood. All group homes that are backed by your state or county government are subject to inspection in order to maintain their licenses. These reports are public information.

There are also many nonprofit organizations that target their services to foster youth and they search for mentors just like you. To find foster youth to mentor, check out these websites:

www.mentoring.org
www.volunteermatch.org
www.idealist.org

Runaway and Throwaway Youth

Many children who are abused and neglected fall through the cracks of the foster system. Their perpetrators may not be reported to the authorities. These kids often run away from home. It's estimated by the National Runaway Switchboard that between 1.3 and 2.8 million runaway and homeless youth live on the streets of America. Thousands of these kids die every year from assault, illness and suicide. These youngsters come from every kind of neighborhood: rich, poor, suburban, rural and urban.

It's important to understand that a youth's reason for leaving home is unique to that individual. There's no such thing as a "typical" runaway. Some may also be "throwaways" or "push-aways" – kids kicked out by their families. Because they are left to fend for themselves, these youth really need mentors who can give them guidance.

To find runaway, throwaway and homeless youth, check the local shelters in your community. There might be drop-in centers for kids to stay temporarily, or to just get a hot meal and a shower, as well as some counseling and opportunities to find more stabilized living arrangements.

Homeless Youth

According to a study by the Better Homes Fund, 40 percent of America's homeless are women and their children. Every night, more than one million children face the dark with no place to call home. They live in abandoned cars and buildings, churchyards and temporary shelters where they wait on lists to be able to transition into more permanent, affordable housing. These kids often deal with depression and post-traumatic stress disorder.

Homeless kids live in cramped surroundings, if they're able to even get a real bed. They usually don't know from day-to-day where they will be sleeping next. Often, one of the parents abandons the family, seeking greener pastures.

There's also a new population of homeless youth that has grown from the economic recession. Many families have lost their homes and are forced to live in shelters. Sometimes these shelters won't allow teenage boys to live there, because there is concern that younger children and teenage girls might be vulnerable to attack.

As a result, the families move into the shelters, but their teenage sons are forced to fend for themselves on the streets. These young men suffer from trying to survive, and also from being separated from their parents and siblings.

Another type of homeless children are victims of domestic violence. Studies have shown that as many as 50 percent of homeless women and children are fleeing from abuse.[3] At least 3.3 million children between the ages of 3 and 19 are at-risk of exposure to parental violence very year.[4]

Children who are witnesses to violence in their homes are usually more aggressive than other kids. They are often numbed by exposure to brutality, which can lead to detachment disorders.

Domestic violence victims live in secret shelters, constantly fearing that another beating may take place or they might be abandoned. They often feel guilty about not being able to stop the violence, or for still loving the abuser. Stress-related problems might

---

[3] National Coalition for the Homeless, 2007
[4] Jaffe, Wolfe, Wilson, Children of Battered Women, Sage Publications 19 (1990)

bother them and they could have difficulties at school. Boys that witness domestic violence are more likely to batter when they become adults.

Domestic violence shelters can be difficult to track down since they need to hide their locations to protect their clients, but most of them publicize hotlines. They also have administrative offices that might be easier to find. Let the receptionist know that you want to be a mentor, and then leave your contact information and ask for someone at the shelter to call you.

Whether runaways, throwaways, victims of domestic violence or just poor and homeless, all of these children are in dire need of mentors. You might be the one person that they feel safe enough to talk with about their feelings. A mentor can show them that not all adults are abusive and many people are very loving and caring.

How do you find homeless youth to mentor? Look through your local phone directory under "Housing Assistance and Shelters." You'll see the names of community organizations that run homeless shelters. Many religious centers have shelters for the homeless. Do some research on the Internet by putting the keywords "Homeless" and "Shelters" into your search engine. You can also add "Children" or "Youth" to narrow the search.

If you have a unique service that you promote, homeless youth might even reach out to you.

That's how I met Luis. He was a 21-year-old man from the Bronx, NY who was living at *Covenant House*, a shelter for homeless youth in Hollywood. Luis had been abandoned by both of his parents when he was born. The woman who raised him had neglected Luis and used him for the welfare money that she received as his guardian. When he was 15, her boyfriend threw him out.

Luis lived on the rough streets of N.Y. with one goal that kept him going: to become a filmmaker. He struggled to survive in abandoned buildings and worked in factories to scrape together enough money to make it to Los Angeles so that he could follow his dream of becoming a writer, director and actor. Luis discovered **Create Now** on the Internet and asked me if we could help him.

At the time, I had met some filmmakers who operated a Digital Video workshop on the weekends. They had offered to give scholarships to some of the at-risk youth that **Create Now** served. I arranged for Luis to take one of their workshops.

The next week, I received a beautiful letter from him telling me that his experience at the workshop was the best thing that had ever happened to him since he was born.

I was able to find Luis a terrific mentor named Max Joseph, who was an up-and-coming writer and an editor. Max grew up in N.Y. not far from the Bronx. He helped Luis to write his stories and taught him editing. Max told me that he was surprised to discover that his mentee was actually very talented.

I also bonded with Luis. He had a hard time trusting people, which is totally understandable considering his tragic past. He often acted aggressive and put up strong defenses with people, yet we developed a special connection. We helped each other in many different ways and I'm so grateful to know him. I still hear from Luis from time to time, which is always delightful. I try to reach out to him too, especially around the holidays.

Substance Abusers

High-risk kids can be at higher risk for alcohol and drug abuse. Many youth in our society are substance abusers for a variety of reasons, including peer pressure. Just as *Alcoholics Anonymous* and other twelve-step programs have sponsors for their clients, mentors can serve a similar purpose – being a positive role model, someone trustworthy that a youngster can contact when they are thinking of falling off the wagon.

You can find these youth by contacting local substance abuse rehabilitation centers. The facility might already have a mentoring program in place, or you could volunteer to start one. If mentoring youth who are struggling with addictions is of interest to you, also try reaching out to 12-step programs in your community.

Juvenile Delinquents and Gang Members

Adolescents often become rebellious and get into trouble with the law. As you probably remember from your own youth, kids listen much more to their friends than any authority figures. Peer pressure can be intense and hard to resist. If some youth encourage their friends to help rob a store or commit another crime, they will often comply just to fit in.

These vulnerable youngsters can really benefit from mentors. Check with your local police and sheriffs' departments, as well as detention facilities like boot camps, juvenile halls and other youth prisons to see if they can refer you to a mentoring program for kids in the juvenile justice system.

In many communities, gangs are rampant and kids are recruited to commit all kinds of crimes. Is it any wonder that impressionable youngsters look up to local drug dealers and gang leaders as role models? They see the "bling," as they drive around in expensive cars flaunting their money. These thugs are usually affectionate and generous toward the youth, luring the kids to do their dirty work, such as delivering drugs, or worse.

Children need mentors who can steer them on the right path. Many youth are "jumped in" to gangs as young as six or seven years old; therefore early prevention is essential. Mentors can really make the difference. Contact your local elementary and especially the middle schools, since youngsters ages 11-14 are at a tender age when they're more prone to join a gang.

Some people claim that once kids reach their teenage years, there's no way to turn them around or to get them to leave their gang. In fact, gang members must usually endure a heavy beating by other gang members, as well as their enemies. They can even risk death if they try to drop out.

I don't believe that these kids can't be reached. I've personally helped youth to leave gang life and have seen it done numerous times. Everyone deserves a second chance.

Gang interventionists are usually former gang members who are hired by police or other agencies to keep peace in their communities. Some of them even volunteer their time to mentor youth in their neighborhoods.

Jason, a 38-year-old ex-convict, was released from prison after serving time for two killings. He was a conflict mediator on Kansas City's gang-infested east side.

He became a mentor through *Aim4Peace*, a program that sends reformed criminals into some of the city's tensest neighborhoods to calm disputes before they erupt. Police credit the program with reducing violence on the east side, where most of the city's homicides occurred.

Jason said, "A lot of these dudes that I work with, they've got family histories and I try to break the cycle. That's like the situation I was in. My dad was a heroin addict and used to rob people. My brother's in prison for murder."

In 1999, Jason was sentenced to 10 years on two second-degree murder counts. He had pleaded guilty to the fatal shootings of two men: one stemming from a bar fight in 1998 and the other a confrontation in which the victim was gunned down in his car in 1997.

Jason said that he left prison determined to use his street influence to help heal neighborhood problems. "I've done everything they're thinking about doing," he said.

His mentoring worked. John, age 17, lived in one of the east side neighborhoods that Jason patrolled. He said he respected Jason and the other interventionists in *Aim4Peace* because they were not afraid to "roll up on you" to make sure there was no trouble brewing. "They really be out in the 'hood trying to do something about the violence," he said.

Jason and the other half-dozen or so *Aim4Peace* street intervention workers, who are also known as "violence interrupters," say they resolved 22 conflicts during one year in Kansas City. The east side no longer led the city in killings, according to crime data.

If you want to mentor high-risk delinquent youth who are already in a gang or are in trouble with the law, check into local gang intervention programs. They are probably listed in your phone directory or you can find them online.

As mentioned, call the police or sheriffs' departments or the Department of Probation in your city and ask if they have a mentoring program. You can also track down the detention facilities in your community, often listed as "Boot Camps" or "Juvenile Halls." Ask the receptionist if they have a Volunteer Coordinator, or request the Activities or Recreation staff. They often call this department "Program Services."

Whatever the terminology, if you persist, then you'll reach someone who will put you in touch with the right person. This individual will probably be thrilled to know you, since more and more community, educational, religious and governmental agencies are out there searching for mentors just like you!

At-Risk Youth

Many people want to mentor, but they are uncomfortable around troubled youth. They might worry about being attacked or robbed, or that they'll say the wrong thing about a sensitive matter and do more harm then good. These are perfectly valid sentiments and nothing to feel badly about. Mentoring should be enjoyable for both the mentor and the mentee(s).

There are millions of kids who have never done anything wrong in their lives, but they really need someone to look up to. They might be latchkey kids who are forced to stay at home most of the time since they live in a bad neighborhood. Perhaps they're just shy and have a hard time making friends. They can use some help learning how to break out of their shell.

Schools

Many schools already have programs in place for mentoring. This type of mentoring will likely be academic in nature. The school administrators might seek mentors to help their students learn how to read and write, assist with math and science homework, as well as other subjects.

Remember that tutoring is different than mentoring, because it's only focused on academics. Check with the school to see if their mentors are allowed to develop a personal relationship with mentees. If their program is restricted to academic learning only, but you want a deeper relationship with a youth, then find out right away so there are no miscommunications later.

Religious Centers

Churches, temples, mosques and other places of worship are excellent places to mentor. You already have a location that is accessible to the mentors and mentees, as well as a shared interest in spiritual pursuits.

Families tend to be more open to socializing with members of their religious community, since there's a common set of values and beliefs. It's somewhat easier to establish trust. Mentoring in places of worship may revolve around or include promoting religious beliefs.

Sick and Disabled Children

Another group of youth who need mentors are those who are sick and in hospitals, hospices or bedridden at home. There are 3 million children hospitalized in the U.S. each year. These kids not only suffer from physical ailments that create pain, but their illnesses can also be emotionally detrimental.

As mentioned, I was sick with a kidney condition called Nephritis as a child and was bedridden at home for months at a time from ages 9-13. Whenever I returned to school, I was picked on and bullied by the other kids. They said I had "cooties" and many avoided me. The experience has left me with emotional scars to this day.

Youth who deal with illnesses are often frightened about their condition, but they have no one to turn to when they want to share their feelings. They may not want to worry their parents. They could be afraid to talk about things with their doctor for fear that they will be given another injection or bad-tasting medicine.

A mentor can help sick children during this difficult time. For these kids, just knowing that someone else cares about them who doesn't *have* to because they're not directly related can be very soothing. These youth will look forward to your visits with great excitement, which accelerates their healing process.

It's been proven that the mind can heal the body with positive thoughts and emotions. Having a mentor can make sick children want to get better quickly so you can take them to visit a special place, or attend a unique event.

To find sick children to mentor, contact your local hospital and ask to speak to their Volunteer Coordinator. Especially seek out children's hospitals, which probably have special programs for volunteers. Hospices may also need volunteers for terminally-ill children.

Disabled youth are in vital need of mentors. They have to deal with physical challenges that restrict them and might also cause pain. These kids are often bullied or avoided by other children because they are different. They can't join in on activities that require any physical senses or motor skills that they might lack.

A mentor can show these kids that they are important and valued in spite of their challenges. A mentor can bolster their confidence and be a sounding board when they need to express their hidden emotions.

Karen was a blind 8-year-old who grew up with many limitations amongst her family members in Southwest Washington. Her two older sisters and mother were also blind and her father suffered from cerebral palsy. Karen became increasingly shy and often heard that she was "stupid" and wouldn't amount to anything. Frustrated and sad, her life was filled with physical restrictions.

Then she met her mentor and everything changed. Beth an outgoing, successful trial lawyer, became Karen's Big Sister. Due to a nerve disease in her legs, Beth used crutches or a wheelchair to get around.

Beth and Karen learned to adapt their special needs to help each other. The mentor got her mentee to promise that she would always keep a hand on Beth's wheelchair when they were out together. That way, if there was a problem, they could work it out together. They did, becoming sisters in every sense of the word and forming a tight bond.

Beth and Karen did everything that sisters do together — they explored the world of music, attending concerts ranging from classical to jazz and rock. They ate at ethnic restaurants, visited museums and zoos, and even embarked on rock-hunting expeditions. Gradually, Karen's beautiful personality and self-confidence emerged. Beth always encouraged her mentee to excel in school and to follow her dreams. Karen graduated from college and Beth was in the audience cheering her on!

You can find disabled youth to mentor in your community by contacting the National Organization on Disability at www.nod.org. Also, search the Internet for organizations that serve handicapped youth, such as Junior Blind of America (www.juniorblind.org), United Cerebral Palsy (www.ucp.org) and the Muscular Dystrophy Association (www.mda.org).

Special Needs kids also benefit greatly from mentors. Youth who are dealing with Downs Syndrome, Autism and other developmental disabilities need mentors to provide them with love and encouragement. A mentor's guidance might help them to build their confidence and become more self-sufficient. They can enjoy delightful new experiences, especially having a good friend.

Best Buddies is an organization that matches mentors with youth who have intellectual and developmental disabilities (IDD) at more than 1,500 college, high school and middle school campuses across the U.S. and internationally (www.bestbuddies.org).

Mentoring Programs

Whether you want to mentor high-risk or at-risk youth, there are probably organized mentoring programs in your community that can help you find the perfect mentee(s).

Recreation centers in your neighborhood might have such a program. This is often a good place to do sports mentoring, such as helping out with the local baseball team. They usually offer other activities, like arts and crafts, swimming and a variety of games.

You might start out assisting someone in the activities department, but discover that you have bonded with several of the youth. Mentoring can evolve in a more organic manner by just being present on a regular basis. Some of the kids might open up to you in a way that they can't with other adults in their lives.

There are also large mentoring organizations throughout the country with chapters in most communities.

For One-on-One mentoring, Big Brothers/Big Sisters of America (BB/BS) is the largest youth mentoring organization in the United States. Founded in 1904 by Ray Coulter, this organization is credited with having developed modern mentoring. With more than 400 affiliates across all 50 states and U.S. territories, BB/BS is probably close to your home. They will match you One-on-One with a mentee based on your interests (www.bbbs.org).

If you want a structured program that serves groups of at-risk youth, contact your local Boys & Girls Club (www.bgca.org), YMCA (http://ymca.org), Boys Scouts (www.scouting.org) and Girl Scouts (www.girlscouts.org). If you're into sports, try the Little League (www.littleleague.org), the Junior NBA (www.jrnba.org), NFL Youth Football (www.nflflag.com), and also the American Youth Soccer Association (www.soccer.org) to find local chapters in your area.

There are also hundreds, if not thousands, of smaller community-based mentoring organizations all around the country. Just like my own organization **Create Now**, these nonprofits have been founded so they can match people like you with kids that need mentors.

Community-based organizations (CBO's) with mentoring programs search for volunteers to develop a relationship with their mentees, since that has the most impact on youth. They usually want "General Mentors" to teach social skills and to expose youth to the joys of life.

However, **Create Now** focuses on arts mentoring. Some community organizations might look for sports mentors, literacy mentors, or those who can introduce youth to the great outdoors. They might target a specific population, such as children of prisoners or foster kids. They could also serve youngsters in a particular neighborhood.

CBO's with mentoring programs might be part of a larger agency, like a family center that provides counseling services, anger management classes, legal advice and other types of assistance. Mentoring could be just one component of a multi-layered approach to addressing core problems. That means the mentors could be on a team with attorneys, therapists and other service providers.

Here's the best thing about mentoring through an established program, whether it's large or small, through a school, faith or community-based organization: their staff can match you with youth in need of a mentor, and give you training, as well as materials that you might need.

If a problem develops with your mentee or his/her family, having someone at a mentoring organization to intervene can be invaluable. Also, mentoring through a structured program often gives you added benefits, such as special outings with your mentee(s), the chance to share ideas or issues with other mentors, networking and additional opportunities.

If you are looking for a place to mentor in your neighborhood, then I highly recommend that you contact Mentor. Founded in 1990 and based in Virginia, Mentor has become a clearinghouse for mentoring organizations. Their extensive website also offers online resources and guidelines about mentoring that you can download for free.

Mentor has established a top-notch database of hundreds of mentoring organizations around the country. To find a mentoring organization in your neighborhood, visit www.mentoring.org and put your zip code in the search box. This will give you a list of mentoring organizations in your community.

After you go through all the possibilities, choose a mentoring group that interests you and contact them. They are seeking out volunteers and their staff will be thrilled to hear from you. This Volunteer Coordinator will meet and interview you, then later place you as a mentor with a youngster.

Each agency has its own protocols to process new mentors. If for some reason you have a negative experience with a particular mentoring organization, then don't give up. There are plenty of kids out there who need mentors, and other places to find them.

BENEFITS TO MENTEES

When at-risk youth are asked why they like to have a mentor, they often respond about how meaningful it is that someone volunteers their time to be with them. They can't believe that their mentor isn't getting paid to help them, and that they support their mentee simply because they care about them.

Most of these kids feel unwanted, especially children who have been abused and abandoned by their families. They may feel unloved, and guilty and responsible for what has happened to them, even though it wasn't their fault. While their teachers, social workers, therapists, counselors and other adults that they interact with may have their best interests in mind, it's their mentors who support them without receiving any monetary gain. It's a powerful feeling to know that someone cares about you just because of who you are, without having any obligations or ulterior motives.

It's important to track the results of mentoring, so that best practices can be improved, funding can be raised to expand mentoring programs, and at-risk youth can benefit as much as possible.

Academic or school-based mentoring is relatively easy to measure, since the focus is on academic achievements. Teachers can calculate grade changes, as well as differences in the mentee's attitude and behavior during classes.

Unfortunately, relationship-based mentoring is more difficult to evaluate. Mentees may not show any visible signs of change for years to come.

You may meet with your mentee regularly for a period of time and feel frustrated that she or he doesn't seem to have improved. You may both eventually decide to terminate the relationship. Ten years later, your mentee might say to someone, "You know who really made a difference in my life? My mentor, when I was in the seventh grade."

Mentors plant seeds in their mentees. Something you say casually may be buried deep into the psyche of your mentee, whether you are consciously aware of it or not. They may or may not physically react to your words of wisdom, but the meaning behind your guidance is implanted. Years later, the significance of what you said might finally sprout. It can take time for mentees to blossom.

During 1992 and 1993, *Public/Private Ventures*, a Philadelphia-based national research organization, looked at 959 boys and girls, ages 10 to 16, through *Big Brothers/Big Sisters* agencies in Phoenix, Wichita, Minneapolis, Rochester, Columbus, Philadelphia, Houston and San Antonio.

Of the young people taking part in the study, more than 60 percent were boys, and more than 50 percent were minorities. Most came from low-income households, and many lived in families with histories of substance abuse and/or domestic violence.

Approximately one-half of the children were matched with a Big Brother or Big Sister. The others were assigned to a waiting list (control group). The children were randomly assigned to one group or the other.

The matched children met with their Big Brothers or Big Sisters about three times a month for an average of one year. Researchers found that after spending time with their "Bigs," the Little Brothers and Little Sisters were:

* 46 percent less likely to begin using illegal drugs.
* 27 percent less likely to begin using alcohol.
* 52 percent less likely to skip school.
* 37 percent less likely to skip a class.
* More confident of their performance in schoolwork.
* One-third less likely to hit someone.
* Getting along better with their families.

Big Brothers/Big Sisters volunteers had the greatest impact in the area of alcohol and substance abuse prevention. For every 100 youth between ages 10 and 16 who start using drugs, the study found only 54 similar youth who were matched with a Big would start using drugs. Minority boys and girls were the most strongly influenced; they were 70 percent less likely than their peers to initiate drug use.

Many mentors reported seeing their mentees change in regards to school. The mentored youth who participated in this study:

* Were happier in school.
* Participated more in school activities.
* Took more healthy risks in class and with friends.
* Had fewer trips to the principal's office.
* Had reduced school detentions.
* Had improved academic performance.

As if that's not enough, youth who are mentored often show tremendous improvement in changing their negative attitudes and behavior through:

☆ Increased communication.
☆ Improved eye contact.
☆ More smiling.
☆ Improved interactions with peers.
☆ Better appearance.
☆ Increased consideration of others.
☆ Decreased hostility.
☆ More enthusiastic.
☆ Improved attitude.
☆ Paying attention more.
☆ Greater self-acceptance and care.
☆ Opening up to the mentor.

While the advantages to mentees are tremendous, it's important to remember that mentoring takes patience and commitment. These benefits may not be apparent for a long period of time, but if you remain dedicated to your mentee(s), learn to listen to them and let them know that you are there to support them, the results will be astounding.

Samuel Merritt University (SMU) students enrolled in the Doctor of Podiatric Medicine (DPM) and Bachelor of Science in Nursing (BSN) programs spent their summer mentoring more than four dozen middle and high school students from the Oakland, CA Unified School District.

The *Youth in Medicine* program allows at-risk students between the age of 11 to 15 to have an up-close look at human anatomy and clinical skills as part of academic programs at the university. It was created to provide an opportunity for students living in low-income areas to get acquainted with different careers in healthcare and to encourage them to pursue college.

The teens spend part of their day working on their English and math skills, tutored by SMU students. Then the entire group goes to the university's main campus in Oakland to learn about basic vital signs, treating patients, diabetes, anatomy, and healthy living.

The program not only benefits the youth, but also SMU students. One DPM student said that working with the teens and explaining anatomy, podiatry, histology, and operating room situations allowed her to practice communication and teaching skills.

"I like learning from the university students because they don't lecture or make me feel dumb," said 15-year-old Mimi Le. "They help explain things a little easier then in a regular classroom and it's more personal."

Paul, 15, was considering a career in medicine. This was his second time in the *Youth in Medicine* program. "It's great because it gives you a bunch of opportunities and opens a lot of doors."

CHAPTER 3

MENTORING BASICS

There is a process to becoming a mentor, since youth are not only at-risk because of their environment and home life, but also because there are sick predators who prey on innocent children. You can see this almost daily on the news. These monsters are drawn to vulnerable kids just like moths to the light, and mentoring is a way to reach them.

It's the job of those who are the guardians and protectors of children to safeguard them by making sure that anyone who comes in contact with youth has a clear background, with no instances of criminal behavior, especially inflicting physical or sexual abuse.

Some mentoring programs may not realize that it's their duty to vet mentors, but most of them follow certain protocols. They must obey government regulations that protect our children or they risk losing their licenses.

Each mentoring program has its own system for screening volunteers, then training and matching them with their youth clients. Once you've gone through their mentoring process and have been matched with your mentee(s), it's helpful to draw up a "contract" for the relationship. This document (also known as an "MOU" or Memo of Understanding) outlines such details as when and where you and your mentee will meet, and what your goals are (if any).

Don't limit yourself with the MOU so that you're too restricted. However, you could tailor it to your needs. For example, you might list any topics that you prefer not to be discussed, like your personal finances. Your mentee might write that she doesn't want to talk about sex.

Discuss this contract with the Volunteer Coordinator before you present it to your mentee. They may have their own contract that they prefer you use instead.

I've included a template of a Mentor/Mentee Agreement in the Appendix. With this contract (which you can customize), you're able to evaluate your progress and pitfalls on a regular basis. When going over it with your mentee, accentuate the positive. When discussing the negative, use constructive suggestions and ideas, and always end on a positive note.

SEVEN STEPS TO MENTORING

You might already be in a mentoring relationship or have access to a youth that you want to mentor. This could be a friend's child, a neighbor or relative. Perhaps you're a Girl Scout Leader or baseball coach and you currently mentor a group of kids. If not, then here are some basic steps that you will need to take in order to start mentoring. I've already mentioned some of them, but this is a good opportunity to review the information.

1. Determine Your Mentoring Type:

The first step to becoming a mentor is to decide what type of mentor you want to become. Will you be mentoring a group of youth or One-on-One? Will you mentor as part of a team of work associates or family-to-family?

Think long and hard about the commitment you plan to make, since this can impact your mentee(s) as much as you. If you know that your life is stable and you can easily make consistent appointments, then a long-term One-on-One mentoring relationship would be ideal. Your mentee will know that he or she can count on you to be there every week, and that builds trust.

If you can donate your time for at least one year (which is usually the minimal time requirement for One-on-One mentoring, unless it's academic), then this type of relationship will be greatly beneficial. The bond you form with your mentee will hopefully endure for a lifetime, but I have found that even if One-on-One mentoring takes place for less than a year, it still has a powerful effect – *as long as the youth knows before the mentoring starts that your relationship will only last for a specific time period.*

It is very important to establish this "deadline" from the beginning and to remind your mentee of an approaching termination, so they are prepared when it comes to an end. This way they won't take anything personally.

If you travel a lot or your schedule is erratic, then consider a mentoring relationship that is more flexible, such as mentoring kids at a temporary shelter for homeless children or domestic violence victims, since they are in frequent transition.

Lakenya served as the primary life coach or mentor at *F.A.M.I.L.Y. Movement*, an organization that provides educational opportunities to over 150 women in the Boston area. Their workshops focus on a wide range of topics including self-esteem, professionalism, parenting, and financial education.

Lakenya said, "Back in 2000, I was transitioned in a local shelter after traveling from home to home due to my mom's substance abuse and an unstable environment. Recently I decided to visit my old shelter, *Bridge Over Troubled Waters*. Speaking to the moms there about how I was in their shoes once and how now I'm able to aim higher taught me a valuable lesson about how important mentoring is. I now mentor at over five shelters in Boston."

When asked what a typical mentoring session is like, Lakenya responds, "My mentoring sessions consist of parenting, role-playing on relationships, and games on building up character traits and self-esteem. They usually take place on weekday evenings in group sessions at local shelters.

"All participants have my direct contact info in case they need guidance or direction. I even spend time with girls One-on-One and maybe bring them to church with me or to my own mentoring session. Yes, I have a mentor! I need to be empowered as well."

You can make a big impact on these youth, even in a short period of time. You might say a word of encouragement that they will always remember. The next time you volunteer at the shelter, there will probably be some new children that you can help. If you have to miss out on mentoring for a period of time, it won't negatively affect the kids, since they will not have bonded that deeply with you.

If they *have* become attached to you, then just let them know that you're taking a short break and you will see them again when you return.

If your time commitment is short, you can also consider mentoring as part of a project that has a specific goal. This could be coaching a sports team for a brief duration, or working on an arts-based project with one or more kids.

You might decide to help a group of kids organize a special project that everyone works on together to complete. That way if you have to miss a few sessions, there are other team members to move it forward.

Once you determine what type of mentor you will become, then you can take the next step.

2.   **Decide Who You Want to Mentor:**

In Chapter Two, I detailed many different types of high-risk children and youth who are facing great challenges in their lives, such as foster youth, homeless kids, juvenile delinquents, gang members, substance abusers, teen parents and children whose main problem is the lack of a positive adult in their lives.

There are also millions of "at-risk" kids who are relatively "normal," yet they still face challenges, such as coming from a poor family or feeling isolated.

It's important that you know which type of child(ren) you want to mentor, since there are millions of kids who really need support. Does it tug at your heartstrings when you learn about kids who are Autistic or who are suffering from a life-threatening disease? Do you fantasize about helping a youth with a substance abuse problem overcome his addiction because your brother died of an overdose, or you are a recovering addict? Do teenage mothers pop into your thoughts, since you had a child at a young age and know how difficult it was?

The age of the child or group of youth that you want to mentor is also a determining factor. This will ideally be a long-term commitment, so you want to make sure that you're comfortable and enjoying your mentoring relationship(s). Do you love playing with toddlers and younger children? What about hanging around teenagers?

Each age group has its pluses and minuses: younger mentees will require a deeper commitment, but you can see them mature and blossom over a longer period of time. Teens are at a vulnerable moment in their lives, when they are about to become independent.

For youth without much (if any) family support, a mentor can make a huge impact on their lives, which can bolster your good feelings.

If you're stuck about knowing whom you want to mentor, think about what you envisioned in your mind when you first had the goal to become a mentor. What was the age of the mentee that you visualized? Were there any special qualities that she or he possessed?

Follow your instincts and you will choose the perfect mentee(s). The Volunteer Coordinator at a mentoring program can also give you guidance in this area.

3. Initiate a Mentoring Relationship:

Now that you know what type of mentoring you want to do and whom you want to mentor, you can initiate a mentoring relationship. This might take some research, but you have a clear direction in which to move forward in order to start.

By following Step # 2 and discovering *who* it is that you want to mentor, you can narrow your search. If you want to mentor sick children, then contact your local hospital to find out about volunteer opportunities. If it's homeless kids that draw your attention, call the shelters in your community. You'll find these institutions listed in the phone directory or by doing a search online.

When you have identified this information, make the call. Ask the operator to connect you with the Volunteer Coordinator, or the Community Resource Department. Most people are familiar with the term "mentor," so if you mention that you want to volunteer in this capacity, they will probably put you in touch with the person in charge of finding someone just like you.

If the facility, school, mentoring program, community organization, shelter or institution does not respond to your offer to help, please don't give up! It took me a year to make the right connection for my own mentoring program, and some mentors have had to wait for two years or longer for the right match. You won't need to be that patient. If it doesn't work out at one place, simply try another.

You might also consider starting your own mentoring program if none exists in your area, since there are probably other people just like you who would love to help youth. Think of the large numbers of needy kids you could reach by assisting others to also become mentors! This is what inspired me to found **Create Now**.

4.   Visit the Facility or Mentoring Program:

Once you have established contact with the right person at the facility or program of your choice, set a time to meet in person and arrange a tour. Mentoring is a commitment and you want to make sure that this environment will be mutually beneficial.

Write up a list of questions before your meeting. Some examples are: How often am I expected to mentor? Where will the mentoring take place? How do you make your matches? How long am I expected to mentor? Are there any restrictions?

When you visit the place, make sure it's located in a neighborhood that you can easily get to. Is it safe? Will you be comfortable going there every week?

Are the kids the right age and type that you want to help? For instance, if you feel more at ease working with younger children, then don't be coerced into mentoring teens, unless you're willing to change your goals. It's better to make these choices up front than to wait until you're mentoring. If you break off a relationship later, then it could damage the self-esteem and confidence of that youth.

Before you commit to a mentoring relationship, be sure that it is exactly what you want. Find out how to reach the staff person you meet, in case additional questions come to mind.

5.   Application Process:

During this visit, you will likely be given a formal application to complete and return. You'll need to fill out your contact information, details about your education and work background, personal interests, hobbies and references (names and contact information of people you know well).

The staff will reach out to your references to get their feedback on whether you would be a good mentor, so you should let your family, friends and associates know ahead of time that they will probably be contacted.

Fill in the application form as clearly as possible. Include any additional documents requested. For instance, many facilities will require a copy of your driving record, even if you don't plan to drive your mentee(s) anywhere. This document will alert them to a DUI, which might prevent you from mentoring at that facility. Each mentoring program has its own rules about this.

You will be interviewed to make sure that you are a suitable mentor. You'll probably be asked why you desire to mentor. Be honest and answer all the questions as frankly as possible, and don't be afraid to query them, too.

Every mentoring program is different and during this interview, you might be asked what type of youth you want to mentor. Other facilities could wait until you are accepted as a mentor before suggesting potential matches.

Generally, children are matched with mentors of the same gender. However, since there is a shortage of male mentors, some mentoring programs match women with boys who have lost their mothers or who are in need of additional female influence. Those facilities with youth who are gay, lesbian, transgender and bi-sexual may match female mentors with male youth and male mentors with female youth.

Other criteria for mentoring matches will hinge on which youth are most in need, their ages, locations, schedules, hobbies and interests.

6. **Prerequisites:**

Most states require that anyone who works or volunteers with youth must undergo a security clearance, which includes being fingerprinted. There are state and national databases that are used to make sure that all people in contact with children do not have a criminal history, especially as a child abuser.

This research might bring up past activities that took place many years ago, such as substance abuse or petty crimes. During your interview, when the security clearance is mentioned, let the staff know of any infractions or past problems that might come up during the security clearance. The staff might advise you not to waste your time and the money that it takes to pay for this investigation, which can cost anywhere from $10 to $100. Usually, the facility needing volunteers will pay for this process, but they might ask you to cover the expense. Regardless, if you have a questionable history, it's important that you mention it during your initial interview.

Don't despair if you aren't able to pass the security clearance. While one program or facility may not allow you to mentor through them if you fail, there might be other facilities willing to take you on as a mentor.

For instance, a homeless shelter might not care that you had a DUI twenty years ago, as long as you are not going to drive their children anywhere. While a foster group home might not allow you to mentor if you were previously arrested for using drugs, a substance abuse rehabilitation center might relish the fact that you're a former user who has overcome an addiction. You could be a terrific role model for their youth.

No matter what kind of shady past you might have, just be up front and honest about your background right from the beginning. It can prevent a lot of grief later.

I wish that one of our **Create Now** mentors had followed this advice. I met "John" at a large event where people were sharing their dreams. John told everyone that he was an artist with many years of experience. His dream was to be able to teach art to kids. I gave him my **Create Now** card and we met and communicated during a period of several weeks.

John said that he didn't have much money since he earned his living as an artist and business was slow. He didn't want to spend a lot of money using gas to travel anywhere. I found a group home with six teenage foster boys right up the street from his home. It turned out that they had one youth who was a very talented artist and the boy wanted to learn more techniques.

John met with the owner of the group home, who had him fill out an application. The owner introduced him to the boy and they immediately clicked. John gave the youth a lesson in art during their brief meeting. The owner told John that he would need to have the security clearance before he could mentor, and he would have to pay for it himself.

John contacted me and asked if **Create Now** could pay the $50 expense. He told me that he was concerned that he might not pass because years ago, when he broke up with his girlfriend, she got angry and accused him of something minor at their workplace. From his description, it didn't seem like any type of legal situation and no arrest had been made, so I told him that my organization would pay his fee.

It took around two months for the results to come back. John didn't pass his security clearance. There was no reason given, but he finally told me that around 10 years earlier, his ex-wife had argued with him and kept pushing him, so he hit her in the face. As if that wasn't bad enough, he had also thrown a rock at his son! John had been arrested for domestic violence.

I was furious that he wasn't upfront about this situation. He had wasted my time and **Create Now**'s money, but I was especially horrified because John had met this boy and helped him with his artwork, and now the boy would be disappointed to lose his mentor. Luckily, the owner of the group home had never told the youth anything about having John as a potential mentor, so he didn't expect anything more than a one-time art lesson.

The security clearance system is there for a reason. I'm very grateful that they caught someone who had been a batterer, and that this youth was not negatively impacted.

Security clearance can take anywhere from a few days to months. It will depend on the system used and the backlog of applicants. For instance, the "Livescan" process is an electronic system used by many law enforcement agencies in the U.S., as well as a number of mentoring programs. Since it's computerized, the clearance might only take a few hours or days for them to complete it.

However, government agencies that oversee youth institutions, such as juvenile detention facilities, could be affected by budget cuts, which is the case in California. With a lack of employees to verify the applications, the process can take awhile. Just be patient and follow up periodically with the staff person who interviewed you, but don't be a pest.

Many youth facilities require a TB (Tuberculosis) test in order for you to mentor. With this disease now resurging, they might insist that you go to your doctor or a clinic to take an exam, which involves getting a vaccine with a miniscule amount of tuberculin injected under the surface of the skin. It takes 48-72 hours to get the results. There is a lot of information about this test available online. If you're absolutely against having the test, then seek another youth mentoring program that doesn't require it.

7. Acceptance:

You will be officially accepted as a mentor when: (a) Your application has been processed; (b) Your references have been checked; (c) You have passed your security clearance; and (d) You are proven clear of TB.

In all likelihood, you will be called by a staff representative at the youth program, or will receive notification in the mail with a security badge or pass.

Many youth agencies also require an orientation and training sessions, which might be held at your first interview or during a scheduled time. Orientations usually give an overview of the mentoring program and often include a tour of the facility.

Sometimes, the mentoring program might offer additional training and specific advice on how to work with their clients. Don't miss out, since the more knowledge you have, then the better for you and your mentee(s).

If other mentors attend the orientation and training sessions, this is a good chance to network and connect with additional people who are also becoming mentors, for more support.

That's it! Once you complete these seven steps, you will most likely be allowed to mentor at-risk or high-risk youth.

MENTORING MATCHES

If you are going to mentor One-on-One with a youth, you may still be wondering which specific child you will be mentoring.

Every mentoring program has their own unique system for matching mentors with youth. If you didn't discuss potential mentees at your initial interview, the staff might ask you to meet with them again to find your match.

The Volunteer Coordinator probably already knows which kids would benefit the most from having a mentor, and those children will be at the top of their list. Based on the way you have responded in their application and during your interview, they will determine who to pair you with. For instance, you might be a professional computer programmer and they may have a youth who loves computers.

If during the matching process, you find out about a child that needs a mentor, but for some reason, you're just not interested in mentoring him or her, don't feel obligated or pressured to accept that match. Let the staff know that you're not comfortable and would prefer to know of alternative matches. It's important that you do this before you actually meet the child or they will feel hurt and rejected if the truth comes out later.

You might be given the opportunity to select your own mentee. Some mentoring programs arrange a special event, like a carnival or a picnic. They bring busloads of kids and the new mentors get to mix and mingle with all of the children. Some mentors and youth are naturally drawn to each other.

Children Uniting Nations is a Los Angeles organization that screens, trains and matches mentors with foster youth. They hold an annual event called "The Day of the Child," where hundreds of foster children are invited for a day of fun activities, including rides, games, performances and celebrity appearances. Hundreds of mentors are also present. Throughout the day, adults and children have the opportunity to connect in a natural manner.

It can be challenging to pick your mentee if given a choice. How can you discover the best match?

In some respects, finding the right mentee is similar to going to an animal shelter to pick out a new pet. Obviously, this analogy is not to say that finding a youth to mentor is equivalent to rescuing an animal, but in both cases, your gut feelings are an important detector.

Most of the animals at a shelter are precious. However, there is probably one that impacts you in a special way. You know in your heart that this is the pet you're meant to adopt.

Although there is a very big difference between picking a mentee and selecting a pet, both processes tap into your feelings. Allowing your intuition to work could help you to know which youth is the right one for you to mentor. Choosing a mentee is such an important decision, and you would do well to use all of your resources to make the right choice.

Schools and other mentoring programs might have a list of kids who need mentors. They narrow down the search by comparing these mentee candidates with your pre-written preferences.

For instance, you might have said that you want to mentor a girl between the ages of 9-12 years old and your favorite pastime is scrapbooking. They may have four girls in that age range who need mentors, but two are really into sports. One girl loves to go camping and the other enjoys making arts and crafts projects. The logical match would be to have you mentor the girl who enjoys making things, since she would probably enjoy learning about scrapbooking. You would both have more things in common to talk about, so your relationship would get off to a better start.

When you are matched with your mentee, find out about their background, or as much as the Volunteer Coordinator is allowed to tell you. Most of the kids that you will be matched with will be "normal," but there could be a child who has endured horrible abuse. They might have issues that you need to know about, such as self-injury or low self-esteem. Perhaps a parent abandoned them and they are very sensitive when talking about it. You can gain by being compassionate and more aware upfront.

When mentoring troubled kids like this, you can greatly impact their lives. You could be that special person who turns their life around. However, if you know from the minute you're told about the child's background that you'll be uncomfortable with them, or if your gut tells you that there's something about the youth that you just don't like, then it's important to let the Volunteer Coordinator know right away, before you meet the child.

When a Volunteer Coordinator finds a match for you that you are happy with, then your mentoring can begin. If you haven't already met your mentee, then the facilitator will probably arrange a meeting at their location, at the child's home or a neutral place, such as a school, restaurant, bowling alley or a park.

If you are going to mentor a group of youth, then the process is usually easier. The group might already be organized, such as a Girl Scouts troop or a baseball team. They could be members of your local Boys & Girls Club or in the school activities program. Your church, temple or mosque might have a youth-group program that needs mentors.

These kids are already familiar with each other and comfortable at their location. They know the rules and what to expect from the activity that you're going to share. All you need to do is to meet with them regularly to help carry out the activity, get to know the youth and be available to support them.

If you're going to mentor at a place where the kids are not already involved in a particular activity, then you will need to work with the Volunteer Coordinator or other staff to get youth interested in participating. They might already have a bunch of youngsters who would be very interested in your program, or know of individual youth who would greatly benefit.

The staff might ask you to put together a flyer that they will post in a central area or promote in other ways to let the kids know about the opportunity to be mentored by you.

Putting together a flyer to promote your project is easy. Just write the basic information: who, what, where, when and why. It might say something like,

"Come have FUN as you learn how to DRAW and PAINT! Starting March 3rd, join artist Charles Johnson in the Teen Lounge on Tuesday nights from 7:00 to 8:00 PM for this exciting workshop. Sign up with Ms. Smith in the office."

You might include a photograph of you, and a drawing or painting as a sample of what they'll be learning. Print the flyer on colorful paper and it will get the attention of the kids. This type of flyer can be adapted for whatever you're going to teach: sports, writing, cooking, etc.

When you start a group mentoring project, you will probably attract kids that share your interest. They may want to attend based on their own desire to learn more about that topic. They could be encouraged or even forced to be there because of a therapist or social worker's recommendation. Their best friend may be taking your workshop, so they don't want to miss out.

Even if only one or two youth sign up to take your workshop, these are the kids that you're meant to be working with. The numbers will likely change, as some will drop out due to boredom, transportation challenges, family commitments, etc. Don't be discouraged if your mentees disappear, since there will likely be new kids who want to join in as they learn about your program from others.

HOW MUCH TIME MUST I VOLUNTEER?

It's been proven that the more time you put into mentoring, the better the results. This makes perfect sense, because it takes time to build trust with people, which is what develops a relationship. Think of your own life. When you meet someone for the first time, you generally don't rely on them immediately, nor confide your darkest secrets.

When you first mentor a child (unless you know them already), you are a stranger to them. It's going to take time for them to know that they can depend on you to be there when you say you will, and to follow through on all of your promises.

Ideally, mentoring works the best when you meet every week on a regular basis for at least one hour. It's also important that you are consistent with the day and time.

Before Elias became a patrolman with the New Mexico State Police, he was a devoted father — something he tried to pass on to young boys as a mentor with the Taos group *Men Engaged in Nonviolence ("MEN")*.

"This year, I took my mentee to his first varsity football game. He'd never been to a football game!" Montoya said. "They matched him with me because he wants to be a cop. I hope I can help him reach his goals."

MEN Program Director Fritz Hahn remarked, "Some of these kids are so hurt they've shut down. After a while they can develop an abnormal detachment from people. When a mentor shows up on time, every week, regardless of the kid's behavior, they start to learn that they are important and that not all adults are inconsistent."

Your mentee will be counting on you – and probably counting the days and hours until you meet with her again. She will know that every Thursday at 6:30 PM, her mentor Jessica comes to spend time with her. By Monday, she'll be looking on the calendar to see how many more days are left until that meeting. On Thursday morning, she'll be marking the hours until you arrive.

If you're able to meet more frequently, that's even better. And by giving two or three hours of your time, or an entire day, then you'll get to bond even more: the longer you mentor, the better.

A mentoring relationship should endure for a lifetime. It's a special friendship that evolves. Through mentoring, you learn a lot about each other and become like extended family members. You might be a surrogate parent, or an older sibling. You could become buddies, even best friends, as you both grow older.

What a beautiful thing to have someone that you've mentored into adulthood who looks upon you as part of his or her extended family. Wouldn't you feel blessed to have your mentee tell their family and friends that you've been the one person in their life who really made an impact? Couldn't you relish being invited to their wedding or named as the Godfather or Godmother of their child?

I have been mentoring Demond for five years, since he was 16, and also his wife Virgina, They asked me to be the Godmother of their daughter Destinee. I'm so honored and I can't wait to experience the joys of being a Godmother and helping Destinee as she grows up.

However, it's perfectly fine if you want to mentor for a shorter period of time. Even just one meeting with a needy child can trigger a transformational impact.

Most One-on-One mentoring programs require a minimum of a one-year commitment. When that year is complete, it's up to the mentor and mentee on whether they should continue meeting. This issue may never come up for discussion if the relationship is going well, but if there is a review at the end of the year, then you'll need to decide if you want to keep going. I hope that you will!

You may decide that once the time you have committed to mentoring is completed, you can't meet on a regular basis any longer. In Chapter Ten, I discuss how to end your mentoring relationship, but I urge you to stay in contact with your mentee even if you don't continue to meet. By calling him or her every now and then, plus giving them your email address or phone number, that lets your mentee know that you still care about them and they can turn to you in the future if they need some help.

SHORT-TERM MENTORING

Some mentors can't commit to a weekly schedule, or for an entire year. They may only be able to mentor every other week or once a month. That's okay. You may not have quite as profound a relationship as those mentors who meet more often with their mentees, but you can still have a solid connection and you will do a lot of good. I think it's better to give something than nothing at all!

I have found that as long as the mentee knows well in advance (and is occasionally reminded) about what to expect in terms of your time commitment, then they are usually not disappointed or let down by irregular visits.

If he knows that his mentor Rick travels for his job and can only meet with him every once in a while, than he will understand that his mentor can't make it to his soccer match on Saturday. However, if Rick calls his mentee after the soccer match to hear about the game, this phone contact can have the same benefits of him being there.

High-risk youth are usually in-and-out of group homes, detention camps, homeless shelters and the streets. A challenge that some mentors must deal with is that their mentees might be transferred, released or have gone AWOL from their youth placement agencies. Just as the mentor begins to connect with a youth and feels like he or she is making progress, they're gone.

One way to remedy this situation is to quickly give your contact information to a youth that you bond with. Write down your email address, cell phone or voice mail number. If they disappear, at least you know that they'll be able to reach you if they want.

Since you might only have one or two meetings, it's important that you make them worthwhile. Don't waste your time watching TV or playing videogames when you could be introducing your mentee to the wonders of your community. Take him on a hike in the park, which might be the first time that he's experienced the great outdoors. Invite her to visit your college campus.

Every association is unique and a mentor might be able to bond deeply with a child in just a short period of time. You might say something encouraging or share an experience that plants a seed in the child's fertile mind. It could sprout into the dream of going to college, or traveling to distant places they had never even heard of before.

The rules for short-term mentoring are the same as long-term:

(1) You must honor your commitment;

(2) Let your mentee know when and how long you will be mentoring; and

(3) Give closure when it's over.

It's easy to maintain contact with your mentees, especially in this technology-driven age. You can talk on the phone, send emails, text message each other and snail mail to fill in the times when you can't physically be together.

PROPER BEHAVIOR

Mentoring involves common sense. You are a role model for your mentee(s) so you need to act mature. It's okay to be silly or goofy to have fun, but no matter what your age, you should always act like an adult with your mentee.

Children need guidance and discipline to mature and to assimilate into society. They must have someone responsible in their lives to teach them right from wrong.

Unfortunately, many at-risk and high-risk youth lack positive adult role models in their lives. More than 25 million children in the U.S. don't have a father living at home. Single mothers struggle to raise their kids. Even with both parents in the house, many mothers and fathers must often hold two or three jobs to pay the bills, so an adult is rarely around.

Drug and alcohol addiction is rampant in our country, which leaves many children without parents, and 2 million kids have at least one parent in prison. Millions of youngsters must fend for themselves with little, if any, adult supervision, including those from wealthy homes whose parents work a lot or travel frequently. In disadvantaged families, children as young as seven or eight years old often end up being the guardian of their younger siblings.

Many well-meaning parents just don't know how to do their job. They may spoil their kids, or turn the other way when their son or daughter misbehaves because they don't know how to discipline them correctly. Parents might also react to their children's poor behavior by being too strict and unfair with punishment, which can anger and alienate their child, so they rebel in a worse manner.

Parenting is an art that requires particular skills, but *a mentor is not a parent*. You are not there to discipline and chastise your mentee, but rather to be a guide and a role model.

A mentor is the voice of reason. You are the one person that the youth can look up to in order to learn what's acceptable in society and what is not. You are the person that can inspire them to complete their education and follow their dreams to build a career.

Your behavior is going to be observed in subtle ways. Most kids are very attentive. They're like sponges and they pick up on things quickly. Many youth can tell when you're being false or if you're fearful and anxious. This sharpened sense is especially acute with street kids, since it's essential for their survival skills. They can develop animal-like instincts that give them an instant evaluation of who you are and what you're like as a person.

As your relationship develops, your mentee will be silently observing how you behave in different situations. When you drive, do you get angry and scream at the other drivers? Is your tone of voice warm when you meet a new person or do you act a little distant?

Here are some things to be aware of with your behavior:

A. Don't be intimidated or self-conscious. It's important that you be true to yourself and not pretend to be someone that you're not. Be glad that you have something special to offer. Your mentee(s) will sense that and feel more respect for you.

B. How do you shake hands when greeting someone? Handshakes are an important form of communication and it varies greatly within sub-cultures. Most youth today share unique handshakes that include various ways of bumping their fists. This could be a fun icebreaker when you meet your mentee(s). Shake their hand in a professional manner, and then find out if he or she has a special handshake that's used amongst friends. They'll enjoy teaching you.

C. If you indulge in what are considered to be negative behaviors, then it's important that you follow certain parameters. For instance, if you smoke cigarettes, then don't smoke in front of your mentee. Ask to be excused and go outside. He or she will probably know that you're smoking and you should be honest if they ask. But you can also let them know that it's a terrible habit that can lead to death and you hope they won't follow in your footsteps.

D. Let them know about the negative effects of smoking (lung cancer, emphysema, lingering smell, costly, etc.) and that you are trying to quit, but you're human and it's difficult to stop. Seeing how you're challenged with trying to quit may encourage them to not start smoking.

E. If your mentee also smokes, maybe you can both make a pact to quit together and have a contest to see who can stop smoking cigarettes the longest. Hopefully you will both win.

F. If you like to drink alcohol, then don't do it in front of your mentee. They will want to mimic you and unless they're legally allowed to drink, you don't want them imbibing alcohol. Wait until you get home to drink. If you had some alcohol before meeting with your mentee, be sure to clean your breath so they don't smell it. You obviously don't want to be with them if you're intoxicated! If that happens, either call or have someone else call your mentee to reschedule your meeting.

G. Don't ever purchase alcohol or cigarettes for your mentee, even if they beg you to or you want to be "cool." Not only would you be a terrible role model, you could be arrested for buying illegal substances for a minor.

H. It's also important that you don't take your mentee to an R-rated movie, or rent an R-rated DVD or videogame, without first getting parental permission. With younger kids, ask first about PG and PG13-rated content.

I. Don't feed your mentee foods such as candy, caffeinated drinks or foods that commonly cause allergies (like peanuts) without first checking with his or her parents. They may be diabetic or could be negatively impacted by them.

J. Don't impose your personal habits on your mentees. It's important that you're aware of whether or not your routines and habits are excessive. If your family and friends tease you about your idiosyncrasies, then it's a safe bet that you might be somewhat compulsive. If so, don't pass that on to your mentee.

We have a volunteer through **Create Now** who mentors a 10-year-old homeless girl. This mentor is very successful in her career. She loves mentoring and regularly takes her mentee on outings, like bowling or hiking.

I joined them at one of their bowling games where they had a wonderful time. Afterwards, in the restroom, the mentor asked the girl, "What did I tell you about washing your hands?" The child automatically recited, "I have to put soap on my hands and then rub them while I count slowly to 30. Then I wash the soap off and I do that two more times. 1… 2… 3…"

I was horrified as the child counted slowly to 30, then washed the soap off and repeated this long ritual two more times. I immediately called the Volunteer Coordinator at the homeless shelter where the girl resided. I told her that I was sorry because it seemed that our mentor was dealing with an Obsessive-Compulsive Disorder (OCD) and that she was inflicting it on this poor child.

The Volunteer Coordinator laughed. She said that some of the families at their shelter had very poor hygiene and that occasionally the caseworkers even had to vomit when visiting their rooms. She thought that the mentor was compensating for this by giving her such a lengthy process to stay clean.

I personally think that the mentor has some serious issues and that she should not be enforcing these beliefs on an innocent child.

If you have been told that you are OCD or neurotic about certain things by your family and friends, *please* don't inflict your neuroses on your mentees. They have tender young minds and are vulnerable, so you don't want to give them even more challenges in life.

This includes following certain health regimes. If you run five miles daily, it's not fair to enforce this practice on your mentee. It's okay to encourage exercise and a healthy lifestyle, but don't nag or try to control them.

Maintain proper physical and emotional boundaries until your mentoring relationship develops. It's important that children (especially younger ones) learn to be wary of strangers. At your initial meeting, you will probably be a stranger to your mentee. Therefore, you don't want to give them a warm hug or kiss right away, unless they initiate it. If your mentee reaches out to hug you, then by all means do hug them back.

A handshake is a great way to reach out and touch your mentee without crossing any boundaries. It teaches proper etiquette and can be very expressive. Later, as you get to know each other better, your greetings can become warmer.

When mentoring children that are victims of physical, sexual and emotional abuse and neglect, you need to show even more reserve when you first meet. It's best that you don't hug or touch the child until a great deal of trust has been established. Again, if the youngster initiates the move to embrace you, then by all means respond, but do so in an appropriate manner.

I met Julia at a group home for teenagers dealing with mental health challenges called *Project Six*, in Van Nuys, CA. Our mentor Talyn was teaching an arts and crafts workshop. Julia was around 16 years old, and she approached Talyn while sobbing in hysterics. She was going to be leaving the group home the next day to live with her mother because her treatment at the facility was completed.

This change was traumatic for the girl, since she had bonded deeply with another young lady there, as well as other kids and staff, and she didn't want to leave her friends.

She asked Talyn if she could have a hug and Talyn embraced the girl. A little later, Julia was still very depressed. My heart went out to her. I gently touched the top of her arm to try to comfort her. She suddenly screamed at the top of her lungs, "Don't touch me! Don't touch me!"

Immediately, I backed away and apologized. I felt terrible for having upset Julia even more. I should have known that all the youth at this facility were living in the group home because of emotional and behavioral challenges, some due to abuse and neglect. I had overstepped my boundaries.

After Julia calmed down and left, I related the incident to Talyn. She told me that the girl always acted that way with her and even with other staff and kids. Yet she would often approach Talyn to ask for a hug, which her mentor gladly gave her.

Another form of behavior that you must always keep in check is advocating your religious and political values, as well as your beliefs about hot-button issues like abortion and homosexuality. It's okay to share your views and feelings about these topics *within limits* during a normal conversation. You can express yourself briefly, but don't go on and on about your personal beliefs, and certainly don't force them on your mentee!

In return, it's very important that you also listen to your mentee's point of view. Create a balanced dialogue. Her or his attitudes toward religion, politics and other issues may differ greatly from yours, but it's not up to you to convert them to your way of thinking.

If you raise controversial matters and find resistance from your mentee, then quickly change the subject. If you don't, then you may lose their respect. This could even destroy your relationship.

WHAT SHOULD I WEAR?

It's important that you dress comfortably, yet professionally. As a role model, you want to leave a good impression. However, you don't need to get "dressed up" to do so. Wear comfortable clothes that look "normal." Follow the style worn by the majority of people in your community, particularly of your age group. Don't try to imitate the kids' clothing styles by wearing garments that are popular with a younger generation. The key word is "comfort," both physically and emotionally.

Avoid torn jeans and clothing with holes or stains. However, if you're working on messy arts projects like painting or sculpting, then do wear those old clothes because you don't want to ruin your good ones. I've lost some of my favorite shirts to **Create Now** arts workshops because they got stained.

Wearing T-shirts with negative icons (like a marijuana leaf, sexual or violent images) will obviously send a bad message. If you have sports shoes or sneakers, make sure they don't look dirty or sloppy.

Ladies, try not to overdo it with your make-up. Be careful not to wear seductive clothing, such as low-cut tops and jeans or short-shorts, bare-midriff shirts, tight mini-skirts and stiletto heels. These are not the images that we want to project to easily influenced youth.

Some facilities, like detention camps, will prohibit you from entering if you wear provocative clothing, or any open-toed shoes and sandals.

Create Now had a mentor who didn't wear proper attire. "Linda" was a very successful businesswoman who worked as the vice-president of a small corporation. She was also a single mother with two teenage children. She taught an arts and crafts workshop at *Children of the Night*, a shelter in Los Angeles for teenage prostitutes.

Linda wore a very low-cut top to her workshop and she was well-endowed. While nothing happened during her program, I sensed that the staff at this facility wasn't thrilled with her clothing, since they were working hard to change these young ladies' self-images. They were helping them to not prostitute any longer, so they weren't pleased that a mentor wore clothes that were promiscuous.

This isn't to say that you should be prudish or conservative in the way that you dress while you're mentoring. Just remember that the clothes you wear will reflect many things and leave a lasting impression on your mentee(s), so be aware of how you look.

Use common sense when dressing to mentor. Think about how you will appear to your mentees, through their eyes.

If you are mentoring in a neighborhood that feels risky or dangerous in any way, then don't bring expensive jewelry, purses and other accessories. Ladies, leave your heels at home, unless you want to use one as a weapon. You need to think of safety in regards to your clothing.

CHAPTER FOUR

What Can I Expect?

Mentoring is a scary prospect. You're committing to meet on a regular basis with a total stranger, the goal being to help them to enhance their life. That's a pretty tall order! Also, you probably don't know much about your mentee before you meet, so it can be nerve-wracking.

You'll probably wonder what he's into: videogames, sports or math? Is she going to like you or think that you're boring? Will you make a fool of yourself in front of a whole group of youngsters while trying to mentor them?

These feelings of anxiety are perfectly normal. You're embarking on a new adventure that can impact others' lives, since not only will mentoring influence your mentee, but it will also ripple down to the rest of his family, friends and neighbors. Not only will your mentee learn how to sew, cook, draw or improve her grades through mentoring, but she may remember things that you casually said to her for many years to come.

DIVERSITY

Your mentees will probably differ from you in regards to age, their ethnic/religious background and their socioeconomic status. Don't be afraid of diversity. As you get to know your mentee, then his or her "differences" will no longer be apparent. Besides, part of the excitement of mentoring is that you can learn more about someone whose life is dissimilar from yours.

Diversity is a two-way street. To your mentee, you also represent someone from a very different world.

My first mentoring experience was at *Optimist Youth Home*, where I taught my Screenwriting workshop. As mentioned, this is a detention facility for teenage boys who are locked up for a variety of crimes.

One young man named "George" was a talented writer and he wanted my guidance. He was African American, from Oakland in Northern California. I would often chat with him during our dinner breaks or after the workshop. He seemed to be at ease during our talks.

Wanda Patterson, an African American artist, helped me get my program started at *Optimist*. One day she took me aside. George had told her that whenever he spoke with me, he would tremble from nervousness because he had never met a white person before.

It's natural to feel some anxiety when you mix with people from different worlds. You might worry that you'll say the wrong thing and offend someone. Perhaps you're concerned that they might do you some harm.

Be aware that these youth are equally nervous, since most of them have never been to your community either. I've met kids who have no problem committing a robbery, yet they're terrified to go into "mainstream society," since they feel so out of place. They sense that many people are scared that they'll rob or hurt them. They worry that everyone will ridicule them for the way that they dress.

At the same time, they're also curious to learn more about you, to share your culture and interests. Young people are inquisitive. Answer their queries with candor and patience. Use questions and answers as a means to build trust. If a child asks you something that is too personal, just let them know in a kind manner that some things are private and better left unsaid, and that you will show them equal respect. They will appreciate your honesty.

Be understanding and nonjudgmental. Don't be critical. Show compassion and empathy for your mentee's situation and learn to appreciate what makes you both different.

FIRST MEETINGS

Initial meetings can be a little frightening, just like when you meet anyone new in your life. They can also be exciting, stimulating and extremely rewarding. You could feel an instant connection with your mentee, but it's more likely that your relationship will need to evolve. It takes time to get to know someone and to build trust.

In your first meeting, you want to learn about your mentee(s) and vice versa. On the other hand, you can't force friendship. It's best to be open about yourself and share as much as you can personally. This will encourage your mentee to also open up.

Your mentee may initially be unresponsive. Many youth are accustomed to disappointment when dealing with adults. As a result, they may not seem enthusiastic upon meeting you. It will probably take some time to develop trust, so please be patient.

When kids meet you for the first time, they might feel as nervous and intimidated as you do. They could wonder if you're really some authority figure that they need to be wary of, like a social worker, teacher or a probation officer, perhaps working undercover.

They might be curious about how much money you earn and also your personal life. They could hope that you'll help them out with a job or money. They might wonder if you'll lie to them or hurt them, like so many other adults have done throughout their young lives.

Your mentee may be shy. New people could intimidate her. He might wonder what to say to you, or be concerned that you won't find him interesting.

To initiate a conversation, it's all right to ask simple questions like, "How many brothers and sisters do you have?" and "What's your favorite TV show?" These questions are icebreakers, but they can also lead you to a dead end. Try not to engage your mentee with inquiries that require just one-syllable responses or that's all you will get back.

For instance, you might ask, "What's your favorite sport?" When they respond, then inquire, "What do you like about it?"

If you ask, "Do you like basketball?" then he will probably just respond "Yeah." That's pretty abrupt and not very conducive to a good conversation, but by following it with, "Did you see that crazy rimshot Kobe made in the fourth quarter?" you'll probably get a very enthusiastic and detailed answer that will give you more fuel for your conversation, and you'll instantly form a bond.

If possible, find out about your mentee before your initial get-together. Learn what their hobbies and favorite activities are so that you can share your mutual passion when you first meet. Chances are that you have been matched with this child or group of kids because of your common interests, so that's the first place to start.

One idea is to bring a survey for them to fill out, which you also have the option to complete at the same time if you want to make it reciprocal. I've provided a sample in the Appendix that you can customize for your needs. This questionnaire will help you to collect more information about your mentee, like their favorite color, food, sports, movies, etc.

Be sure to include a space for their birthday. You might be the only person to remember their birthday when it comes, which can have a tremendous impact on a young life.

With this background knowledge, you will be able to focus your activities toward doing things that your mentee enjoys, while also exposing them to new experiences.

Remain patiently committed. In some instances, it could be months, perhaps even a year or more before your mentee fully opens up. By repeatedly showing your commitment, you'll gain his or her confidence.

Charlie's experience of being a mentor to Justin was tough, but at the same time exciting. They met through *Friends of the Children* in Portland, OR.

Justin was an exceptionally bright child but felt the need to have a "bad" attitude. He honestly believed that he was a bad child.

The first month of mentoring Justin was difficult. When Charlie visited in class, he was not acknowledged. When Charlie picked Justin up at home he did not want to go, and when they did go out, all Justin wanted was to get something to eat and go home.

Justin's walls were strong and Charlie was sensitive to the fact that there was a trust issue. Everyone who had dealt with Justin had given up on him and literally left him alone. He was expecting Charlie to do this too.

> After the first month, however, Justin opened up. He told Charlie that he wanted to go bowling, paint and walk dogs. Justin finally began to trust his mentor after they spent more time together.

Ask questions to give your mentee every opportunity to communicate, but be careful not to pry. Also, don't force discussions about personal issues.

This also works in reverse. It's important for you to set boundaries right from the start. Let your mentee know that you won't talk about certain personal matters, if that's the case. You might say that you'll be open with them about everything, but you don't want to talk about _____.

Let them know if they can phone you and how late to call, or any other issues that are important to you. It's essential that you detail this information right up front. You must set your boundaries.

It's important to be yourself. You don't need to learn your mentee's "language." However, let them know that you're there to offer assistance as a friend. Ask questions about family traditions. Find out about their religious beliefs and share your background and feelings, too.

Most kids will open up pretty quickly and you'll soon have a new friend. However, if your initial meetings become uncomfortable and you feel like there's a block, ask a staff member, teacher, parent or someone else close to the youth for support. You may not be aware of some extenuating circumstance that's causing your mentee's reaction.

APPOINTMENTS

After the initial meeting, it's essential to maintain your commitment. Prove that you're dependable. Take the time to meet with your mentee every week or whenever you're scheduled to get together. They're going to be looking forward to it and probably even counting the hours until you get there.

Don't make promises that you can't keep, especially when it comes to appointments. For instance, if your mentee asks you to attend their high school graduation ceremony and you don't think you can make it since you have an important meeting scheduled that day, don't say that you'll try to be there. Your mentee will assume that means "Yes, you'll be there."

It would be better in this situation to apologize and let them know that you have a conflict and you're really sorry that you can't attend. Then if you are able to make it after all, it will be a very happy surprise, rather than a big disappointment.

Try your very best not to break appointments unless it is absolutely essential. If you have to cancel, then be sure to let your mentee(s) know as soon as possible that you can't make it. If possible, give the date and time when you'll return.

If you don't speak with your mentees directly, they may not get the message, even if the staff, teacher or parent says they'll pass it on. At your next meeting, be sure to mention that you felt bad you had to postpone and you tried your best to reach them to let them know.

I can't stress enough how important it is to be dependable when mentoring. These kids look forward to your visits and they are devastated when you miss a meeting. Many of them have been abandoned by their families and when you let them down -- even once -- it can bring back those painful emotions of being let down by someone else they trusted.

Many of these children's stories are heartbreaking. One 14-year-old teenager who participated in our program was even left on the side of the freeway and told by his parents that he was on his own.

If you constantly change the time and date of your meetings or miss appointments, your mentee(s) will feel that you don't value them. This is also why it's important to maintain consistency with the same date and time of your get-togethers. They appreciate that you've set aside a special time in your schedule just to be with them.

One of the mentors in our program had been meeting regularly with his mentee. He suddenly became ill and went to the hospital. Even though his illness wasn't that serious and he was able to communicate by phone or to send a message to the youth through **Create Now**, the mentor never bothered to call his mentee again.

The young man was disappointed. The boy ended up misbehaving and was sent to Juvenile Hall to serve time at a detention facility and the mentor never contacted him again.

If you're conscious and able to communicate, then please call your mentee, or ask a relative or a friend to make the call for you if you can't make it to your appointment.

Let's look at this from the other side of the fence. You're taking time out of your busy schedule to meet with your mentee(s). You prepare your afternoon activities, drive over to the meeting place and then discover that your mentee isn't there. He forgot that he was meeting you and went to the movies with his friends. Or she suddenly got a toothache and went to the dentist, but forgot to let you know. Or the detention camp is on lockdown because of a fight that took place earlier, so all of the activities are canceled, but nobody called to notify you.

A lot of things can come up, especially when working within an institution, shelter, school or other youth facility. Because of the different schedules of teachers, parents, administrative staff, Volunteer Coordinators and everyone else working directly with the kids, you may be the last person they think of to inform about a change that occurs.

I encourage you to always call before you leave to meet with your mentee(s), particularly if they're in an institutional environment where sudden cancellations can take place. If possible, get the name of a supervisor, therapist, school official or recreational coordinator who is reliable and always knows the status of the kids. It's good to develop a relationship with this staff member, because they can make your time there easier. This is especially true when mentoring troubled youth.

If you're working one-on-one with a youth, you might want to set up a system with your mentee so that he learns responsibility and how to keep to a schedule. This is especially helpful if you find that he's missing some of your appointments. Give him a calendar and ask him to call you the night before you're scheduled to meet in order to confirm the meeting. Or you can have her send you an email a few days before to verify that you're getting together.

The most important thing is for you to be dependable when keeping appointments with your mentee(s). You can do far more damage than good if you're not a reliable mentor.

SOCIAL SKILLS

Many at-risk and high-risk youth have not had any social skills taught to them. They may have grown up in a home where they were totally neglected and left to fend for themselves, or been continually moved from different foster families to group homes to detention camps. Perhaps they've been homeless and don't know proper hygiene. Maybe their parents never taught them manners. As a result, they could have a hard time fitting in with mainstream society.

As a mentor, you can help to bridge this gap. You could be the one to gently teach them how to say "Please" and "Thank you," since these simple words are so essential in our communication. You might be the one friend who can teach them how to brush their teeth, or to act properly at a public event, such as the theater.

The way you go about this can determine the child's receptivity to your guidance. If you sound too demanding or forceful, they will probably rebel and shut you out. Try to make your comments more of a suggestion, and be their role model. Act the way you want them to act and they will subconsciously mimic you.

For instance, if you're at a restaurant and your mentee is wolfing down the food, instead of saying, "Katie, don't eat like a pig. And you're holding the fork like it's a shovel," try softening the advice by making it more positive. "Katie, I know you're hungry, but you might want to slow down a little. And if you hold your fork the way I'm doing, you'll find that you can control it better and it looks more elegant."

Social etiquette is very important for people to succeed in our world, and as a mentor, you can teach your mentee(s) how to use these silent rules to progress in life. As another example, you could spend time helping them to create a thank you card for the college representative who gave them a tour of their campus.

You could invite them to the theater for a cultural experience and demonstrate the proper way to dress and behave in this environment. There are countless ways that you can effectively give your mentee(s) guidance on how to fit into society, and these tips will make a big impact on their lives.

LIFE SKILLS

Most at-risk and high-risk youth also lack basic life skills, such as how to open a bank account, cook, balance a checkbook, rent an apartment or apply for college.

Some high-risk and at-risk youth have never even met anyone with a real job before. Their families, friends and neighbors may survive on welfare or through illegal activities. Inviting your mentee to spend time with you at your job can be a powerful experience that helps guide their future.

English is a second language for Monica, who was born in Mexico. Therefore, reading was once one of her more difficult subjects, but with her mentor Lynn's help, she now reads and speaks with ease.

Monica and Lynn met through *TeamMates* mentoring program in Grand Island, Nebraska. Lynn learned that Monica had a career interest in becoming a dental assistant. She arranged a job shadow opportunity for her mentee to observe at a dental office and ask questions about the profession.

Lynn says of her relationship with Monica, "During our five-and-a-half years as friends and *TeamMates*, we shared the ups and downs of life. We acted as true and dedicated teammates would. When one struggled, the other was there with strength and insight to back them up. We developed a friendship that will carry us far into the future."

Monica agrees, "I remember laughing together, but also crying on her shoulder. I trusted my mentor and opened my heart to her. She won my respect and a special place in my heart."

"Monica's graduation day was one of the happiest days of my life," said Lynn. "We are so proud that she is the first person in her family to graduate from high school. She has a new goal now. She is studying at Central Community College to become a dental assistant."

Many youth have no idea about how to prepare a resume or to go on a job interview. As a result, many of them, particularly foster kids who are "aging out" of the system, will end up permanently homeless, in prison or on welfare if we don't do something to help them.

When I was growing up, I depended on my parents to teach me these things. They gave me every opportunity possible to attend college and to have all of my needs taken care of by them. However, most of these at-risk youth are not as fortunate.

As a mentor, you can guide your mentee(s) to fend for themselves and to become independent. They might think that higher education is just like high school, and so they may not be interested in attending college. Take them to visit local campuses to give them a taste of college life. By experiencing universities or community colleges first-hand, it could change their negative ideas and put them on track for a college degree. With your help, they can learn how to find the right college, research potential scholarships and complete the applications.

You can also assist your mentee to develop a resume. There are many online resources for this type of help. Once they have their resume, give them tips on how to look for a job. Show them the classified ads, employment agencies and online resources for finding employment. Help them dress properly for a job interview. Maybe you can go through their wardrobe with them to find the right outfit, or visit a thrift store to buy something inexpensive that they can wear.

Then hold a mock interview where you're the employer and they're interviewed for a job. If you're working with a group of kids, it's a fun exercise for everyone to take turns doing. Afterwards, give constructive criticism and try it again.

You could also switch roles so that your mentee pretends to be the employer. That way he/she can see how you would respond to the employer's questions, as well as gain some appreciation for being in charge of hiring. As your mentee becomes more comfortable in these employment role-playing games, it will be much easier for them to go on actual job interviews.

Money issues are hard for most people, let alone kids who have never had much (if any) money. You can help them to learn money management in a variety of ways. One is to assist them to set up a budget that they can easily follow.

Another technique is to use money-related games like "Monopoly" or "The Game of Life." By playing these games, kids have a chance to invest money in different properties, learn about student loans and purchasing stocks without actually risking a penny, while having fun in the process.

A great resource management tool is the series of city or civilization building games, like the SIMS.

Another idea is to give your mentee empty jars for saving their money. As an example, one jar could be for a computer they want to buy. Another could hold money for entertainment. A third jar could be allocated for charitable donations and a fourth could be for another of their goals, or to buy gifts. You can help your mentee decide what's important for them to save for. Then whenever they get money, it can be divided and put into their various money jars.

There are many other topics that youth need to learn in order to navigate through life. Finding a place to live can be very challenging for older kids. It's something that should be taught at an early age so they know what to expect. Learning about healthy eating and how to prepare food is also essential.

It's important that you listen to what your mentees say about what they want to learn. Perhaps his dream is to be an auto mechanic, but he doesn't know where to get that training. You could help him to research vocational schools, or give advice on how he might be able to find an apprenticeship with a local mechanic.

Maybe she's thinking that nursing would be a good career, but she doesn't know exactly what she wants to do. You might arrange for her to visit a hospital where she can decide if she's comfortable in that environment. Direct her on where to find out more about nursing, as well as other jobs in the healthcare industry.

Think about your own life and what areas you felt that you needed help with in order to make it on your own. You probably had the support of your loved ones, and now, as a mentor, you are the loved one who will hopefully provide support to your mentee when it is needed.

FAMILY MATTERS

Yes, family *does* matter. Your mentee is probably going to have at least one parent or a guardian who is in charge of his or her welfare. This could be birth parents, foster parents, adoptive parents or others.

Most parents are very protective, so giving a total stranger access to their child might be a challenge. They could worry that you're a predator, out to abuse or kidnap their loved one. Perhaps they're concerned that you're not responsible and their kid could be harmed in an accident. Just put yourself in their shoes and imagine what it would be like to send your beloved child off with someone you just met, hoping that it will work out.

To alleviate these fears, I recommend that you plan a private get-together with the family member(s) before you start mentoring, even if you've had a formal meeting through the mentoring program, school or other group that has brought you together. Of course, if you have been matched through a third-party, be sure to check with them and find out if you are allowed to arrange a private meeting with your mentee's family.

If so, I would suggest that you contact the parent(s) and suggest that it could be beneficial to meet so you can get to know each other and thereby better serve their child. Tell them that you'd like to learn of any special issues you should be aware of, like food allergies or schedules, and you just want to have an opportunity to learn more about your mentee, since it's such a precious relationship and you want it to be as beneficial as possible.

Ask if you can stop by their home at a convenient time when your mentee is at school or another activity. This will give everyone the chance to speak openly. You might bring a small gift, like flowers or something to eat, such as pastries. Another idea is to invite the parent(s) to meet at a restaurant for a meal, or at a café.

The point is to be in a relaxed environment where you can get to know each other. Be yourself and share your story: your background, what kind of work you do, hobbies, special relationships, etc. They're giving you permission to take their child into your world, so it's only fair to paint them a portrait of how you live. Don't go into details or get too personal. You just want to get to know each other so that you're more familiar and comfortable.

You should also be asking your mentee's parents different questions. The more you learn about them, then the brighter the light will shine on your mentee, since it will help you tremendously to have more knowledge of their family history.

Don't pry, and be very sensitive. If they hesitate to respond to a question that you pose, then quickly change the subject so there's no concern that you're a snoop.

Another fear that can arise is when a parent might worry that their child will favor you over them. The green-eyed monster of jealousy could rear its ugly head. This is a natural tendency, especially if the child has been matched with a mentor because there's tension at home and another adult is needed to provide balance.

You don't want to get into a fight for control. This is why I think it's important to meet the parents when your mentee is not around, so that you can assure them of your good intentions. If they understand right from the beginning that they are still the boss and you're not going to take away their power, then they can relax and appreciate you more. Let them know that you'll follow any rules they might have, such as meeting a curfew or providing only food that is permissible. You can also check with them before arranging activities.

I recommend that you don't become so close to the parent(s) that they start to confide in you about their problems and ask for your advice like a close friend, unless you feel qualified or willing to respond. You're really not there to help them -- just their child -- and if the parent doesn't like something that you say, it might reflect on the relationship with your mentee.

Also, unless it's the love of a lifetime, don't get involved romantically with your mentee's parent. If it doesn't work out, it could destroy your mentoring relationship with their child.

If you're in a One-on-One Mentoring relationship, be careful not to let the parents impose on you. They might want you to mentor their other children, but you are not responsible for your mentee's siblings. That doesn't mean that you can't invite them to join you every now and then, but make it clear that your primary purpose is to mentor their one child.

Carl volunteered with Chicago's *Cabrini Connections* for many years. His mentee Roman was a 9th grader. While their relationship started with an academic focus, it evolved into mentoring. They saw each other often outside of their tutoring sessions.

> Carl also made an effort to reach out to Roman's family, with whom he talked at least once a week, just to see how things were going. His relationship with Roman's family began a few years previously when Carl chaperoned a trip to Ireland with the boy's older sister, Tatianna, who was also a student at *Cabrini Connections*. While Carl was close with the whole family, his special relationship was with Roman.

If you find that your mentee's parent(s) or guardian(s) become overbearing and demanding, then talk to an intermediary who can resolve the problem. This would ideally be the Volunteer Coordinator. In case there is no coordinator, then ask a neutral person to mediate on behalf of your mentee. This might be a teacher, neighbor or mutual friend.

Another challenge that can come up with parents is when they use the time you spend with your mentee as punishment. In frustration, they might say, "If you don't clean your room, then you can forget about going out with your mentor!" Not only does this penalize you, as well as your mentee, but having you there as a positive influence to encourage your mentee to clean his room might be exactly what motivates him to do it.

If this type of threat is used, I would suggest contacting the parent as soon as possible when your mentee is not there. Tell them how difficult it is for you to do your job as a mentor when they use your relationship as a weapon. Not only does it break down the connection that you have built with their child, but it also means less time spent with your mentee when you could be providing positive reinforcement of the parents' values.

Your time is precious since you plan your schedule around mentoring and it's disappointing to have things changed at the last minute. The parents need to have consideration for you, too.

If a parent "grounds" their child from going out after school, then ask if you can still arrange to meet with your mentee at their home or school, so that there is more consistency and support for their child.

Finally, when speaking with your mentee's parent(s), don't let things that your mentee told you in confidence slip out. Even if she didn't specifically say, "Don't tell my mother this," you must be very careful not to reveal anything that was said to you in confidence. It may seem small and meaningless, but sharing this information with a parent (or anyone else) could upset your mentee to the point where the trust you have built is totally destroyed.

BULLYING

The 2009 National Youth Risk Behavior Survey found that about 1 in every 5 teens had been bullied at school in the last year. The government's "Find Youth Info" web site also reports some bullying statistics:[5]

Bullying is most common among middle school children, where almost half of students may be bully victims. Between 15 and 25 percent of students overall are frequent victims of bullying, and 15 to 20 percent of students bully others often;

About 20 percent of students experience physical bullying at some point in their lives, while almost a third experience some type of bullying;

Females may be the victims of bullying more often than males; males are more likely to experience physical or verbal bullying, while females are more likely to experience social or emotional bullying.

The Cyber Bullying Research Center's[6] statistics on bullying from 2009 show that between 20 and 25 percent of students have been the victims of cyber bullying, with about the same number acting as perpetrators.

Bullying takes place in communities around the world. There are three types: physical abuse (hitting, kicking, pushing, choking, punching), verbal abuse (threatening, taunting, teasing, hate speech) and psychological or social abuse (isolation, exclusion from activities, spreading lies and rumors).

These vicious acts of aggression can take place anywhere, such as schools, churches, neighborhood streets and on the Internet. Bullies attack at all hours of the day and night, alone or with groups of friends.

Being victimized by bullying can devastate a child, regardless of their age. They must endure public ridicule, while living in constant

---

[5] www.bullyingstatistics.org
[6] www.cyberbullying.us/research.php

fear of being attacked again and again by their perpetrators. They can suffer from long-term emotional and behavioral problems. Kids who are bullied may feel depressed, anxious, lonely and have poor self-esteem. They are at-risk for suicide.

Kids who are bullied often have nowhere to turn for help. While many schools try to stop bullying, others ignore the problem. Bad schools deny that these aggressive acts exist, or they rationalize them. They might even blame the victim for bringing it on himself or herself.

Children who are bullied could be reluctant to tell their parents because they may feel their child is complaining too much or being weak. Siblings and friends possibly don't want to get involved. They could also be so embarrassed about the problem that they hide the abuse, like a dark secret.

In Jay McGraw's book "Life Strategies for Dealing with Bullies," (as seen on *Dr. Phil*), he lists some warning signs that could indicate if your mentee is bullied:

- Makes up excuses not to go to school;
- Is often angry, sad or depressed, withdrawn, self-loathing and emotionally erratic;
- Frequently hurt by a particular person or group of people;
- Frequently picked on in the presence of other people;
- Mistakes are turned into a big deal by someone;
- Belongings are often stolen or taken;
- Always being confronted with lies/rumors.

If you suspect that one or more people are bullying your mentee, try to get him to open up without prying. Maybe you can share your own experiences of when you were picked on by kids when you were younger.

Jay McGraw suggests that if a child is being picked on by a bully, sit down with him or her and go over this list of Do's and Don'ts to keep them safe:

1. Don't get into a fistfight with a bully or try to retaliate in other ways;
2. Don't believe the insults about you;
3. Don't overestimate how much power a bully has over you;

4. Don't think that bullying will stop if you ignore it;
5. Don't waste time in places online where bullies target you;
6. Don't be afraid to think of new ways to solve the conflict;
7. Don't believe you deserve to be picked on;
8. Do get real about bullying and how it makes you feel;
9. Do get angry, but keep your anger under control;
10. Do write down how you feel;
11. Do learn to say and believe good things about yourself;
12. Do speak confidently when telling a bully not to physically touch you;
13. Do work on developing at least one good relationship with a classmate, neighbor and/or an older child;
14. Do walk or run away if a bully tries to hurt you.

There are a number of mentoring programs around the country that focus on the issue of bullying. Here's an example of one:

Beyond Bullies is the first online program in the U.S. dedicated to helping teenagers who are the targets of bullying and cyber bullying, primarily through online and offline help from peer mentors. Bullied teens have access to peer mentors online they can chat with in real time using a computer or other electronic devices at www.beyondbullies.org.

Teen mentors specifically train to understand what bullying is and how to prevent it. They help targets of bullying to clarify their concerns, point them to pertinent resources and respond to messages with an open mind.

The program allows teenagers who are targets of bullying and cyber bullying the ability to reach peer mentors online in private chat rooms, discussion boards and through e-mail. The program provides a safe space for teens to communicate what it's like for them to go to school and be teased, physically intimidated, beaten up, socially excluded from their circle of friends or tormented online, through social networks, texts or the internet.

As mentors, you're already serving a valuable purpose by being a sounding board for your mentees, so they can vent their feelings to someone who is sympathetic and a good listener. Your compassion and encouragement is priceless, whether your mentee is being bullied, or if he or she is the bully, since bullies have feelings too, including anxiety, fear and guilt.

Imagine if you're basically a good kid but in order to fit in with the crowd, you have to go along with bullying another child. If you don't, then your friends will think you're weak and a coward. You really don't mind the poor victim and you might even like her a little. When you hesitate to beat her up, spread a vicious rumor or taunt her when you're with your friends, they threaten to dump you and pick on you, too. You're very torn about what to do.

Perhaps your mentee isn't a bully who harasses other kids, but he witnesses their aggressive tactics, yet does nothing to stop them. Maybe she saw other children bullying a child and even though she had nothing to do with it, she's afraid to tattle on the bullies. These situations create all kinds of mixed emotions that can torment a youth who has witnessed bullying.

What creates a bully? In the article "The Secret Life of Bullies: Why They Do It—and How to Stop Them,"[7] James Lehman, MSW, suggested that perhaps the parents or older siblings of a child may use aggression or intimidation to get their way. The youth may have a mental and/or an emotional disorder, or have learning disabilities that inhibit the opportunity to learn social skills.

James wrote that kids use bullying primarily to replace the social skills they were supposed to develop in grade school, middle school and high school. As children go through their developmental stages, they should be finding ways of working problems out and getting along with other people. This includes learning how to read social situations, make friends, and understand their social environment.

Bullies use aggression, and some engage in violence and verbal abuse, to supplant those skills. They don't have to learn problem-solving because they just threaten the other kids. They don't have to figure things out because they just push their classmates or call them names. They don't have to get along with other people. They just control them. The way they are solving problems is through brute force and intimidation. So by the time that child reaches ten, bullying is pretty ingrained. It has become their natural response to any situation where they feel socially awkward, insecure, frightened, bored or embarrassed.

---

[7] www.empoweringparents.com

When the bully feels powerless and afraid, he's much more likely to be aggressive, because that makes him feel powerful and in control. It's very hard for bullies to let go of that power.

Jay McGraw writes that parents might encourage bullying in their own children when they exercise absolute control over their child, or threaten them with spankings and other violence. They may humiliate their child as a way to punish them. Perhaps they push competitions too much, or teach their kids that mistakes are unacceptable. They rule by fear and tell their kids what to say, do or think. Children who have been exposed to domestic violence sometimes turn to bullying as a way to lash out.

Regardless of the reasons why kids bully, as a mentor you can try to reason with your mentee to explain logically why it's wrong to bully other kids, but you shouldn't be disappointed if a heart-to-heart talk doesn't stop the bullying. These issues go much deeper and it's not your job to try to psychoanalyze your mentee or fix the problem.

If your mentee is a bully, it can be very challenging for you, especially since you're not their parent. Be careful not to offend the child's family by accusing them of creating the problem. If her parents are doing nothing at all to stop their daughter from bullying, then don't interfere with the way they are handling the situation. Their values might be so different from yours that they even consider her aggressive actions as positive, showing strength and power.

What you can do is to tell your mentee that you certainly don't approve of his negative behavior and that you think he should imagine what it would feel like to be in his victim's shoes. Try some role-playing, where you pretend to be the bully and you pick on your mentee as the victim. Afterwards, have him identify what emotions he felt, and as a victim of bullying how he would react.

Try to get him to talk about what's going on in his life. Let him know that he matters and he's loved. It's safe for him to tell you what he's feeling and/or experiencing, whether it's good or bad.

Intervene when you see bullying happening or bullying behaviors developing. Make sure your mentee understands that you will not stand for bullying. Perhaps a consequence might be that you will not come to your next mentoring session. Maybe you won't take him to the movies like you promised. However, if you threaten to withhold something (including your time together), then be ready to follow through. You can't make a threat and not carry it out. Also, you don't want to suffer from the consequences.

Be a role model for your mentee in how to be empathetic and kind to others. When you talk about the needs and sensitivities of other people, then you help them to understand emotions, feelings and differences.

As a role model, think about how you treat other people. Reflect upon how you express your anger. Remember the things you say when you're upset or a situation is not going your way. You are your mentee's role model for how to behave socially. If you're not practicing the behavior that you're asking your mentee to use, then it may be difficult to get them to behave appropriately.

SEX AND DRUGS

These two subjects seem to be prevalent in many youths' minds, even younger children. With sex and drugs prominent in our media and society, children are curious. They might experiment without knowing the repercussions of their actions, so a mentor can be a valuable guide. If they ask for your opinion about these issues, then give them your feedback and try to steer them in the right direction.

I would find out from your mentee's parent(s) or guardian(s) what their philosophy is in regards to educating their child about sex and drugs. You need to respect their beliefs. If they are truly adamant that they don't want to have their child learning about these topics, then you need to respect their wishes.

If this is the case, then what do you say if your mentee wants to know about sex and drugs, or other controversial issues like abortion and euthanasia?

You certainly don't want to go against their parents' wishes. If you were to give your mentee any information and the parents found out, they might ban you from ever seeing their child again. My advice is to redirect their questions by encouraging them to talk to their parents. If that doesn't work, then suggest they approach their teacher or guidance counselor.

Another way around this sticky issue would be to encourage your mentee to use the library – not specifically to look up information about sex and drugs, but for them to learn about this fantastic resource that they can tap into for school and to satisfy their curiosity about all kinds of different topics.

This will take the pressure off of you, since if your mentee is really motivated to learn, then he'll take the initiative to go to the library. I also don't think a parent can blame you for encouraging their child to use the local library, as long as you don't tell them to specifically go there to research sex, drugs or any other taboo subjects. You are just showing them another tool that can benefit them for learning about many diverse subjects.

It's also possible that your mentee's parent(s) might actually ask you to teach their child about these subjects. For instance, a single mother might feel strange talking to her teenage son about sex. If you're a male mentor, it might ease her burden to have you explain things to her son.

Let's assume that there's no conflict with a parent and your mentee is a teenager who is old enough to learn about the birds and the bees, as well as drugs. She asks you some touchy questions about these topics. How do you respond? I think that you should be honest and forthright.

You could encourage your mentee to attend a class in drug education. Find out if there are any community or school projects that teach youth about the dangers of drug and alcohol addiction.

The same goes for sex education. Take your mentee to a seminar that includes instruction about preventing STDs and unwanted pregnancies.

Naomi was the deputy editor of the "Taste" page in the *Wall Street Journal*. She mentored a girl named Veronica through *Big Brother/Big Sister* in New York.

"When Veronica was about 13, I got a flyer for a seminar led by a representative of *Planned Parenthood* on how to talk to mentees about sex. It started as you might expect: Give them all the information they want about birth control, emphasize the importance of safe sex, tell them where they can get tested for STDs, and so on.

"When the discussion turned to what the appropriate age is to begin having sex, the woman explained: 'You should tell your Little that they shouldn't have sex until they are in love.' I nearly fell out

---

of my chair. Veronica had been in love seven times during the last school year alone.

"Veronica and I have never discussed birth control or STDs, but about five years ago, she told me she wanted a baby. I told her that I didn't think that was a good idea yet, and that she should finish high school, go to college, start a career, find the right guy, get married, and then have a baby. She nodded and said that seemed like a long way off. I assured her that she wouldn't regret waiting.

"This past June, I attended Veronica's high school graduation. Her record wasn't stellar, but she's attending Kingsborough Community College this fall. She has learned something about discipline and hard work. She has had some good teachers. Her classmates have been a good influence... And there's no baby."

Another option is to borrow some books on these topics for your mentee to read. She might be embarrassed to talk about it with you, but reading the information in the privacy of her room could be more comfortable.

The goal is to let your mentee know that he or she can come to you for guidance if they need to, and that sensitive topics like this are okay to discuss with you (*if* that's the case.)

You might actually feel awkward discussing these things with your mentee, and that's perfectly all right. Just let them know right away that you're not comfortable discussing this matter and then suggest they approach a teacher, guidance counselor or other positive adult role model to get the information.

If you do take on the task of enlightening your mentee about sex, drugs or anything else that's a hot button issue, be sure that you are clear in your communication and thorough in your delivery. You don't want to leave anything out, especially when talking about HIV/AIDS, other STDs and the importance of always using condoms.

This can be very challenging for those mentors who believe in abstaining from sex altogether. What do you say when you think it's a sin to have sex before marriage? I would suggest saying exactly that, if it's what you believe. Just tell your mentee that you can't respond to her questions about sex because you believe in abstaining.

Don't lecture or be judgmental. Suggest that if they want these questions answered, then they can ask their parents, a teacher or another adult who would be more comfortable in responding to their questions, and then move on to another topic.

<u>CONFIDENTIALITY</u>

Confidentiality means that information about your mentee and his/her situation is private. It's important that you let your mentee know that whatever he or she wants to share with you will remain confidential. This helps develop trust. However, stress that you'll maintain their confidence as long as what they tell you will not harm them or anyone else.

Your mentee(s) might confide things to you about her or his past, or discuss tough issues that they are dealing with currently. Some of their confessions might shock you or raise your concern.

This could create a difficult situation. For instance, your mentee might confide that she's pregnant and she seeks your advice about what to do. Regardless of your personal feelings and whether you are pro-choice or pro-life, it is your obligation to safeguard this girl's confession.

The right to privacy and confidentiality is a human, as well as a legal, consideration. While confidentiality laws vary from state to state, as a mentor, it's totally your responsibility to maintain your mentee's privacy.

There's an important exception to this rule. You have a moral responsibility to violate a confidential agreement if you believe that a youth is engaging, or is going to engage, in a behavior that's dangerous for themselves or to others. Then you must notify the proper authorities.

For example, if your mentee confides that he intends to commit suicide, you have no choice but to alert his parent, guardian, teacher and staff at the youth facility.

If your mentees tell you there's a big gang shootout that's going to occur at a certain time and place, then you need to notify the police.

If she tells you that she plans to attack or kill her rival, that's definitely cause for alarm.

If you suspect that your mentee has been physically or sexually abused, it's essential that you report this immediately to the appropriate authorities.

While it's a rare occurrence, you might be required to be a defendant in a civil, criminal or disciplinary action that relates to your mentee. If so, you will need to share all information that your mentee confided to you, as it relates to that case.

Other than these extreme situations where you think that harm may come to your mentee(s) or others, then you should keep all confidences that your mentee shares with you a secret. If you are unsure if he or she wants you to maintain their privacy about something they tell you, just ask them. They will really appreciate it.

SAFETY

In the fifteen years since my organization **Create Now** has been in existence, we have never had an assault or traumatic event occur to any of our mentors. This includes serving youth in high-security prisons, as well as kids who are emotionally-disturbed due to abuse and neglect.

Generally, the high-risk youth whom we serve are so appreciative of the time and attention that's given to them that they would never want to hurt their mentors. They think of their mentors as friends and allies. They also don't want to lose the many benefits that mentoring brings.

However, there is always the possibility that something dangerous might occur, particularly in prisons and detention camps, and also in poor neighborhoods where crime is rampant. It's important to take precautions and to be prepared – just in case.

If you're mentoring within an institution like a school, clinic, group home or shelter, sometimes there will be a security guard present. This person helps to keep troublemakers in check. Learn how to reach this guard quickly, just in case a fight breaks out or you're in need of immediate help.

In detention camps, juvenile halls and prisons, there will probably be many probation officers ("P.O.s") and guards who are trained in suppression tactics. Fights could break out in these environments, particularly between rival gang members or when there's racial tension.

If a fight between youth occurs while you are in the process of mentoring, don't try to break it up on your own. You're not there to be a hero or a mediator and you certainly don't want to get in the line of fire where you could be hurt. Immediately call for help or run out and find a probation officer or guard to handle the situation.

In Chapter Seven, I share a field-tested technique for breaking up a fight. Most mentors will never have to deal with this problem, but it's good to be informed. As they say, "Better safe than sorry."

The same holds true when you mentor kids in a poor neighborhood. You could be vulnerable to attack, especially during tough economic times.

I don't want to scare you or to insinuate that you'll always be at great risk of attack whenever you go into a disadvantaged community. In fact, *every* community in the world is at risk of escalated violence and crime these days. Unfortunately, it's a reflection of humanity. With guns readily available, gangs spreading like a disease, crazy lunatics massacring innocent people and drugs and crime on the rise all over the world, you would be foolish *not* to be cautious.

Basically, just use common sense. This means that you should always be alert. If something doesn't feel right to you, then follow your instincts. Be sharp and aware of your surroundings wherever you go in life, and take precautions.

If you are mentoring in an impoverished community where crime rates are high, then try to arrange your schedule so that you can meet during the day, rather than nighttime when most crimes take place. If you are a woman, I'd recommend mentoring with a partner so you don't walk around dangerous streets all on your own.

Be sure to ask the school, facility, religious or community-based organization that is arranging your mentoring program where the best place to park is, since you would be a lot safer if you could drive into a secured parking lot.

As mentioned, don't wear expensive jewelry or designer clothes. Make sure your shoes are comfortable and, if it became absolutely necessary, you could easily run. Ladies, leave the spiked heels, low-cut tops, bare midriffs and mini-skirts at home. These clothes send the wrong signal and leave you wide open as a target.

If you don't feel comfortable going into a risky neighborhood, then see if your mentee can meet you at a safer location, like a public library or a park. If they are old enough to take public transportation, this will be a good education for them on getting around, and you'll feel better in a more secure place.

Whether you're mentoring in a poor or rich community, through a church, school or another institution, you must safeguard your personal property. Don't leave your purses, laptops, briefcases, cell phones or other precious possessions lying around where someone could easily snatch them. Don't carry large sums of cash or other valuables with you.

Most people who live in poor neighborhoods are honest and hardworking individuals. They wouldn't hurt a fly or steal from anyone, but there are always a few unscrupulous individuals who don't share those values. Protect yourself, but also don't be overly suspicious and accusatory unless it's absolutely warranted.

I made this mistake when I visited a **Create Now** TV Writing workshop that one of the Producers and also a Writer of *Buffy the Vampire Slayer* gave at Camp Joseph Scott, a teenage girls' detention camp. For the final workshop, I had organized a party to celebrate that these 12 incarcerated girls had worked together and completed a class, which was a major accomplishment for them.

The party went great. They ate special treats and I gave each youth a gift bag filled with goodies, such as CDs and a "Certificate of Completion." The mentors also gave the girls souvenirs from *Buffy* and they were all elated. There was such wonderful energy and a feeling amongst the mentors and mentees of love, respect and gratitude. I was so happy that I had helped to bring them together to manifest this successful project.

When I got home, I discovered that my wallet was gone. I was horrified, since I had been so busy organizing the party that I had left my purse out. One of the girls could have easily taken my wallet. Since they were all locked up for a variety of crimes, shoplifting and theft were high on the list of common offenses.

I checked my car and my home, but the wallet was nowhere to be found. I called the person on duty at the camp and reported that my wallet was missing. They immediately gathered the 12 girls from the workshop and searched them thoroughly. The girls continually claimed they were innocent. They were angry and hurt that they were being accused of theft.

The camp reported that they couldn't find my wallet anywhere. I searched my home again and went back to my car. I found my wallet there, tucked in a corner after it had fallen out of my purse.

Mortified, I called the camp back and let them know that I had found my wallet. I felt terrible (and I still do) that I had wrongly accused these girls of stealing my wallet. I had spoiled their joy from the celebration and taken something from their success. I have tried to be very careful with my possessions since then, and also not to make any wrong accusations.

GIVING GIFTS

Some mentors like to give gifts to their mentees. They might celebrate their birthdays by bringing them presents, or buy them things just for the heck of it. They may give them cookies, candies and other special treats.

I think it's great to be generous to your mentee(s) by giving them presents, but I recommend that you first check with the child's parents, guardians or the staff at the shelter, group home, detention camp or other youth facility before you spread your generosity. Find out their boundaries ahead of time.

Parents may not want you to spoil their child with gifts for any number of reasons. It might feel like charity to them, or perhaps giving presents to your mentee could make his or her siblings jealous.

At the same time, they may feel thrilled that their child has a wonderful advocate like you, someone to buy him the things they can't afford. They'll probably be delighted with what you give their child, but you should always check first.

The same holds true with schools, shelters, group homes and other youth institutions with mentoring programs. They may not want the children who aren't being mentored to feel left out. Also, if the other mentors don't buy their mentees gifts, then that could cause problems. Ask the staff about their gift-giving policy.

The same rules apply with providing food. You might want to treat your mentee to an ice cream sundae, but that could make his mother angry when he's too full to eat his dinner. You could bring your mentee to eat at a restaurant and not know that she's allergic to certain food. It's best to ask the parent or guardian of your mentee(s) before indulging them.

If you are working with a group of kids and you give out gifts or treats, don't show any favoritism. Even though you really adore one child and secretly have a hard time dealing with another, you must treat them equally.

If you start off your mentoring relationship by immediately giving your mentee(s) a gift, then they may anticipate receiving presents each time you meet. I caution you to only use gift-giving for special occasions. If you don't associate the gifts with a special event, like a birthday, graduation or a unique accomplishment, then they will just become meaningless. It's not necessarily the material value of a gift that has impact, but rather the meaning behind it.

You can use gift-giving as a reward for accomplishing challenging tasks, like getting a good grade or completing a tough assignment.

If you give something, then don't expect anything in return. You have to give from your heart and have no expectations. This means that if you give your mentee a birthday gift, then you can't feel upset if he or she doesn't reciprocate with a card or gift for your birthday.

Giving gifts as an incentive to inspire your mentee to accomplish something can be tricky. You don't want to motivate them to complete their tasks simply because of greed. Also, if you give them the gift up front, before the undertaking has been completed, then don't be disappointed if she or he flakes out and doesn't follow through.

Create Now had a mentor who paid for six months of rent for her mentee's apartment, with the understanding that the girl would get a job and become self-sufficient. When the six months were over, the girl never even tried to get a job. She also left the apartment a total mess, thereby losing the security deposit and forcing the mentor to pay reparation costs.

Her mentor was upset, but it was really her own fault for having expectations about what this girl could or would accomplish. The girl did finally get her life together. She was so grateful to her

---

mentor for the support she had provided that she made her the Godmother of her two children.

The mentor's gift ultimately paid off, but the frustration she had experienced was the price she paid for having expectations.

Kids will sometimes hint or directly ask you to buy them gifts, especially if you have been generous in the past. This is especially true with younger children, but even teens and young adults can be brazen about asking you to buy them things. Many of these kids have never been taught manners. They probably don't even know this is not polite.

They may also assume that you're rich and have lots of money to spend on them, because compared to them, you *are* rich. When you're a child and very naïve about financial matters, you might think that someone who drives a good car and has nice clothes is also a millionaire who lives in a huge mansion. Since many inner-city youth have never been outside of their own neighborhood, they often assume that the rest of the world looks like what they see on television or in the movies.

You might also be matched with a youth who was spoiled by a previous mentor. It can be hard to follow in someone else's shoes.

Angela was a **Create Now** volunteer who mentored a 12-year-old girl we'll call "Debbie" in a mentoring program for children of prisoners. At their first meeting, Angela took her mentee to the local mall to hang out. Debbie instantly asked Angela to buy her something.

Apparently, the girl had a previous mentor who spoiled her and bought her presents every time they got together. After consistently meeting Debbie for a couple of months and buying her gifts, the previous mentor just totally abandoned her mentee. This obviously had a negative impact.

Angela told Debbie that she wouldn't buy her a gift. The girl kept whining and demanding that her mentor buy something. Angela threatened to take Debbie home if she asked again, since she and her sister Skylar (who was mentoring Debbie's brother) had already taken them on a fun outing and treated them both to lunch. Debbie complained again, so they immediately took her (and her brother) home.

The following week, the same thing happened. The girl kept begging her mentor to buy her something, but Angela refused. Debbie continued to whine and complain, so they quickly took her home.

After that, Debbie never asked for another gift. She finally got the message. Angela bonded with her by gaining her respect and letting her mentee know that there were boundaries that she couldn't cross.

If your mentee asks you for gifts, respond by letting them know that gifts are special and not to be expected all the time. Don't feel obligated to give things.

It's not your job as a mentor to provide gifts. However, if you want to give things, finding the right present can be totally free and will show your mentee(s) that you care about them just as much.

Perhaps during a hike you'll come across an interesting stone, seashell or pinecone that you can give. These can be treasures for a youth who has never been out in nature before. It also teaches kids that beauty is all around and we need to protect it.

If you find a fascinating article related to one of your conversations, cut it out and bring it to them. When you discover a cool photo of a hot new car that would pique your mentee's interest, make him a copy. Search for a poem that expresses an experience that your mentee told you about during your last mentoring session and share it with her.

These gifts don't cost anything and yet they have deeper meaning for your mentees, since it shows them that you were listening to what they shared with you and thinking about them during the week. It also demonstrates that you cared enough about them to take time out of your busy schedule to bring them those items.

Giving gifts involves learning how to receive gifts. Whether you give a gift to your mentee(s) or not, your mentee(s) might present you with something they bought or made. This could be a bouquet of flowers they picked, or a group project, such as a poster they all created to show you their appreciation, or something special that they saved up to buy you.

Regardless of what the gift is, be gracious and appreciative of the love and effort that went into giving you this present. For disadvantaged kids who don't have a lot of money, their gifts can come in small ways. They might seem insignificant, but the emotion behind them is certainly not. They will probably look for something easily available to express their love and affection to you. So even if it's just a clump of weeds thrust in your direction with nothing more said then, "Here," you should gush at their thoughtfulness and let your mentee know how much their gift means to you.

This is an excellent "teachable moment" – the chance to show youth that when receiving gifts, it's polite to express thanks verbally and also with a card. Either make a card by hand or buy a special thank you card to show your mentee(s) what their gift meant to you. It will make you all feel good, while they will learn how to show their appreciation in a positive manner. This is an important lesson for them to succeed in the future.

LOANING MONEY

At-risk and high-risk youth usually come from low-income, disadvantaged families with barely enough money for basic necessities like food and shelter. Your mentee may even have to work to help support his or her family. Money is almost always tight.

Your mentee might think that you're rich, even if you don't have a lot of funds. What you may consider a small expense, like tickets to the theater or eating at a decent restaurant could give them the impression that you are "loaded."

If he or she is desperate for money, they will possibly turn to you for help by asking for a loan. It could be a small amount, like $10 or $20, or a lot more, depending on their needs.

It's entirely up to you as to whether or not you should loan them money. However, be prepared that if you do, then you might never see it again.

One of my mentees called me a few days before Christmas, sobbing on the phone. She worked in a fast food place and someone stole her wallet with all of the money she was going to use to buy her three year-old daughter Christmas gifts. She begged me to help her with a loan of $100. She promised to pay me back the following week when she got her paycheck.

I was torn about whether or not I should give her the cash. I could afford to lose the money if she didn't return it, and I hated the thought of her child going without Christmas gifts, so I loaned her the money. She promptly returned it the following week, and I was pleased and relieved.

However, a couple of weeks later, she called again and asked me to help her with another loan so she could pay a bill. I told her that I couldn't. She had to learn that I wasn't a bank and she couldn't always lean on me.

On three other occasions, young men that I mentor have asked me to loan them $20. One needed it for rent, another for food and the third for diapers for his baby. They all promised to pay me back the following week. Each time, I felt that $20 was low enough that I could afford to lose the money, and I wanted to help my mentees through their crises. I have yet to receive the money back from any of them.

Perhaps I should have just given them the $20 as a gift, but if I had, they might assume that in the future, asking me for a loan could be a great way to receive more gifts. At least by lending them small amounts of money, there was hope that I would get it back.

WHAT IF IT DOESN'T WORK OUT?

Most mentoring organizations, schools, religious centers and other agencies that seek mentors for youth have their own system for matching mentors with their young clients. This could depend on a variety of factors, such as age, gender, location, schedule, hobbies, interests, needs of both the youth and mentor, and more.

When you meet with the person in charge of screening volunteers, they will probably ask you questions about your preferences as a mentor. They will do their best to match you with the child (or group of kids) that will benefit the most from being mentored by you, while also giving you pleasure from the experience. The match needs to be a win-win for everyone involved.

However, in spite of all efforts, it's possible that your relationship with your mentee(s) just doesn't work out. For example, there could be a lack of chemistry between you. This happens all the time in life, where two people just don't click for some unknown reason.

You could be appalled by your mentee's lifestyle. Perhaps she dresses promiscuously and talks about having sex with many different boys. Maybe he uses too much profanity or chain smokes. These may not fit with your personal values and you have a hard time mentoring them.

In these situations, try to be more open-minded. You're there to assist your mentee to follow their dreams, not to change them or mold them to the way you think they should be. If you try to force your beliefs onto them, they will just shut you out. They don't want another parent or an authority figure telling them what to do or how to be. They want a friend who can listen to them and then assist them to fulfill their needs.

If you just can't tolerate their lifestyle, then I recommend you tell your mentee that you find these behaviors offensive. Ask them to please respect you by dressing with more modesty, watching their language, refraining from smoking, or whatever it is that bothers you when they're with you.

No matter what the issue is that bothers you, be open and forthright with your feelings. Honesty is the best policy, but don't give ultimatums. If you do, they might feel defensive and rebellious.

If you find that you still don't like your mentee in spite of all your efforts and you just don't want to mentor them anymore, then talk with the Volunteer Coordinator or other staff that matched you with your mentee to see if they can resolve the problem.

Another challenge is if your mentee is unresponsive to everything you try to do. It can be frustrating to spend your valuable time organizing an outing or preparing an activity for you to share with your mentee only to have him or her refuse to participate, or to remain cold and sullen.

If this is the case, then find out why he or she acts this way. You might discover that it's something simple and easy to fix. Perhaps he feels like you keep taking him to places that you want to visit, but which don't interest him; or he misunderstood something you said and was feeling angry in response.

Maybe she thinks that your tone of voice is demeaning, even though you weren't aware that you came across that way; or she was so upset that her father left home that she took her anger out on you.

Kids in a workshop might stop attending or be indifferent because they feel that you give so many assignments, and now the fun workshop they had signed up for is like school; or perhaps they are into a totally different activity that conflicts with your schedule. These are things that can be easily remedied. Make the workshop more interactive, entertaining and less academic. Rearrange your schedule so there are no conflicts. There is usually a way to fix everything if your intention is good.

Your mentee may also have been forced into a mentoring relationship by his or her parents, counselors, a judge, school officials or others. They could be resentful about this and might be unresponsive to your efforts as a mentor because they are rebelling against authority.

Perhaps your mentee stands you up for appointments or never returns your calls. You might feel like you're doing the best you can to reach out, but it feels like you're talking to a wall and just wasting your time.

You need to find out from your mentee why he or she acts this way. You might discover that they don't know how to keep track of time and they simply forgot that you were supposed to meet. You can give them a calendar to write in your appointments and circle them in red.

Maybe you're leaving messages for them that aren't being delivered. You can find an alternative way to connect. Texting on cell phones works great, since that's how most kids communicate.

Having an intimate talk with your mentee about such reactions and behaviors could also help them to air their buried feelings. You might be the catalyst to assist them in processing deeply buried emotions, especially if they relate to their family members. They could realize that it's safe to share these feelings with you, since you will maintain their confidentiality and give them solid advice.

James was 7-years-old when his mother died. He had no contact with his father, so he lived with his grandmother. As he grew older, his grandmother realized that he needed something more. "He seemed lonely," she said. She contacted *Denver Partners*, a mentoring organization in Colorado. They matched James with Matt, a real estate professional.

"That first meeting was real quiet," said Matt. "James just sat back and listened. He didn't say much at all!"

"That's just the way James is," his grandmother replied. "He just listens and takes stock of a person, but I knew right from the start that Matt would be someone he could count on, trust and talk to."

Within a couple of weeks, James came out of his shell. "Matt is a positive person," says James. "He has taught me that even though there may be tough times, you have to remain positive and I like that."

James said that he and Matt talk a lot about college plans. He hopes to study business management at either Louisiana State University or Syracuse. But, he admits, Matt is most helpful when it comes to talking about a particularly important and sensitive issue: "Girls!" says James. "It's kind of awkward to talk about girlfriends with my grandma."

Don't force your mentee to open up. You can try to find out why they're being unresponsive or apathetic and offer to help by listening to their problems, but if they still don't react well, then step back.

If this occurs, contact the Volunteer Coordinator or staff in charge of matching mentors with youth and explain the situation. Since they know this child, it's possible for them to get to the bottom of the problem. Let them mediate and determine the next step to take, so that you won't be put into an uncomfortable position.

I discuss this issue in more detail in Chapter Ten (Ending Your Mentoring Relationship), but I'd like to emphasize now it's important that you try everything possible to maintain your mentoring relationship. However, if you decide that you definitely need to end it, then have closure with your mentee by letting her or him know that there are no hard feelings and you wish them the best. If possible, leave the door open and offer them the chance to contact you again in the future if things change or they need advice. You don't want to say anything hurtful, even if you feel angry.

It's essential that you don't take the blame or feel guilty if your mentoring relationship doesn't work out (unless you are at fault).

Things happen and they usually work out that way for a reason. Consider it another valuable lesson in life and just move on.

Even if the relationship with your mentee doesn't endure, that doesn't mean that he or she didn't gain some wonderful benefits from your mentorship, and hopefully you have profited as well. They just might not have been ready for what you had to offer. However, things you said and did might impact them later in their life.

It also signifies that it's time for you to move on to another child in need. There are millions of kids out there who want mentors, so even if it didn't work out the first time, get back out and try it again. Find another youth who will thrive with a mentor and reach out. You won't regret it.

CHAPTER FIVE

Do's and Don'ts

Mentoring is like a voyage into unknown territory. You embark on a journey with a stranger who's probably very different than anyone you've ever met before. Friendship develops and an adventure unfolds as you share new experiences. Diverse food, language, cultures and perspectives of life become topics of mutual interest. But if the road becomes rocky, will you crash and burn or will you traverse the bumps and ride on to a successful mentoring relationship?

No written rules exist about what a mentor should or shouldn't do when they're with their mentees. If you're mentoring in a program, such as through a school or a community organization, you will probably receive a manual, guidelines or an orientation from someone like the Volunteer Coordinator. With or without support, just be sure to use common sense at all times. Remember, you're a role model!

DON'TS

Here are some things that you should *not* do when meeting with your mentee(s).

1. Don't Interrupt Them:

Have you ever tried to share your feelings with someone, but they constantly interrupt you? Frustrating, isn't it?

Now imagine if you have a difficult time communicating in the first place and you're continually being interrupted. Don't do it! Even if you are excited to chime in, be patient and respectful to let your mentee finish his or her thoughts.

You should pay attention and encourage your mentee to express all of his or her feelings, negative and positive alike. When young people are allowed to share their emotions, particularly negative ones, it offers them a safe outlet. If they're not allowed to communicate these negative feelings in words, then they'll act them out in some form of antisocial action.

Kids want desperately for us to understand how they feel. Many never receive this empathy from their parents, teachers or staff at schools and other institutions. As a mentor, you can help your mentees. The technique is simple:

a. Establish eye contact;

b. Listen carefully to what the youth is saying;

c. Formulate in your mind what the child is expressing;

d. Repeat back to him or her, in your own words, the feelings that they have just communicated to you.

By using this simple technique, the mentee will really know that you understand, because they will hear their own feelings coming back to them through you.

Be careful not to repeat the exact words your mentee has used, so you won't sound like an echo. Paraphrase the child's feelings in your own words.

For example, you might say, "Let me get this straight. You feel angry with your mother because she wouldn't let you go to the party on Friday night even though you did your homework and chores. Is that right?"

This may not lead to a dramatic change. However, it's the most effective way of keeping open the lines of communication between you and your mentee. It lets the child know that you understand how he or she feels and that their sentiments are valued. It also helps to promote mutual respect between you.

2. <u>Don't Be Close-Minded</u>

Maintain an open mind. Your mentees may tell you things about their lives that might shock you.

Since many of them have suffered from all kinds of abuse, this is the violent world that they know. They may confide about terrible acts that have been done to them, and/or horrible things that they may have done to others.

It's important that you're not judgmental when listening to their confessions. Sympathy and empathy is more appropriate. Instead of saying, "Your father is a psychopath," you could reply, "That must have been very difficult for you to endure." Rather than saying, "How could you have done such a disgusting thing to your cousin?" you can say, "How do you feel now about the way that you acted?" or "What can I do to help you?"

Accept the youth's description and perception of his or her life encounters. Be aware that every person has different experiences and don't be critical.

Your mentee may confide a deep secret to you. Perhaps he or she is a lesbian, gay, bisexual or transgender (LGBT) and they haven't "come out of the closet." Their families might disown them when they reveal their sexual preference. LGBT youth often end up on the streets or in the child welfare system, where staff and other kids frequently abuse them.

One such youth, Joel, had been in the foster care system since the age of nine, when he already considered himself gay. At thirteen-years-old, Joel was the lead plaintiff in a Federal class-action lawsuit filed on behalf of gay, lesbian, and bisexual youth in foster care in the New York City child welfare system.

Joel testified that at a series of group homes and large residential treatment centers, adults rarely intervened when other kids made him the target of constant harassment. Among numerous incidents, he was thrown down a flight of stairs, had his nose broken twice, was hit in the face with a broom, and had his shoulder blade broken. All the youth who filed this lawsuit were allegedly abused by their peers, foster parents, and even the staff members of child welfare agencies because of their sexual orientations.

You never know what's behind the sadness or anger of a mentee. It's important to be compassionate. You are there to help the child develop into a responsible adult. If you're close-minded, you will only alienate them.

Don't freak out if your mentee tells you something shocking. Stay calm and use common sense. Also, know that sometimes children exaggerate or lie about things. They could be making up stories just to impress you.

When I worked with the group of incarcerated teenage boys at Optimist Youth Homes, they told me all kinds of stories about how they killed people, attacked rival gang members and jacked cars. I realized that while some of them were telling the truth, others were "posturing" or "posing" and trying to look tough for my benefit, as well as their peers.

Take these kinds of accounts with a grain of salt. As I mentioned in Chapter Four, if you think there really is the potential for danger, then alert the proper authorities.

If you feel that you're really unable to be open-minded about your mentee for whatever reason, then discreetly express your feelings to the staff so that a better match can be made for both of you.

3.   Don't Expect Perfection:

Nobody is perfect, so it's unfair to expect your mentee(s) to reach your ideal. Doing so imposes what you personally want onto someone else. You might think that perfection is graduating from college and having a lucrative career, but your mentee might think of perfection as getting married and raising a family. That idea might be repugnant to you, since you were married young and had a bad marriage and you want her to wait until she's older to have a child. By imposing your ideals onto your mentee, you are creating unfair expectations.

You can't have *any* expectations when you're mentoring. You are not a parent or guardian, and even if you were, your mentee must make his or her own decisions. They have to discover their strengths and weaknesses and learn to accept their flaws.

Maybe you always eat a healthy diet and you work out at the gym regularly. You're in great shape and you want your mentee to also be conscientious about his health. But no matter what you say and do, he eats way too much junk food and has become obese. You suggest going for a long walk to get some fresh air, but he just wants to hang out, eat candy and watch TV.

This can be a very frustrating situation. You want so much to help your mentee improve his health and appearance, but you feel like you're just spinning your wheels. It creates tension in your relationship and you wonder if you're just wasting your time.

You're not! Hopefully some day your words will make an impact, but sometimes we don't take advice to heart until we have heard it a dozen times from different sources. Urging your mentee to exercise and eat well might click in a few years down the line, when he hears it again for the umpteenth time. One day, he could look in the mirror and hear what you told him echoing in his thoughts. It could suddenly spark him to get into shape.

Regardless, you have to let him be who he is, without imposing your own values and making him live up to your idea of perfection.

You might find that it's your mentee who demands perfection. If she gets frustrated because she doesn't look as ideal as she hoped, convince her that flaws are natural and beauty is subjective. Beauty comes from inside. Girls are particularly conscientious about their appearance and there is strong peer pressure to look a certain way. This can lead to eating disorders. As her mentor, you can be the voice of reason and help to build her self-esteem.

4. **Don't Get Frazzled:**

You might be the first person in your mentee's life to show an interest in their growth and progress. As a result, they may test you to see how much they can get away with, and if you will still come back. This can manifest in many different ways, such as refusing to participate in an activity, or talking back in a nasty manner.

Remember that many of these kids are going through a lot of difficulties, plenty more than the average child. They can be hungry or perhaps they don't know where they're going to sleep that night. They may be fearful for their safety and that of their family members.

Perhaps your mentee's parent(s) are working multiple jobs to support their large family. They could be drug addicts or alcoholics. More than 2 million children in the United States have one or both parents in prison. With no adults around for supervision, then kids who are just children themselves can often be responsible for the well-being of all their younger siblings.

Many of these at-risk and high-risk kids are teenage parents who don't have a clue about how to raise their child. These are all very heavy burdens to bear.

Even if your mentee comes from a decent home with two loving parents, all youth today are faced with the lure of drugs, alcohol and sex. They may have to deal with such hot-button topics as abortion and homosexuality. If they open up and talk to you about these issues, or anything else that's controversial to you, don't get frazzled because you may not agree with what they are saying.

If they tell you that they just met someone new and had sex, but you're very much against pre-marital sex, don't freak out. Not only will you upset your mentee by stirring up guilt and shame, but they will also hesitate to ever confide in you again. Listen carefully to what they tell you, accept it and then share your own opinion in a respectful manner. Don't be condescending or patronizing in the way that you speak to them.

The best thing is to *respond* rather than *react*. When you respond, you listen to what your mentee has just shared and digest it. Reacting is saying the first thing that comes to your mind, which might be judgmental or hurtful to your mentee. A better way would be to respond with, "How does that make you feel?" or "Tell me more."

5. Don't Underestimate Your Power:

Children care about adults' opinions. They often worry that they are disliked or not respected by their elders. Even though teens may occasionally seem nonchalant in their attitude, your opinion is always important. Recognize that your mentee has come to you for guidance. Always take their concerns seriously.

Use praise and censure only as appropriate. Compliments can be a powerful tool, such as, "That's a great idea. You're so creative," or "How clever of you! You're very smart." These words will stick with them for a long time.

The reverse is also true. A casual remark might slip out of your mouth and be totally meaningless to you, but it can deeply hurt your mentee. For instance, you might say, "Can't you do *anything* right?," which is something that you say jokingly to your spouse, but it won't be funny to a child who feels like a total failure.

Your mentee may not show any outward enthusiasm about having you as his or her mentor. This can make you feel like it doesn't really matter if you're there or not. Remember that these kids are great at hiding their true feelings for fear of being hurt again. You have a lot more influence on them then you probably realize, so be careful how you use it.

6.   Don't Overestimate Your Knowledge:

Your mentee may have a serious problem. You could be asked to help him or her with something for which you're not qualified. Recognize your limitations and don't exceed them. You are not a psychiatrist, drug counselor or a social worker.

If your mentee seeks help and you're not qualified to provide it, connect him or her with experienced specialists. When working with high-risk institutionalized youth, there are usually staff members at their school or facility to handle these situations. Recommend that your mentee speak with one of his counselors. If she's uncomfortable doing this on her own, you can suggest that you'll contact the program specialist on her behalf, or attend the session with her.

7.   Don't Dump Your Problems On Your Mentee:

Sometimes, life becomes challenging and we need to vent about things that create tension. Your partner could be cheating on you, or your son is driving you crazy. Maybe you've lost your job and you're worried about how you're going to pay the bills.

When we become close with people, it's natural to share our personal concerns. This helps to release stress, and the people that we confide in can sometimes suggest solutions to our problems.

You might become so intimate with your mentee that they become a good friend or an extended family member. It's very tempting to open up and share your problems with him or her, but don't do that.

Remember that you became a mentor so that you could help your mentee to handle her own challenges, not to burden her with your own. She might be facing homelessness, teen pregnancy, drug cravings or struggling to graduate from high school. It's not fair to add more pressure to her life when you speak about the challenges you personally face, because then she will feel obligated to help you.

If you start complaining to your mentee about how much you hate your boss or that you're worried you'll be fired, then how is he going to respect you? You're supposed to be his role model, but instead of looking up to you, he's going to be concerned about your well-being.

There is a fine line that you must walk as a mentor. Be open about yourself to show that you're human and that you are also vulnerable, but don't be *so* honest that you blur the line between being a positive role model and a negative complainer.

8.   **Don't Force Your Beliefs:**

You may have been raised in a religious household where your parents taught you to follow a particular spiritual doctrine. It's natural that you would want to share your beliefs with your mentees, but it's important that you don't force them on anyone.

The same goes for your political views. You could feel strongly about certain issues that affect your community. Perhaps you support the Republican Party. Maybe you are a liberal Democrat or an Independent. You have always been politically involved, attending rallies and meetings to fight strongly for your beliefs.

While it's fine to talk about your ideas and perspectives with your mentees, it's not okay to keep repeating them. Don't push your opinions to the point where you're lecturing and trying to force your mentees to follow your beliefs. Not only will you turn them off so they won't want to talk with you anymore, but you would also be overstepping your boundaries.

9.   **Don't Give Up:**

There will probably be times when your mentee just doesn't feel like communicating. He might miss a few meetings because he decided to go to the movies or attend a sporting event. She might feel depressed because of family problems and just not want to see you.

They may create some distance between you when you start to get close. If they push you away, say, "I think you're pulling back because you're afraid to trust me." They'll respect you for being perceptive and honest.

During group workshops, some of your mentees could feel intimidated by the scope of the creative project that you're working on. The idea of creating a mural from scratch or putting on a play for their family and friends is just too daunting. Perhaps they think that the project is boring. They could also be worried that you'll scold them for not completing their assignments.

Maybe the story they are writing isn't turning out the way they had hoped. Perhaps they're upset because the art project is bringing up some of the deeply-rooted emotions that they have managed to hide for so many years.

The key is to be patient. If your mentee won't meet with you, then try to talk with them on the phone. Ask gently to find out what's troubling her, without seeming like you're prying. She might not be in the mood to tell you for a while, but if you're persistent, then she will probably open up.

It might be easier for him to communicate through writing. You can try sending your mentee a letter or emailing him if he has access to the Internet.

If your mentee is high-risk and living in an institution, you can try to contact his or her therapist, probation officer or social worker. They might be able to shed some light on the situation and help figure out a way to deal with it.

There could be times when people close to you pressure you to give up mentoring. Perhaps your family members don't want you to be away from home. Your boss might ask you to work extra hours. Even the staff at the mentoring program that matches you with your mentee may suggest that you quit. But, *you* need to decide what's right (within reason, of course).

That's what happened to Patricia in Washington, D.C. Although the ten-year-old girl that Patricia was matched with through Fairfax County's mentoring program was nothing like the ideal mentee she had requested, they got along fine. It was her family that was the problem. They couldn't keep schedules straight; they lived in utter chaos and neglected their children. It created a great deal of frustration and added responsibility for her mentor. The Volunteer Coordinator of the mentoring program that matched Patricia with her mentee suggested that Patricia should let this girl go and find another child to mentor.

But Patricia couldn't bear to desert her mentee. She stuck it out and did everything she could to help the child, which included finding places for her to sleep and warm clothes when it got cold. They grew very close over the years and Patricia was amazed that the girl's whole family also seemed to benefit from her influence.

10. Don't Forget to Have Fun:

Spending enjoyable time together is a vital part of the mentoring relationship. In fact, for some kids, the time with you might be the only moments when they get to enjoy the company of an adult. Try to achieve balance. Don't feel guilty about taking in a movie instead of researching colleges. It's okay to go on a shopping spree (if you can afford it) every now and then. If your group program allows for field trips, see if you can arrange to take the kids somewhere fun and interesting.

As long as you don't let any goals fall entirely by the wayside, then take pleasure in your time together. After all, mentoring isn't just work. It's also play, so enjoy it. Have a blast!

DO'S

Here are some things that you *should* do when meeting with your mentee(s).

1. Listening Is More Important Than Speaking:

Listening is hard. Many of us (myself included) are great talkers, but when it comes to listening, we sometimes fail miserably. Kids need to be heard, especially youth who are in trouble. Listening isn't just being quiet. It's hearing and caring. It's having an active interest in what is being said. Give your mentee reassurance that you are listening with an occasional nod, a smile, or "I understand."

Be empathetic. Let your mentee know that you not only comprehend what they are saying, but also that you're sensitive to the feelings they're communicating. Saying things like, "I can see how that would be frustrating," or "It's okay to be upset. You have a right to be," are simple ways to show your concern.

At the same time, it's important not to be phony. Kids quickly pick up on fake empathy and you can end up doing more harm than good.

Sitting down with a child to talk about the day can be a challenge. They might jump from subject to subject, not finish their thoughts and quite often, they will avoid talking about whatever it is that's really bothering them. This is where the skill of good listening becomes even more important. Kids will often drop hints at what they really want to talk about, so be quiet and listen carefully to pick up on the cues.

Plenty of people have difficulty communicating, but at-risk and high-risk youth have an even harder time. With 25 million kids in our country living without a father at home, these youngsters often lack good role models. It's usually the gang-bangers and drug dealers who teach them from a young age not to be emotional. In order to survive on the streets, they quickly learn to cover their real feelings, so they can appear tough.

Kids might clam up simply because they're shy. They may take their time to carefully observe someone before they share themselves.

Sometimes it's difficult to get one of these kids to even smile, but if you develop their trust, they may soon open up and pour their hearts out.

My friend Rafiki Callixte works with homeless kids in Rwanda, many of whom were victims of the genocide. These orphans barely survived on the streets. They were fearful and would lie about their families. He taught me a technique to get them to open up and tell the truth. Rafiki would sit with them and play a game, usually cards. While the youth were distracted with the game, he would casually ask them questions about their backgrounds and they would open up to him about their pasts. Rafiki jotted notes down later and used this detailed information later during counseling sessions.

Be patient with helping your mentee to communicate. He might not be good at putting his feelings into words, but underneath that tough shell is a kid who just wants to be heard. The key is to stay responsive and dependable. Build their trust.

Jessica, a fifteen-year-old freshman at a high school in Missoula, Montana, had a problem communicating. She hung out with a bad crowd and got into trouble with the law. Jessica kept ditching school and her teachers didn't expect her to make it through the year. So when Allison, a sophomore at the University of Montana, was matched with Jessica as a tutor, several of the troubled girl's teachers actually laughed, confident that she'd never turn up for her tutoring sessions.

When they met, Allison and Jessica immediately clicked. The college student had a warm heart and a good ear. She listened carefully to the girl as she began to open up. Their relationship quickly grew to encompass more than just tutoring. Allison was serving as Jessica's mentor.

It turned out that Jessica was suffering from Post-Traumatic Stress Disorder as a result of being raped when she was 13. She also witnessed the killing of her friend during a drug deal, which greatly compounded this tragedy.

In spite of the efforts of her parents, teachers, probation officer, school counselor and other adults in her life, Jessica's mentor was the only person she trusted. This is all because the university coed knew how to actively listen without placing judgment on what she heard. Allison was able to impact Jessica's life in a way that no other adult could up to that point.

At first, you may not quite understand what your mentees are saying. They might use slang terms or mumble incoherently. Don't be afraid to ask what a word or phrase means. These kids usually get a kick out of the fact that you're interested in communicating with them at their level. They also enjoy being able to teach you something. It builds their self-esteem to know that they can share information.

Think of it as if you were visiting a foreign country and learning about their local culture. If you traveled to China but didn't speak Chinese, then you would expect there to be communication difficulties. That same curiosity about a different lifestyle and a desire to connect can be transferred to your mentee, as long as it's not forced or intrusive.

If your mentee appears to be frustrated or uncomfortable expressing himself, ask some simple questions to help him get started. Sometimes youth just can't find the right words to tell their story.

You might suggest that she write a letter to you or create a fictitious story to get her point across. She could also draw or paint a picture to communicate, since creative expression often unlocks buried emotions.

2. <u>Mind Your Body Language:</u>

Listen with your eyes as well as your ears. Tone of voice, eye movement, posture, hand gestures and facial expressions can convey what these kids may be trying to hide. There are many books and online information available about body language, which is always a good thing to know, especially when trying to communicate with a youth who might be reluctant to speak.

Eye contact is especially important. Gang wars can start when rivals "mad-dog" each other. If two gang members meet and look directly into each other's eyes, one might confront the other by saying, "What are you looking at?" (peppered with a lot of profanity), and then violence follows.

Street language can be rich, with terminology that's unique and creative. "Mad-dogging" came about as gang slang because wild dogs always have one alpha dog that communicates with the rest of the pack through eye contact. All of the submissive dogs must look down or away from the leader to avoid a fight, and direct eye contact is taken as a challenge.

As the old saying goes, "The eyes are the windows of the soul." Use direct eye contact to express love and friendship to your mentee. They may resist looking back at first because of ingrained fear of being attacked or exposing their true feelings to someone else. If this happens, then continue to look into their eyes when you communicate. With time, you may be able to help them overcome their fears as they change their negative associations about direct eye contact.

If your mentee is smaller than you, then come down to his or her level when you look into their eyes. Squat, stoop or bend to become equal in height, especially when making a point.

Also be aware of your own body language. Are your arms always crossed, indicating defense and self-protection? Do you frown a lot? When you meet, do you stay far away, at a "safe" distance, which prohibits any kind of real intimacy?

Your mentee might feel threatened by sudden hand movements. In some poor communities, one has to be alert at all times to the possibility of being attacked by drive-by and "walk-by" killers, or crazy and desperate people who will shoot anyone around them without even needing a reason. At-risk youth are particularly vulnerable to potential attacks because of the prevalence of gangs in our inner-cities.

If your mentee has been abused physically or sexually, it can be very intimidating for them to have another person touch them or reach out too closely, especially someone they are just getting to know. Respect their boundaries and create your own, as well.

3. **Open Up About Yourself:**

Share yourself with your mentee. It's important to be open about your feelings, as well as some of the challenges that you face. This will allow your mentee to see that you're human and that you're also quite vulnerable.

If you keep everything to yourself and don't ever communicate about problems that you have to deal with, things that you find upsetting, or any emotions that you have ever experienced, then your mentee might feel intimidated to open up to you.

Put yourself in your mentee's place and imagine what it would be like for her to meet with someone who always seems perfect. Her mentor seems to have an ideal life with the best job in the world, along with a loving family and everything she could possibly desire. From your mentee's perspective, her mentor has probably never experienced a bad day.

Yet here she is, a youth dealing with all kinds of physical, mental and emotional challenges, including deep feelings of anger, frustration and loneliness. She desperately needs someone reliable to talk to about these things, but her mentor seems so flawless that she thinks you would never understand what she's experiencing.

She could also be afraid that if she tells her mentor what's really bothering her, then you won't want to spoil your idealistic life by wasting time with her, so she might clam up when you're together. She could be afraid to tell you the truth about anything.

It doesn't take much to fix this situation. When I say to open up to your mentee, I'm not suggesting that you whine or complain about things that you don't like. As I already mentioned, you don't want to dump your problems on your mentee. You should always try to stay positive and not dwell on any negativity. However, you could share some intimate experiences that show your humanity.

For instance, perhaps your mentee tells you that he's in love with a certain girl and he can't stop thinking about her. He could be unsure of how to approach her. You could tell him about the first time you fell in love. Give him some guidance from your own experience, maybe even about a time when you failed. Let your mentee see a warmer, more vulnerable part of you. This will make him feel more comfortable about expressing himself.

Even just admitting that you are having a rough day can help your mentees relate to you more. If your car broke down and it's going to cost you a small fortune to fix it, then let them know how tough it can be to maintain a vehicle. Allow them to see that you are human and you have to deal with challenges and feelings, just like they do.

If you have experienced abuse, neglect, addiction or other challenges in your life, it's important to share this information with your mentee. She or he might be going through the same thing, yet they could feel totally alone with their problem. By meeting someone who has overcome the same challenges, you allow them to be inspired, open up and release their buried feelings.

Fashion designer Cassie Betts joined **Create Now** as a mentor because she was sexually abused throughout her childhood. She wanted to help foster girls who were experiencing the same thing.

We found several of these girls who had aged out of the system and they jumped at the opportunity to intern with Cassie. She enlists their help to put together fashion shows, which gives these young ladies valuable life experience and career support.

"I share my story about sexual abuse with my mentees and they *instantly* share theirs with me," said Cassie. "Some have told me that I was the first person they ever told about their abuse. It always shocks me how easily they open up."

Always end your conversations with a feeling of gratitude and appreciation for the wonderful things in your life, including the relationship with your mentee(s).

4.   Choose Activities, But Follow Their Lead:

Successful mentoring relationships are youth-driven. It can be fun trying to come up with goals and activities. Always be open to your mentee's suggestions.

Select things to do that will be of interest to your mentee, without imposing your own values. If he likes playing videogames but you prefer football, then play videogames. Remember, this is about him, not you. Maybe you can compromise and play a football videogame. That way, you both learn something new and you'll grow closer sharing the experience.

Even if she's shy, include her in the activity-choosing process. Make it a game. Write down different things you can do together on pieces of paper and have her pick one out of a hat.

Find ways to introduce your mentee(s) to your local environment. Every community has something special to offer, or another town or city nearby to explore. Just don't forget that you are there to help the mentees. It's important to be a leader who also follows the lead of the mentees, so let them guide you in what they want to do and don't force your ideas.

5.   Find Common Ground:

It can be hard to connect with someone that you meet for the first time, especially when you're both so unique. Your mentee will be from a different generation, background and culture with a varied lifestyle. Finding common ground gives you something to talk about and opens the door to other subjects that you might enjoy sharing.

You could love a similar type of food, music, celebrity, dream car, TV show or career goal. You would be amazed at how much two completely different individuals can have in common. Find your connection and work that angle.

For instance, you could be a middle-aged gentleman with your own successful business and no children. What can you talk about with a 14-year-old kid who plays videogames all the time?

Perhaps you're a 65-year-old retiree and you want to mentor a young girl and teach her how to sew, but all she wants to do is listen to rap music at ear-splitting levels.

You could also be a college student who plans to mentor a youth by helping with their schoolwork, but your mentee only wants to talk about boys and her latest crush.

In all of the examples that I just gave, there is a disconnection between the mentor and their mentee. Their goals and interests are totally different, which makes it more challenging for them to bond.

You can find common ground in order to build your relationship. Since like attracts like, you need to find out what it is that makes you alike.

In the first example, the businessman who mentors the videogame addict could ask his mentee to teach him how to play the videogames. He might enjoy it and share in the excitement of this activity. He could also expose the boy to other types of thrilling things, such as watching car races or attending a sports event. He should find out what other interests the boy has that he might already share. Maybe they're both crazy for comic books, or eating the hottest chilé.

The retired woman who mentors the girl that prefers rap music to sewing could discover that her mentee loves to cook. Perhaps the girl has always wanted to learn about gardening, which is her mentor's favorite hobby.

The college student may feel irritated that her mentee doesn't want to study for school and seems to be obsessed with chasing boys. However, she may find out that the girl really enjoys bicycling, and that's her favorite activity, too. She could include bicycle riding as part of the mentoring sessions, which will make the time they spend together more fun and help them to bond quicker.

Finding common ground can be easy, especially if you use the Mentee Survey that I've included in the Appendix. You can both fill out this questionnaire to find out what similarities you share.

Perhaps you both adore koala bears, or you love the color fuchsia. You can't get enough macaroni and cheese or you and your mentee love the same magazine. This is knowledge that you can use to initiate conversations, and to find special gifts or reminders that you were thinking about your mentee.

6. Set Goals:

Help your mentee(s) to set goals. This will maximize your relationship, so you can feel more satisfaction as objectives are accomplished.

Some examples of goals might be for your mentee to improve his or her grades at school, to learn new skills that can lead to a career, or simply to expose them to resources and opportunities in your community while having a fun time together.

When you meet with your mentee(s) for the first time, ask them what their goals are. They might shrug and say, "I don't know." That can be the start of a good conversation. Many at-risk and high-risk youth don't even have an idea of what a goal is or the importance of setting goals. Your dialogue will get them to start thinking about what they hope to accomplish with their lives and how to go about doing it, with your support.

David was referred to *Crossroads* mentoring program by a probation officer in Seabrook, TX. The 16-year-old had no goals or ambitions besides being a rapper. He lacked motivation and self-esteem. The probation officer felt he would benefit greatly from a positive adult in his life. David was assigned to a 66-year-old female volunteer.

David's mother abandoned him and his family when he was 4. When he was 14 his father left, too. David was orphaned and put in the custody of Child Protective Services. Looking to belong to a

---

family, he joined a gang. He was put on probation for carrying a weapon to school. This young man needed nurturing.

His mentor saw something in him that many people had overlooked -- his potential for success. She saw how intelligent, funny, compassionate, and incredible this young man was.

With the encouragement of his mentor, David received his GED and signed up for classes at Houston Community College. His goal was no longer to be a rapper, but to work as a drug and alcohol counselor. He wanted to help boys who like himself had made bad decisions. David wanted to give them hope, just as his mentor gave him hope.

Work with your mentee(s) to develop an ultimate goal, and then write a list of necessary steps to get there. For instance, if her or his goal were to go to college, they would have to get good grades in school, take the SAT or other tests and research different universities and colleges. They would also fill out college applications and apply for scholarships. Ideally they would be invited to meet college administrators for interviews, and then have to choose which university to attend. You can continue this list of steps toward their goal: find a place to live, research classes they would like to take, discover different activities they could participate in on campus and places to meet new friends.

Provide explicit directions to help your mentees reach their goals. They may become confused or frustrated if they don't understand certain terminology or ideas. Therefore, if he or she just doesn't seem to get it, find a different way to express that step.

It can be very challenging to not lose your patience when trying to get a point across to someone who has a problem understanding, but it is important not to show any irritation when explaining something to your mentee. They can probably sense your feelings, so keep your annoyance in check. You also don't want to come across as demeaning in any manner, so watch your tone of voice, as well.

As your mentee completes the steps toward his or her goal, mark them off on the list. This small gesture can have a big impact as they realize how much they have done.

While setting goals and working toward them is essential, you also need to deviate a little. You don't want your mentee to feel you are only there to help them with their schoolwork or a particular task. Then you will be a tutor instead of a mentor. But if you find that your meetings are just becoming aimless gab sessions, then let your mentee know that time is precious and you need to get back on track.

However, those gab sessions may be exactly what both you and your mentee need. Don't feel that any particular task or goal has to take precedence over your mentoring relationship. You are primarily there to give your mentee emotional and moral support and to help them reach their objectives, whatever they might be. Try to maintain a good balance.

Be sure to give positive feedback when it's merited. You can remind them about how far they've gotten with your project, and then assign another task for them to complete before your next meeting.

Provide them with small rewards along the way. Something as simple as a special card can be powerful. It motivates them to keep going. They might really appreciate a book related to their college major. Even just treating them to an ice cream can have tremendous impact. When you celebrate your mentees' positive actions, it helps build more confidence.

Many young people lack focus and discipline. They may have diverse interests, but might have difficulty concentrating for long periods of time. Heavy exposure to television with a constant bombardment of commercials and videogames compounds this problem.

Many kids have learning disorders, such as A.D.D. (Attention Deficit Disorder) and Dyslexia. They might be on medications, which can make them drowsy or lethargic. Educate yourself about any disorders that your mentee might have and medications taken. Keep it in mind during your mentoring sessions.

If your mentee has a hard time focusing, then give him or her smaller, simpler tasks that can be easily completed. They will feel successful each step of the way until they accomplish their objective.

Of course, your goal doesn't have to be rigorous; it can be simply to have a fun time together and share new ideas and experiences. The important thing to remember is that if you *do* target a specific goal, then be sure to keep it in mind. Teach your mentee(s) to finish what they set out to do.

7. **<u>Introduce Your Mentees to the World Outside:</u>**

Your mentee(s) may not be aware of career possibilities. Friends, family or peers may unintentionally limit their knowledge of the world. Help broaden his or her horizons.

If you are mentoring high-risk youth that live in an institution, you may be able to get permission to take your mentee(s) on a field trip. Invite them somewhere exciting that will demonstrate potential careers. For instance, you can tour college campuses to expose them to higher education.

If your mentee fails at school but is technically capable, explore vocational training at alternative schools, as well as possible apprenticeships in your community. "Job Corps" is a great resource for these kinds of opportunities. Visit www.jobcorps.gov to learn more.

A mentor may make the mistake of trying too hard to push a mentee in a particular direction. Don't dictate your mentee's career. Listen to what they want to do and then help develop their strengths, not impose your values.

Your mentee can be interested in a specific career but may not know how to pursue it. As her or his mentor, you may be able to open doors. Use the contacts you have and find new ones. You can teach your mentee how to research for prospects on the Internet or at the public library.

Naval Academy midshipmen, U.S. Military Academy and Air Force Academy cadets introduce at-risk youth to the opportunities available in the world today through a mentorship program called "Heart to Heart."

Through this program, Midshipman 1st Class Brianna was matched up with a Dallas, Texas high school mentee who needed guidance. Brianna said, "Her family life wasn't that great and one of her parents was in jail. A lot of the times, kids just need a role model better than the one they have in their immediate families, someone they can look up to and ask questions of without being afraid of getting laughed at or yelled at."

Darryl Smith, who trained "Heart to Heart" volunteers, explained, "The idea here is that by exposing some of these at-risk youth to midshipmen and cadets, maybe they might have hope and some much needed role models to deal with life issues they are going through. Any level of the military can do it from a mentor side. We can take cadets and midshipmen from all over the country."

Many at-risk and high-risk youth have never been outside of their neighborhoods. This is particularly true of gang members. They have their "territory" and a rival gang whose turf is nearby will probably attack them if they step outside their bounds.

Thousands of gang members in the Los Angeles area have never been to the beach or the mountains that are close by, because they fear getting killed if they leave their particular "hood" or "barrio." Even going ten blocks away could be asking for trouble. They only feel comfortable going out with some of their "homies" or "dogs."

At-risk youth from the inner-city who are *not* in gangs often feel terrified to leave their limited area. They are sometimes more comfortable hanging out with friends in their dangerous community than mixing with others in mainstream society, since they think that people will laugh at the way they look or treat them negatively. When they leave their neighborhood, they often experience racism and discrimination, even in large cities.

Imagine what it must be like to be a perfectly good kid with lofty goals about going to college or making something out of your life. You walk around in a nice neighborhood that's predominantly Caucasian and you notice that some women clutch their purses when they walk past you. Men eye you with great suspicion. If you're driving, cops pull you over and interrogate or arrest you for no reason. This isn't paranoia. It has been proven many times that racial profiling exists in our country.

Create Now arranged for 12 teenage foster boys from a group home to visit a prominent museum of art. They lived in a desert community called Palmdale, located at a distance from the city. These youth were Latino and African-American. They were good kids who had suffered tremendously since they were removed from their families because of abuse and neglect, or they were orphaned.

The boys were excited to go to the museum, since they had never been to one before. Even though they were accompanied by adult staff and were very well-behaved, two security guards at the museum were immediately suspicious of them. They followed the small group around and intimidated them to the point where the boys were forced to leave, even though they did absolutely nothing wrong!

The next day, the owner of the group home contacted me about what had occurred. He said that the boys were totally embarrassed and horrified by what had happened to them at the museum. Independent witnesses verified the fact that the boys had done nothing wrong. Now these poor youth who had ventured out to explore a museum for the first time think that all White people might treat them this way.

As a mentor, you can show your mentee(s) that not everyone is racist or will discriminate against them because of the color of their skin or the way that they dress. If you want to take your mentee on an outing, but you sense that he or she is nervous about going to a new, strange environment, invite them to bring a relative or a friend along to make them feel more comfortable.

It could be a life-changing experience for a child who has never left their limited neighborhood (especially one that is decrepit and dangerous), to visit beautiful, natural environments. Take them hiking in a park, swimming at a lake, or sledding in the winter

Most at-risk and high-risk youth rarely (if ever) get to attend cultural events, such as a classical music concert, opera or the theater. They may not have ever been to the circus.

Through **Create Now**, every year thousands of high-risk and at-risk kids have been able to attend theater and concert performances at premiere venues, like the Geffen Playhouse, the Ahmanson Theater, Walt Disney Concert Hall, the Hollywood Bowl, as well as Cirque du Soleil and other cultural events.

I sat in front of a group of teenage girls who were experiencing theater for the first time. When the play was halfway completed, one of the girls asked, "What's an intermission?" This is a term that's common knowledge for most people, but not necessarily for at-risk and high-risk youth.

> I could hear their gasps as they watched the sets change and the actors appeared in their period costumes. Afterwards, several of the girls asked me if people could really earn money working in the theater. This was a whole new world for them. I felt exhilarated, knowing that I had exposed these young women to a new experience that could potentially change their lives.

If you can afford it, invite your mentee(s) to experience musical concerts, theater, museums, festivals and other cultural events. There are usually cheap tickets available and many communities offer free entertainment, since every performer needs an audience to make the experience complete. Not only will you be opening your mentee's eyes to new possibilities, you will bond more with them as you share the fun. It will also give you things to talk about in the future.

You will also be creating wonderful memories for your mentee, often replacing tragic ones from their past. Instead of recalling traumatic moments when they suffered from abuse, neglect, homelessness or other challenging situations, your mentee can experience phenomenal, exciting performances, view fascinating exhibitions, meet some interesting people and create new recollections that will remind them of the fun times they shared with you. These encounters will stay with them forever and be fresher in their minds, replacing old, distressing memories.

8.   Look for Teachable Moments:

Many at-risk and high-risk young people lack life skills. Since a lot of them don't have strong adult supervision, they may grow up without learning any manners, practicing good hygiene or understanding how to mix with mainstream society.

It can be awkward dealing with someone who has little or no social skills. How do you politely tell them that they need to show appreciation when accepting a gift? What's the best way to emphasize that it's important to be on time?

Use common sense with your mentee. Without judgment, point out in a kind manner the polite ways to behave in society. You are a bridge for your mentee(s). You might be the only educated person they have ever known.

Money management is another area where at-risk and high-risk youth tend to struggle. Since many come from poor families, money generally goes out as quickly as it comes in. Saving money for the future usually never occurs to them because they don't know how long they will be around. Life in the "hood" or the "barrio" can be dangerous, particularly when you are the member of a gang, or the accidental victim of drive-by bullets.

With homicide as the second leading cause of death amongst youth ages 10-24 in our nation, many of our kids don't expect to live past 21. Their attitude is to enjoy what they've got today, since there probably won't be a tomorrow.

Look for ways to teach your mentees about managing money. When you take them shopping for school supplies and they spot a lovely party dress or a new CD that they're just dying to buy, remind them that they might save their money for the computer they want.

Of course, it's up to them if they want to take your advice or not, and you shouldn't be offended if they don't. Children, particularly teenagers, like to be very independent and make their own choices, which they should do when appropriate. It's a part of growing up. They can develop faster by learning from their mistakes. Offer your guidance and then help your mentee to realize the effects of their decisions by gently pointing out the lessons in a kind and loving manner.

9.   Promote Education:

Around 50 percent of all youth living in the biggest cities in the United States are dropping out of school. This is a tragedy, since bright young minds are being wasted. Plus, without a high school diploma or a GED, there is not much hope for getting a job, let alone having a decent career.

Promote higher education. Don't force it on your mentee, but talk about the benefits and show possibilities, such as different fields of study that might be of interest and potential schools, like community colleges and universities.

If your mentee wants to apply to college, then help her or him to plan it, or seek assistance from someone who can aid them. Inform them about taking the SAT and loan them books that might help them do better on the test. Assist them to get through the application process and to apply for financial aid.

Some youth are surrounded by peers who think of college as "uncool." Determine your mentee's true interest in attending college. Don't push the issue if they are really uninterested. Just try to make them aware of what's possible.

"Sarena" was a sharp African-American girl who grew up in a poor neighborhood. She had problems with her family. When Sarena was thirteen years old, she kept running away from home and getting into trouble by hanging out with boys who committed different crimes.

I met Sarena when she was almost sixteen-years-old. She was at a detention facility in Los Angeles where she participated in a Create Now TV Writing workshop. Sarena really loved our program and bonded with her mentor (who has asked to remain anonymous). When the workshop ended, they continued to meet regularly after Sarena returned home. I also mentored her.

Sarena's mentor encouraged her to apply to college. Although she was very interested in the film and TV industry, she didn't dream that she could ever have such a career. She told me, "I don't think that someone like me can ever be a film director."

Through her mentor's encouragement, as well as my own and that of another **Create Now** mentor, Sarena decided that she would take a chance and apply to USC Film School, rated as one of the top film schools in the world. Around 50 students are accepted into their film program each year.

Not only did Sarena get accepted into USC Film School, but she also received a scholarship from Warner Brothers. Sarena graduated from USC and also completed her first year of law school at the University of Northern Illinois in Chicago. She has found her passion in writing film reviews for the Chicago Drama Film Examiner and performing standup comedy.

Remember that there are many educational opportunities aside from college, including vocational schools, internships, training institutions, seminars and apprenticeships.

10. <u>Provide Reinforcement and Encouragement:</u>

Young people truly need positive reinforcement. They may have suffered neglect at home or in school. As a result, they may not believe they are capable of reaching their potential. Reward each accomplishment. A flattering remark will go a long way, like "I knew you could do it if you tried. I'm so proud of you."

You may want to provide treats like candy or small gifts as an incentive. I'm not suggesting that you should bribe your mentee. However, young people often like competition. They want to be challenged so they can rise up to the occasion.

If you're working with a group of kids, you might want to set up a reward system: Whoever scores the highest gets a prize, or whoever does the best work is the winner and has a special privilege. This type of motivation will depend on the youth that you work with. I suggest that if the kids decide on the winner, then make sure they vote anonymously so no one's feelings are hurt.

Jill Gurr

CHAPTER SIX

20 Amazing Tips

The following tips are some insights from a mentor who volunteered her time teaching a TV Writing workshop at a coed detention facility through **Create Now**. She has asked to remain anonymous. I think you'll agree that her advice is very helpful:

1. Don't judge who will do well by his or her initial application. Some of these kids have had a horrendous education, therefore they have poor spelling and grammar skills, yet they are really bright.

2. Don't judge who is "getting it" by how much he or she speaks up. Sometimes a child has been taught to just shut up, but if you make an effort to call on them ("Ricky, what do you think would make a good ending to this scene?"), they'll surprise you with how much they've absorbed.

3. They are going to talk about a lot of things that might be out of the realm of your experience. Sometimes it's made up, just to shock you and to see if you'll still stick around no matter how "bad" they are. Sometimes what they tell you is the truth. It doesn't matter. Remember, either way, it's their truth. Don't judge, just listen. It's a real temptation to preach, to say, "You shouldn't do drugs," "You shouldn't hang out with gangs," "You shouldn't have sex." Don't say it. They've heard it. Remember what it felt like when your parents preached to you and how little impact it had. Better responses are "That must be so hard for you," "What is that like?" or "Why do you do that?" and "How does that feel?" The idea that someone cares what they think is new to them and gives them the feeling of being worthwhile, which is the whole point. So the most important thing you can do is LISTEN.

4.   When teaching, go in small steps, smaller than you think is necessary. That way they will always have the answer and the experience of succeeding. When they get it right, praise them highly. "You guys are so smart!" or "Jamal, you did it again! Good job!" Don't *ever* make any answer wrong. It's better to respond, "That's a good way of looking at it. Can anyone else think of another way?" Remember, this isn't really about the actual project so much as building self-esteem. It's better to have a line in the script that's not so good and a child who feels like he is finally doing well at something.

5.   They may look like young adults, but they aren't. Although these kids have gone through many adult-type experiences, they usually missed out on the childhood ones. Inside, they are like little kids. They want praise, constancy, hugs, snacks. When I made homemade cookies for them, some of the kids had never had them and didn't even realize you could make cookies at home. One of the boys, who seemed pretty hardened, asked me to tell him the recipe so he could make them when he got out of detention.

6.   Like little kids, they really like structure. This is a hard one for most writers and creative artists who are usually pretty anti-authoritarian. But remember, you're doing it for the kids, not for you. Structure and rules make them feel safe and cared about. They usually grew up with none. You don't have to be too hard on them. I have developed a class structure that starts out with snacks and talking for ten minutes, then work on the script, then about fifteen minutes at the end for more socializing.

If someone's acting up, you can say something like, "I know it's fun to fool around, but you guys are doing such a great job on this script. You're too smart to be spending your time hitting each other with books. I want everyone to stay in the class, but if anyone starts acting up, I'm going to have to send you out. It's not that I want you to leave (*important*), but it's not fair to the other kids who are trying to get something done. So it's your choice" (*also important*). Then, if it happens again, do it in a nice and caring way. Say that you hope that he or she can come back the next week and be able to concentrate on the script. Surprisingly, the kids love this. They love the idea that you have expectations of them.

Of course you have to be flexible, because many of them have deep psychological problems. When they are focusing, or if you send someone out one week and they come back the next and are doing better, praise them for it. "You are doing such a good job this week!"

7.   It's great to have high expectations of them, but sometimes this can feel like pressure. Adults often ask kids, "What do you want to be when you grow up?" Or, they say, "You would make a great lawyer." One kid told me, "I'm just sixteen and I have to make all these decisions. I have to know what I want to be already. Everyone keeps talking about it." I realized then that it's better to say that they have lots of time to decide what they want to do and the main thing is that they can be anything they want. Say, "I have faith in you."

8.   Try to get them to read. It's not even important what it is. I sometimes lend or buy them books on subjects they're interested in. Better to read about basketball or a Jackie Collins novel than nothing. A girl had mentioned a book she'd seen somewhere. After I got it for her, she told me, "I wasn't going to read this. I'm not really into reading. But now I can't put it down. Jackie Collins makes me think about how only you really know what it's like to go through the things that have happened to you, but if you write about it with a lot of details, maybe that will make someone else understand. I'd like to write about my life one day." If a love of reading is all she gets out of the class, that's enough.

As a retired teacher in Pittsburgh, Thomas enjoyed spending his time in the library. One day, a brochure that read "Read Together" caught his eye. It was from *Beginning with Books*, a center for early literacy. He took a brochure and called to see how he could get involved. He went to an interview and completed his security clearance. Three weeks later, he was matched with a 6-year-old African-American boy named Jonathan.

At the library where they meet, they each choose a book to read. At the end of the session, they tell each other about what they have read.

Thomas and Jonathan have now been reading together for four years. Jonathan, who is in 5th grade, is reading at a 10th grade level.

Thomas could not be more proud of him. He loves that he has been able to share his passion for books with a child by volunteering as a mentor.

9. I printed up a form for the kids to fill in with their birthdays, favorite colors, foods and music. This helped me to bring them cards or little gifts on their birthdays. Sometimes you will be the only one who remembers that day.

10. Don't bring up their homes. Some of them don't have one. Some have both parents in jail or parents who have disowned them or who are dead. This is incredibly painful for them. Let them bring it up if they want to talk about it.

11. In some detention facilities, kids get sent to "the Halls" (Juvenile Halls; prisons for youth awaiting trials) if they act up. This can happen between one class and the next, and you probably won't know about it until you show up and the child is gone. You may have formed a bond and then suddenly you will never see them again. You can get home phone numbers in advance if you want to keep in contact (but remember that if you say you're going to call, this is a promise to them and you'd better do it). Just be prepared emotionally for the fact that they can be taken away at any time and you may not even get to say good-bye.

If this happens, talk about it with the other kids. "It's hard that Damien is gone, isn't it? We'll miss him." If it's hard on you, imagine what it's like for them, with this happening over and over to their friends.

12. You can't imagine how important constancy is to these kids. They cannot hold on to the fact that someone cares for them and will be there for them. So if you say you will be there Mondays at 3:00, be there Mondays at 3:00. If you're a minute late, they think you're not coming. I've been teaching the same kids for seven months and they still think every week I'm not coming back. Once, when we were getting ready to go on a field trip, a girl said to me, "You aren't coming back again after this, are you?" She told me that when

something good happens, something bad happens right after. This has been their experience. Don't reinforce it.

They also like you to come the same time and day each week. They think about it all week. So it's better to pick a time you can consistently be there and not change it unless you really, really have to. "Monday at 3:00 is our time." If for some reason, you have to change your time, don't just assume because you told someone on staff that the kids will get the message. Tell more than one person.

Try to find someone at the facility who you can count on to get messages to them. Often this is a secretary or aide or floor supervisor. The kids themselves may be able to tell you whom you can trust with this.

13. Sometimes you will get a sense in the class that the kids can't focus because of something important on their minds. That's okay. It's good now and then to just use a class to listen to what's going on with them. You will be able to tell the difference between them just wanting to goof off and there really being a need to talk.

An individual kid may seem especially sad or like something is bothering him or her, yet not want to talk about it in the group. Take them aside and say that you can see that they have something on their mind and ask if they'd like to stay after class a few minutes to talk. If they say no, say that you are there when they want to talk and to just let you know.

14. Try to let them do as much as possible. Whether it's passing out the pages, handing out napkins, writing on the board, writing down what will go in the script, even cleaning up afterwards, they really like doing this.

Remember, they are in a facility where everything is done for them. They like the autonomy and the feeling of accomplishment and of doing things for themselves. It is especially good for the shy ones to have some kind of responsibility. "Raymond, will you put out the paper plates again? You did that so well last time." "Good job, Michelle. You have excellent handwriting." What we think of as chores, they think of as feeling important and needed.

15. The last thing you say *every week*, after you tell them what a good job they did, should be a reinforcement of when you will

return. "You guys did great this week. You came up with some really funny stuff. Okay, I'll see you next Monday at 3:00."

16.   Whenever you can, find a way to tell them you were thinking about them during the week. "I saw *Boyz 'n the Hood* was on TV, David, and I thought about you saying how much you liked it." "Lucy, I read this article about fashion design in a magazine and thought you might be interested in it."

17.   Make a big effort to keep things equal. Praise, articles, books, snacks, attention, need to be given the same to everyone. Remember, most of them grew up in a family where there wasn't enough (especially emotionally). The things you bring are symbols of caring. If you see a kid hoarding something (for example, taking half the cookies), realize that it doesn't mean they're "selfish." It means they're afraid that they might not get anything again. "There's enough for everyone," and "I'll bring more next week," are good messages applying to things as well as attention. They'll relax once they see you mean it.

18.   It will take a long time for them to trust you. They have been disappointed a lot. Even when they do trust you, they will keep testing you. Tell them "I'm not going anywhere." And mean it!

19.   These kids will remember you forever. That is a huge responsibility. Do not take it lightly. Make their experience with you different than what's gone before. Make it something valuable to remember.

20.   When you get discouraged, rent *Stand and Deliver.* It's really inspiring and you can also get some good ideas from it.

CHAPTER SEVEN

Special Guidance For High-Risk Youth

As mentioned, "at-risk youth" are kids who have the strong potential to get into trouble, while "high-risk youth" are those who are already experiencing difficulties. Some examples of high-risk youth include those who have been abused, neglected, abandoned, orphaned, are left homeless, runaways, substance abusers, teen parents, victims of domestic violence, children of prisoners, gang members or incarcerated youth.

There are millions of high-risk kids all over the world. You can find them in your community by directly contacting local shelters, group homes, detention camps, rehab centers and other youth agencies.

Hundreds of community-based organizations around the country are also trying to recruit positive role models. Volunteer Coordinators, administrators, teachers, social workers and probation officers are searching for mentors just like you, since they know that mentors can often provide tremendous support for their clients.

National CARES Mentoring Movement (NCMM) is an organization founded by Susan L. Taylor, the Editor-in-Chief Emeritus of *Essence* magazine. They mobilize massive numbers of able African-Americans to mentor Black children by connecting caring adults to existing community-based organizations. Learn more at www.caresmentoring.com.

It was through *NCMM* that Phyllis Simon met Mike. Since she has been mentoring him, she's helped the boy transform.

Mike was in the foster care system in NY for most of his life. He had been abused and neglected, and then his mother died when he was 12-years-old. The boy was very distraught, filled with anger and grief. He was difficult to manage. Every person he lived with tossed him out within a couple of months. Mike moved ten times while he was in foster care.

> For six years, Phyllis Simon came into Mike's life as a CASA (Court-Appointed Special Advocate). Phyllis showed Mike that someone cared and was there for him through thick and thin. As a result, he graduated from high school on time, reads and writes well and has a charismatic personality. But like many teens who have grown up in the child welfare system, Mike can be his own worst enemy. Yet there's something about him that keeps adults from giving up on him.
>
> Phyllis considers her mentee to be family, like a son. She said, "I suppose Mike's lucky to have us, but I'm lucky to have him too. In the difficult world of child welfare, Mike has helped me hold on to my humanity and kept me from becoming completely jaded. When I started my work for CASA, I thought I would be changing the lives of children. But I found they have changed my life as well."

DEALING WITH STAFF

Mentors who work with high-risk youth must realize that the kids are in the institution for a specific reason or else they would be living at home with their families. Troubled kids need a lot of professional help in order to rehabilitate and then assimilate back into society.

Their days are filled with school, individual treatment, family therapy, group dorm sessions, Alcoholics Anonymous (AA) and Narcotics Anonymous (NA) meetings, plus tight schedules for homework, meals and showers.

Unfortunately, mentoring is not yet considered a priority when the personnel in charge have to fulfill their responsibilities. Their goal is the same as yours, to help these vulnerable youth, and as a volunteer, sometimes you will just have to take a back seat.

Last minute changes can happen. Maybe one of the kids stole something from another youth, so everyone is being punished until they find the thief. They might cancel your session if personnel call in sick and there's a sudden lack of staff to supervise outside programs. Usually these people are so busy that they will forget to call you to let you know of a cancellation. That's why it's important for you to call ahead of time and check with someone at the facility before you go to your meeting, or you might waste a trip.

Most of the employees that work with high-risk youth are wonderful, loving people who try their best to help these kids. They include therapists, social workers, probation officers, school counselors and teachers, dorm supervisors and administrative staff. They are so dedicated to helping these kids that they work sometimes in dangerous environments for low wages and must carry large caseloads that require a lot of their time. In spite of these difficulties, most youth workers are positive and able to face challenges with a smile.

However, you might come across an individual who has a negative attitude or energy that makes you feel like they are intentionally sabotaging your mentoring relationship. You'll hopefully never meet this type of bitter employee, but if you do, then they could try to ruin your program in subtle ways.

For instance, if students are supposed to be in your workshop at a specific time, they might create an alternate activity that prevents the kids from participating in your class.

If you ask for certain materials or equipment, such as a DVD player or a dry erase board, they will always forget to bring it. Maybe they take such a long time to locate your mentee that when you're finally together, there are only 15 minutes left. Perhaps they punish all the kids for no apparent reason, so they miss out on your art workshop.

When you hit a snag, don't immediately jump to the conclusion that a particular employee is trying to stop you from mentoring. There could be a very legitimate reason why the kids are being punished. Perhaps two rivals at the detention camp got into a fight and now everyone is on lockdown. Another wonderful opportunity like tickets to the circus might have suddenly come up for the foster kids at a group home. Maybe the equipment that was promised to you really is broken.

To avoid these types of problems, be sure to call ahead of time to remind the staff that you will be there and you would really appreciate it if they could make sure that the youth are ready. Also, don't depend on anyone at the facility to supply you with materials. Bring your own equipment.

Dealing with a difficult staff member can feel like you're running into a brick wall. No matter what you need or request, this person will deny it and there will always be a continual cycle of challenges inflicted on you that limits your time with your mentee(s) and spoils your mentoring experience. It may feel like they are trying to drive you away.

The best thing to do is to act professionally and don't be openly upset. Don't take it personally. Try to have a private conversation with this difficult person. Explain your goals and request that they help you to prevent these problems.

If that doesn't work, then share the situation with another staff member who is sympathetic to your cause. They might shed some light and suggest a good solution.

It might help to understand why this person is being so difficult. Perhaps they came from an abusive home and they want to lash out. They might feel jealous of the attention that the children receive. The employee could be miserable due to an unhappy marriage, so he or she takes it out on others.

Unfortunately, many of these people earn little more than minimum wage, which could make them resentful and sour. Some are not well educated.

Maybe they're worried that if the children are healed, they won't be needed any longer and they'll lose their jobs. They might resent that the youth are given a privilege that they don't deserve because they committed a crime or misbehaved in some way. They could also be simply lazy and just not want to put in any time or effort to helping the kids by facilitating a mentoring program.

Whatever the reason, it's a thorn that we sometimes have to deal with. If all else fails, contact the employee's supervisor. He or she might have a talk with the person causing the trouble or schedule them to work at a different time or location.

Whatever you do, don't give up mentoring. If you're having these difficulties with this individual just once a week for an hour or so, imagine what the poor kids have to deal with on a daily basis! At least they have your support, so please be persistent.

FINDING THE RIGHT SPACE

When mentoring institutionalized or "system-involved" youth, finding the right space can be a challenge. The kids may be in a situation where they can't leave the premises, like at a detention camp. You might not have security clearance to take them to other places. Also, many social service agencies struggle for funding just to keep their doors open. They operate in tight quarters with minimal staff for supervision.

Detention boot camps might have just one giant bunkhouse for all their wards, with few private areas. Since staff members are also in low supply, it may not be possible to provide you with a location where you can meet privately with your mentee while also remaining supervised by probation officers.

Emergency shelters also tend to be very limited, since most of the available space is used for cots. Residents usually share a communal cafeteria and bathrooms, but there may be limited room for private discussions or activities.

Foster kids who are younger than 12 years old usually live with foster families. There is an entire industry based around foster youth. As they grow older and become teenagers, it's harder to place them in foster homes. As a result, there are small companies licensed to run group homes for these kids, just as there are people who are licensed to run day-care centers. Those with permits might own or rent one group home, or a whole chain of them.

In a small foster group home, there are generally six boys or six girls living in the house, which is located in a residential neighborhood. The owner of the group home(s) hires staff to supervise the kids around the clock. There are probably a number of these group homes right in your own community.

Whether the foster youth live with a foster family or in a group home, most of these placements have two or three bedrooms, a kitchen, bathroom and a living room. Since family members or other foster kids share the house, it may be difficult to use the living room for a private meeting with your mentee(s). The bedrooms might also be off-limits.

There are larger group homes for foster youth, which are built on big campuses that are tucked away from the public eye. These institutions might have 100 or more residents: foster children ages 6-18. The kids live in dorms, go to school, get therapy and are very protected and isolated from the rest of the world. While there may be more space to meet with your mentee(s) at such a facility, they may be short-staffed and unable to supervise you if you're not (security) "cleared" to take your mentee off campus.

If you find that there is no real space to comfortably meet with your mentee(s), try to find an alternative that will work for everyone. Speak to the person in charge and let them know about your situation. Encourage them to look for a quiet, private space for you to meet your mentee(s).

At a large institution, you could try to gather in the cafeteria when it's not being used to serve meals. This way, you could sit at the table and chat or do an activity, while the kitchen employees are preparing a meal or cleaning up. You would have some supervision, but also some privacy.

Another idea would be to meet in the back yard, porch or the patio of a group home. Perhaps there's a religious center on the premises. Maybe they have a special room for counseling sessions or family meetings. A clean garage could work out.

You might also be able to get permission for your mentee to meet you at a public location, such as a library or a park.

Be careful about bringing your mentee(s) to your home unless you have permission from a parent or guardian to do so. The same goes for inviting them on an outing to any location that is not approved of by the institutional staff or whoever is in charge.

If someone tries to put you into a place where you're not comfortable, don't let him or her force you to go there. Perhaps it's a cold, dank basement or a creaky attic filled with spider webs that they use for storage. The chances are that nobody is ever going to ask you to mentor in these types of places, but if you don't want to meet your mentee in a particular location, then let the person in charge know right away that you prefer a different space. Don't let them pressure you into doing something if you're not comfortable.

I had arranged for an attractive young woman to teach a Screenwriting workshop to a group of teenage boys in a juvenile hall. One of the staff members, a probation officer at the detention facility, found the program to be extra work and an inconvenience.

When our mentor came one day to teach her workshop, this probation officer claimed there was no space for her to work with the youth. He locked this young lady in a pantry with these boys who had been arrested for a variety of crimes! There was no room for them to sit, no ventilation and she was forced into a dangerous situation.

Even though she was nervous and uncomfortable, the mentor went along with this and didn't notify me until after the incident. Luckily, nothing bad happened since her mentees respected her, but this was potentially dangerous and totally unacceptable. She should have refused to be put into such a situation, even if it meant canceling the class that day.

I reported the probation officer to his supervisor. He was reprimanded for endangering one of our volunteers. The juvenile hall then hired a full-time Volunteer Coordinator to avoid future problems.

It's important to make sure that your mentee is also at ease in your meeting space. She may not want to open up and talk with you if she thinks that some of the other girls can hear your conversation. He might worry that his teacher can eavesdrop and he'll be punished later for what he says.

If you sense that your mentee is nervous or ill at ease during your meeting, ask if he or she would like to go elsewhere to talk. Make sure that you find some place quiet and private to ensure an open discussion.

At the same time, you should be aware of your own need to be protected from false accusations. I've never heard of this happening, but there is the potential that your mentee might become angry with you for some reason. He or she could possibly claim that you touched them inappropriately or that you sexually harassed them.

While this is very unlikely, be alert so if you think there is the chance that this might occur or you sense that your mentee has the desire to make up lies about you, then stay in a public space where staff and others can observe that you mean your mentee no harm.

SPECIAL SAFETY ISSUES

When working with high-risk youth, such as those who are incarcerated or struggling with substance abuse, it's essential that you take extra precautions for your security. Chances are that absolutely nothing will happen to you, especially since you are a beloved mentor who is a friend, not an authority figure who is trying to force them to do something against their will. Yet it's always best to be alert, just in case.

There are some extra safety measures that you can take to ensure that problems don't arise. For example, in detention camps, be careful about bringing scissors and paper clips, pencils and pens. These everyday materials can be used as weapons.

In the high-risk unit of Barry J. Nidorff Juvenile Hall in Sylmar, CA, where youth are waiting to be sentenced as adults for very serious crimes, one young man stabbed another youth in the eye with a pencil. As a result, regular pens and pencils are not allowed in the detention camps and juvenile halls. Tiny pencils are handed out to kids, which have to be counted at the end of each class so the staff knows that they have been returned.

If you give writing or art assignments to mentees who are incarcerated, they might have to get permission from authorities to receive pencils. Markers are prohibited since they can be used for graffiti tagging. Ink pens can make gang tattoos. If you are not sure if it's safe to bring something, check with the staff first.

Watch all of your materials and make sure that you get them back. Supplies are easily stolen. One system to prevent theft is to put a number on each item that you give out. Keep a list of to whom they were assigned, so if the goods aren't returned, then you know who has them.

Also know that markers and glue can be stolen for "huffing," (sniffing) since breathing these chemicals provides a cheap high, which greatly damages the brain, eventually causing paralysis. My heart was broken when I met a number of street kids in South Africa who started huffing shoe leather glue at a young age. They're now permanently paralyzed and must crawl or use crutches to get around.

We provided an "Introduction to Art" workshop at a detention camp. Our supplies included a large box of brand new colored pencils and bags of candy. They were stored in a locked closet where our sessions occurred. The pencils and candy were all stolen. We're not sure if the staff robbed them or the kids, although I suspect it was one of the probation officers. They also took my personal pens, which were used for the kids to complete surveys. One girl even tried to hide a slice of pizza down her shirt!

Working with high-risk youth could potentially be dangerous. I wanted to learn more about protecting oneself from violence while working with them.

I was privileged to take an intensive three-day workshop with Harold Robertson, Jr. at Phoenix Academy California in Lake View Terrace, CA as part of their employee training. Harold has worked on the frontlines at Phoenix Academy for many years.

Phoenix Academy is a substance abuse rehabilitation center for 120 teenagers. More than half of their clients are in the foster care system. Most of the boys and girls living there have serious addictions to heroin, methamphetamines and crack cocaine.

Harold gave me some wonderful safety tips:

O When walking to a parking lot, check for shadows;
O Never walk too close to walls or near a blind spot;
O Don't trap yourself in a room;
O Don't touch your mentee or go in their personal space;
O Horseplay and roughhousing can lead to physical violence.

Harold was trained by Pro-ACT® (Professional Assault Crisis Training), which is a risk management, safety enhancement program designed to provide those who work with potentially dangerous clients with the opportunity to develop skills that avoid or reduce the need for physical restraint. If you would like more information, visit their website at www.proacttraining.com.

The many techniques that I learned in this workshop are valuable for everyday life. We live in dangerous times when assaults are too frequent. It's good to learn this safety information because you never know when it might come in handy.

Harold taught us about the five stages of a physical assault in a Stress Cycle developed by Pro-ACT®.

The Stress Cycle is a bell-shaped curve with the assault or aggression occurring at the peak:

1. **Triggering Event** – Something sets off the youth. Examples of triggers might be losing a weekend home pass because of poor behavior, family issues, depression over the holidays, upsetting news about a loved one, rejection from a girlfriend/boyfriend or even just boredom. Nightmares can also be triggers, as well as certain music or movies that bring up bad memories.

2. **Escalation** – Tension increases. The youth might have a loud outburst, make threats or throw things. Her body language changes. She might pout, hyperventilate or bang repeatedly on the wall.

3. **Crisis** – This is when they carry out the assault. His face will turn red. He might throw a chair. She could punch someone, or a brick wall. There will be a lot of negative energy spent intensely for three minutes. After that, the youth will collapse from exhaustion.

4. **Recovery** – Their muscles will relax and they'll regulate their breathing. Their skin color will return to normal. Their speech will be a softer tone and less aggressive.

5. **Post-Crisis Depression** – The youth will want to be in a quiet place away from everyone. They might lay on their bed in a fetal position. Many kids will cry. After the episode is over, they'll remember things that they said and did and will feel apologetic. She might say, "Oh my God! I threw a chair at Monica?" These emotions can brew for hours, even days.

If your mentee experiences an aggression episode like this, my suggestion is to get out of the way and go for help. You're not a trained therapist and it's not your job to intervene. You have to look after your own safety first, since you don't know what triggered the assault or how to stop it. If you wait for three minutes, then the cycle will finish and your mentee will automatically calm down. They might feel embarrassed about their actions. That's when they can really use your support.

Be a friend and just listen. Don't make any threats. Let your mentee tell you what their trigger was, since they will learn more by finding this out for themselves. Be compassionate and have empathy for their situation. Assure them that they can make any necessary apologies later and things will work out.

I hope not to scare you off with all of this safety information, especially since I don't think you will ever need it. However, I think it's good to have these tools in the back of your mind and to be prepared. Here are some more suggestions that Harold gave, *just in case* you are physically threatened:

If your mentee grabs your hair, then hold your hand over his hand and say calmly, "Joe, let go of my hair." Say it firmly so that he can hear you, but without panic.

If you discover one youth beating up another kid, come from behind and make a loud clapping sound or drop a chair to distract them, so the victim can escape.

If two youth are fighting, yell loudly, "Cut it out! Robert stop! Now! Stop it Billy!" If they continue to fight, then go for help.

If there is another adult nearby, signal each other and grab one youth from behind on their belt or by their waistband and swing them around, while the other adult does the same with the other youth, twirling them in the opposite direction. The kids may continue to fight when they meet again in the center, but if you spin around a few times, swirling them away from each other, they will be worn out after three minutes and will finally collapse.

If your mentee throws objects at you, don't close your eyes. Put your palms up in front of your face with your fingers spread out so that you can see. Don't block your view with your wrists. Your palms are cushions.

If someone is going to punch you, quickly move away. Keep your palms up and rush for the door. If you are mentoring in a classroom, try to teach near the door, not at the back of the room.

If a youth tries to kick you, put your palms down with your fingers spread and run behind him. You can also find a table to use as a natural barrier. Talk loudly so that someone nearby can hear and rescue you.

If he goes to a wall and starts hitting it, use some type of diversion to stop him.

If you sense that trouble is brewing, pay attention to signs that your body might give. Just use your instincts and common sense and you'll be fine.

KIDS THAT HARM THEMSELVES

It's estimated that 4% of the U.S. population (12 million people) inflict self-harm.[8] Another report states that 1.9 million Americans mutilate themselves.[9] A third study concludes that 750 of every 100,000 people in the U.S. self-injure.[10] Regardless of which research is correct, they all indicate that a lot of self-harm is occurring.

Those who "Self-Injure" ("SI" for short) do it by cutting themselves with razors and knives, hitting themselves or banging their heads against the wall repeatedly. They might throw themselves through panes of glass. Others punch walls until their hands are bruised and bloody. They pull out their hair or set it on fire, eat glass and needles, expose themselves to extreme weather conditions, break their own bones, continually pick at their wounds to interfere with the healing, and bite and scratch their skin until it is bleeding raw.

You might discover that your mentee tries to hurt himself or herself. Those kids who self-harm are usually *not* suicidal (although a third of them expect to be dead within five years).

The self-injury actually relieves anxiety and deep anguish that could lead to suicide if it's not let loose. Your mentee could physically feel as if he'll explode like a balloon unless he lets go of the pressure and stress that he's experiencing. Self-harm is like a release valve that gives these troubled kids the sensation of control over their lives and their bodies, which they have never really experienced before. *They* decide where to inflict injury, how they'll do it and how deep and long it will be.

There are different philosophies about why kids hurt themselves. Some youth say that they are "numb" and it's the only way they can feel alive.

---

[8] T. Alderman, "The Scarred Soul," 1997
[9] "A Bright Red Scream" by Marilee Strong, San Francisco Focus, November 1993.
[10] "The Plight of Chronic Self-Mutilators" by Armando Favazza, MD., M.P.H., and Karen Conterio.

Another strong belief is that youth who practice SI missed out on having a loving relationship with their mother. Maybe they inflict self-harm because they desperately need attention from a loving caretaker. If that's the case, then perhaps you could be the person to give them that love, so the urge to self-injure could disappear with time.

However, be careful not to let their injuries continue or increase because your mentee craves more attention from you. Be interested in helping, but not *too* interested or it will reinforce their behavior. Find other ways to show your love and affection.

Often, SI hides an eating disorder, like anorexia or bulimia. However, these could be layers that cover the root of the problem: relational deficiency (bonding with a parent). The layers are like an onion, with SI at the top.

I was privileged to attend an intensive all-day seminar on SIV (Self-Inflicted Violence) through Phoenix House, led by Angela Kahn, a Licensed Marriage and Family Therapist who has specialized in SI cases for many years. Much of the information in this section is from what I learned during Angela's presentation. You can reach her through her website: www.angelakahn.com.

Angela stated that SI impacts males and females in equal numbers. The majority are pre-teens and teenagers. It is *not* a personality disorder. She said, While this behavior is obviously not desirable, there's no need to panic. SI actually helps preserve the self. It's finding a way through the pain, which is a statement of survival. It usually starts around age 12-13, although I'm seeing more cases of children doing it at a very young age, including pre-school. SI behavior tends to go away naturally in the mid-20's to the early '30's."

Angela explained that the average youth who does SI is someone most people would never suspect. They tend to be perfectionists, "Teacher's Pet," or the class president who does great at school. They're often outgoing, intelligent and very popular. However, while they're articulate and can talk about many subjects, they can't share their feelings.

If you ask your mentee how he's feeling and you always get one-syllable responses, like "Mad," then try to get him to speak by using his language and culture. Find out what TV shows and movies he watches and use those characters as examples. You could ask, "Are you mad like the Incredible Hulk or more like Homer Simpson?"

Youth who do SI are also hypersensitive to rejection. Angela explained how these kids are often helpful and selfless because they want to be liked. They try to avoid confrontation. They're ashamed of their mental pain and disapprove of their own angry feelings. Their family may have told them that they "over-reacted" to things, so they think that showing any anger at all is bad.

Angela said that SI is very ritualistic, deliberate and calculated. The instruments become "friends," and may be part of a kit, which could include a variety of instruments, such as a shard of glass, a butane lighter and a razor. SI is addictive, since at the moment of pain, our brains give out "enkephalin" excretions that are opium-like. Youth can develop an addiction to (as well as withdrawal from) these endorphins.

One of the phrases that Angela continually hears from her clients is "I'm fine." She showed us these words carved into a youth's arm. She feels that SI is a disorder of relating. "Kids do it to feel pain, control family chaos, to soothe, and to feel alive. They do it to redirect anger, to attack and communicate and to prove resilience. They might also do it to punish someone."

Cutting is probably the most popular way to self-mutilate. The majority of cutters tend to be women ages 13-30, but there are cutters of every age and gender. Most cutters have been sexually molested, physically abused, or are survivors of incest.

Cutters can always find something to cut with: a button, zipper, thread from a shirt, staples, glass and paper. Some cut superficially on the wrist, while the more serious ones cut up the arm to get the vein. Some cut in hidden places, like under their arm, the genitals, the thigh, their pelvis or on their chest.

Don't cringe if your mentee shows you his wounds. One way to get around this natural reaction is to desensitize yourself by watching horror movies. Be strong and speak calmly without fear. Let him know that you are not going to abandon him and you'll try to get him help.

You're not a doctor (unless that's actually your profession), so don't treat any injuries that seem serious. However, tending to your mentee's wounds can bond you more closely. Here are some tips from Angela on treating wounds:

Open wounds require dressing and a possible visit to the emergency room. Make sure there's no infection. For cuts, if the skin comes together by itself, then clean and dress it with antibacterial ointment. If you have to hold the wound closed, then go to the hospital.

When you dress the wound or change their bandages, go slowly. Make eye contact, smile and don't talk. Let it be a quiet moment.

For metal cuts, he'll need a tetanus shot. Lacerations usually take a week to heal, so if the wound doesn't heal, he could be interfering with it (picking at it).

If your mentee tells you that she punctured herself with a needle or other sharp object, there will be minimal bleeding, but the wound will be prone to infection. Don't use peroxide. Soak the wound repetitively for 20 minutes. If she refuses to tell you if the instrument is still implanted, get an X-ray taken.

Burns could be caused by heat, electricity, chemicals, radiation, and friction (from rubbing pencil erasers or the sides of coins against the skin). For deep burns with open blisters, get medical treatment.

Deep bruising might indicate a possible fracture or internal bleeding. If you have any doubts about your ability to treat wounds, get medical help.

As their mentor, it can break your heart to see your mentee suffering and hurting themselves this way. Obviously you want to try to stop them. However, you're not a psychologist. You should encourage them to seek professional help. You can assist by researching therapists with experience dealing with SI.

Here are some more suggestions from Angela:

Ask them to tell the story of the wounds. Give them paper and a pen and have them fill in a timeline.

Do Injury Analysis (like Dream Analysis). Have them describe the SI experience in symbolic language. "This time you cut on the front of the arm instead of the back," or "Why do you use scissors?"

Inject meaning into things. If they SI at night, ask "What is night time to you?" If they use glass or windows, find out if there's hidden meaning in these instruments.

Mimic their language and the terms they use to describe SI. If they say "cutting," use that word. If they say "self-injury, use that same phrase rather than another.

Get your mentee to think about what triggers the episodes of SI. Have them track their episodes by reflecting on what upset them to the point of wanting to self-injure. This could help them to realize why they're doing it, so they might prevent more episodes in the future.

Use art therapy. These kids are *very* creative. Have them draw the cut on paper instead of actually carving it in their flesh. Ask them to write a poem about SI, especially the feelings they have, and then to verbalize it.

Know that just being there to listen to your mentee is a tremendous support for them. It's very possible that they haven't shared their abnormal behavior with anyone else, so having you there to listen to them and to be a sounding board builds trust in adults, and is a huge relief.

Don't ask too many questions, or she may feel that you're prying. Also, know the difference between asking and making observations. If you make too many observations, she may withdraw and think you're a "know-it-all." Find the right balance. Tune in to her needs and perhaps back off.

The issue of who to tell about this can be very challenging. If your mentee is in a facility where the therapists and staff are aware of the self-mutilation syndrome, then you won't need to alert anyone. However, it's a tricky situation if he is living with a family that's not aware of the problem. If you break your mentee's confidence and report his self-harm actions to others, they might put him into a mental institution or hospital. He could be angry with you for reporting him and not trust you ever again.

Also, it might come to light that your mentee is self-harming because a family member sexually or physically abused her. If she is still living at home, that could create a lot of difficulties. Be careful by protecting her confidentiality. Ideally, it should be her choice about who finds out.

At the same time, having professionals in a safe environment to give him the treatment that he needs might be the best thing for him. Perhaps he told you his secret about hurting himself because he desperately needs help and doesn't know how else to get it.

The best thing is for you to have a talk about this with your mentee. Find out what they want you to do and how you can help them. If they get very upset when you mention talking to a parent or guardian about the problem, then ask if they will allow you to speak with a psychologist or a doctor while keeping their identity confidential.

If you think that their health or life is in danger, then you must report it to the authorities even if it means breaking their confidence. Your mentee might be upset and never want to talk with you again, but just let them know that you did it out of love and concern for them. They will hopefully look back on it someday soon and appreciate that you got them help.

Be aware that some hospitals tend to treat this disease with overmedication of tranquilizers and anti depressants. Since the self-mutilation isn't caused by any biochemical imbalances in the brain, these drugs can sometimes do more harm than good.

Don't remove potential weapons, such as throwing away razor blades or hiding knives. If your mentee wants to hurt herself, she will find some way to do that. He can find a clip, piece of paper or other innocuous materials to do SI. If you take away their "friend," it could break the trust you've built.

You can help them to build up an emotional vocabulary. Most kids who do SI don't have any words to describe what they're feeling. Try word games and puzzles, as well as writing exercises to help them learn more words.

Before they can let go of this "coping mechanism," your mentee needs to find healthier alternatives to dealing with the things that have triggered these incidents. They must unlearn what has been the only thing that's worked for them. As their mentor, you can help them find better ways to do this. It could be a long process and your patience will be needed.

Courtney, a mentor in Ten Mile, Tennessee, was honored with an award for mentoring a 17-year-old girl who had been suicidal and inflicting harm on herself. Courtney was trying to form a support group for her mentee and other girls struggling with self-harm and had been working with the girl for almost a year.

"She was struggling with depression, and I have throughout my life struggled with the same thing," said Courtney.

"We talk about a wide range of things," she said. "She's had her phases when she's been suicidal, and if that's the case, that's what we focus on. Right now she's in a very positive state, and we've talked about what she's going to do after graduation, and her friends. Since we've been hanging out, she's been injury-free most of the year."

Courtney said she and the teenager she mentors would stay in touch for the rest of their lives.

"I don't know how I've helped her, but I can say she thinks of me like a sister," said Courtney. "I think she knows I'll be there for her no matter what happens."

One final suggestion that Angela had was to help your mentee create a "white lie" to explain their injuries. It could be very embarrassing for them to tell people the truth, so you could assist them to come up with a plausible explanation. "I was so stupid! I walked through a glass door," or "I forgot that the stove was still on and it burned my hand."

Remind them that the cutting, burning or other form of SI was the best solution for them at the time. They might have killed themselves, so they should be proud that they even survived. Tell them how strong they really are.

If your mentee does well and stops self-injuring, be proud, but also don't be surprised if he relapses. This might be a final test for you as a mentor. Be encouraging and let him know that you're there to help.

You can learn more about self-injury when you visit the website: www.self-injury.net.

Check to see if your local hospital has a program specifically for cutters and self-injurers, including a support group.

Take him to the gym to work out and get him a punching bag. Buy her a big pillow to whack. Take him to a lake or a field where he can throw rocks at a bottle. Find someone to teach her martial arts or gymnastics.

Yoga is a healthy and spiritual way for youth to release stress. Teach them deep breathing exercises, focusing on their chakras and meditation. Check out www.stressfreekids.com to learn more.

Teach him how to write pages of "X's," instead of carving them onto his arm.

Buy her a journal where she can write her secret feelings every day. Get him clay or paints so he can express himself through art.

Keep in close contact through emails, phone, visits and writing. Let her know that she can call you anytime, day or night (if that's okay with you) so that she has you to lean on. If you aren't able to deal with this close contact, then find her a support group in your community where she can be matched with a "Special Friend," "Buddy" or a sponsor, like at AA meetings.

S.A.F.E. Alternatives is a nationally recognized treatment approach for youth ages 12-20 with self-injurious behavior. They have a residential program and also a clinic in Missouri and support groups in North Carolina, Indiana, Ohio, New York, Tennessee, New Jersey and California. You can learn more at 800-DONTCUT or visit their website at: www.selfinjury.com.

SUICIDE

Suicide is a much more serious problem. In 2002, about one in eleven of all high-school students say they made a suicide attempt.[11] Suicide is actually the third leading cause of death amongst all kids ages ten to twenty-four.

Boys commit suicide more often then girls, but no one is immune. One third of all teenagers who commit suicide are LGBT (lesbian, gay, bisexual and transgender).

The American Academy of Pediatrics says that threatening to kill oneself precedes four out of five suicidal deaths. They recommend that if your mentee has been depressed, you should look closely for signs that he or she might be thinking of suicide:

◻ Is he having trouble with a girlfriend or boyfriend, or getting along with friends or with parents?

---

[11] Centers for Disease Control and Prevention. (2002).

- Is the quality of her schoolwork going down?
- Does he always seem like he's bored and is he having trouble concentrating?
- Is she acting like a rebel in an unexplained and severe way?
- Has he run away from home?
- Is she pregnant and finding it hard to cope with this major life change?
- Is he abusing drugs and/or alcohol?
- Is she writing notes or poems about death?
- Is he giving away some of his most prized possessions?
- Does she talk about suicide, even jokingly, and say things like, "That's the last straw," "I can't take it anymore," or "Nobody cares about me."
- Has he tried to commit suicide before?

If you suspect that your mentee might be thinking about suicide, don't remain silent. Suicide is preventable, but you must act quickly:

- ✱ Ask your mentee about it. Don't be afraid to say the word "suicide." Getting the word out in the open may help him realize that someone has heard his cries for help.
- ✱ Reassure her that you love her. Remind her that no matter how awful her problems seem, they can be worked out and you are there to help.
- ✱ Ask him to talk about his feelings. Listen carefully. Don't dismiss his problems or get angry with him.
- ✱ Seek professional help. A variety of outpatient and hospital-based treatment programs are available. Research them to see which would be the best fit for your mentee.

If you think that your mentee is suicidal, then you must report it to their parent, guardian, therapist or another person authorized to help the child. Share any research that you have gathered about therapy programs and support groups.

PREGNANT TEENS

34 percent of young women become pregnant at least once before they reach the age of twenty (about 820,000 a year).[12] The reasons are many. They may have no parental guidance and are uneducated about abstaining or using contraceptives. Perhaps their boyfriends convinced them that it was safe to engage in sex. Many teenage girls want someone to love them, especially those who receive no love from their families. They think that by having a baby, their child will provide them with all the love they need.

If your mentee tells you that she's pregnant, don't freak out or be judgmental. Don't lecture her about having an abortion, raising the child or giving the baby up for adoption. It's not your job to fix the problem, but rather to listen to her and provide support.

Ask your mentee questions so that you are a good sounding board; someone who can help her to think through the situation and to come up with her own solution.

Some questions that you might ask are: How do you feel about it? Have you been to the doctor or visited a clinic? Have you spoken to your parent(s) about this yet? What have you considered doing?

The most important question is, "How can I help you?" That doesn't mean you should try to take over the situation and control it. Your mentee will need to make important decisions. You can help her so that she can tell her parents and also get proper medical attention.

You can assist your mentee to rehearse what she'll say to her family, and give her guidance in what actions she should take, such as seeing a doctor or a school counselor.

My first recommendation would be for you to make sure that you honor your confidentiality agreement with your mentee. It is crucial that you follow your promises.

If you're not breaking your commitment, then (1) Notify the Volunteer Coordinator or other staff in charge of the mentoring program at the school, group home, shelter or youth facility where you were matched with your mentee(s). They will probably know the girl's background, plus they will likely have resources to help youth in this situation; (2) Offer to discuss the situation with the girl

---

[12] Teenpregnancy.org, March 2005

and her parent(s) or guardian(s) if she wants to let them know about her pregnancy, but she's too afraid to tell them herself; or (3) If you are legally allowed and your mentee agrees, then bring her to a clinic like *Planned Parenthood* or a hospital where doctors and counselors with expertise can give her the guidance that she needs.

Remember that as a mentor, you're not there to make any choices for her. You're not a surrogate parent, either. You are there to (1) listen closely to what she tells you that she wants and needs; (2) be an advocate; and (3) give your mentee guidance and support so that she can make her own decisions. After all, she's the one who is going to have to live with the consequences for the rest of her life, whatever they turn out to be.

Judy in La Jolla, CA is mentoring her second teenage mother. "My mentee feels she can only talk to her therapist and me, and I hope she is open to the responses that I give her."

Judy is one of a number of volunteers at *Mentoring Moms*, a San Marcos-based program run by Jewish Family Services of San Diego. The program works with other organizations to provide comprehensive support services, including the YMCA, healthcare agencies, and *The Haven*, a live-in treatment group home for pregnant and parenting teens run by the Salvation Army. Both of Judy's mentees lived there during the course of their mentoring. They both graduated high school.

"In the morning, my mentee can get up and know there are people who care about her, who care that she even gets up," said Judy. "The more people who give her that feeling, the better."

Judy hopes that more women will volunteer their time to help these teens, to stop the cycle that affects these young girls, their families, and their newborns.

If your mentee is male, then he might seek your advice if his girlfriend gets pregnant. Follow the same guidelines, which is to respect his confidentiality and do your best to provide him with sound advice. Listen to everything that he says, and be available to help out as much as you can.

WRITING REPORTS

It's unlikely that anything bad will happen to you while mentoring high-risk youth. However, if you have any personal property stolen or if an incident does take place, then a report must be written and given to the staff at the facility and possibly the local police. This will help to document exactly what happened so that institutional staff can investigate the situation. It will also provide you with legal protection, if needed.

Properly written reports can also safeguard you from someone lying about your performance. What if a youth falsely claims that you initiated an assault? A report will clarify exactly what happened from your perspective. It's essential to have all of the details documented, so if it ever goes through the legal system, you will be shielded from a phony claim.

It is very important that you *don't write the report in front of your mentee(s)*. If he or she finds out that you are writing about them, it could destroy their trust. Wait until your mentee is not around before you document anything. That doesn't mean you should lie about writing a report or hide it, but there's no need to stir up problems by writing it in front of them.

A complete report of a robbery or assault must have six components: who, what, when, where, why and how. In addition to these six components, complete incident reports contain information about injuries, notification and follow-up:

1. *Who*: Accurate identification of all the people directly involved in the incident;

2. *What*: A detailed description of what happened during the incident. This is also the time to list the staff involved and/or outside interventions used;

3. *When*: The time(s) or time frames and date of the incident. Be specific and avoid generalizations like "It happened on Monday evening after dinner;"

4. *Where*: A detailed description of the location where the incident took place;

5. *Why*: Identify the visual, auditory and any signs that might explain the motive of the incident. If the signs weren't clear or not observed, write down what you are sure of. Don't try to guess why the incident happened; and

6. *How*: A description of how the youth carried out the incident and how you, facility staff or any outside help intervened.

You should list the following information in your report to make it complete:

(a) Injuries: Statement of either visible injuries or the absence of injuries.

(b) Notification: Explain who was notified of the incident, like physicians, law enforcement, parents, probation officers, case managers, teachers, dorm staff, supervisors, administrators, etc.

(c) Follow-up: Identify further action. This is the part where you show that you're concerned about the incident.

Remember: If it isn't in writing, it didn't happen. When you write it in a report, then it happened the way you wrote it. Keep your language simple, short and slang-free.

WHAT IF MY MENTEE GOES AWOL OR GETS ARRESTED

AWOL is a military term that means "Absent Without Leave." It signifies someone deserting his or her post without permission. If your mentee runs away ("goes AWOL") from their detention facility, rehab center or foster group home, they might try to return a few days later, but sometimes they just disappear onto the streets forever, or until they are caught. Also, most of the youth agencies that deal with high-risk youth have strict rules that forbid kids to return once they leave.

If these youngsters run away and get caught, they are usually sent to Juvenile Hall ("the Halls"), which are temporary prisons where youth are locked up until their court date. Once they appear in court, the judge will then decide where they will be sent.

If your mentee gets into serious trouble, don't be surprised if you receive a collect call asking for help to bail them out. You are probably one of the few people they can turn to when facing a problem.

Giving them bail money is something that you will have to decide on for yourself. Assume that any money you spend will be lost, since your mentee may jump bail or never be able to reimburse you for the expense. If you can't afford it or choose not to pay for bail, then don't feel guilty. Your mentee created the situation and made a poor choice. He or she needs to learn from the consequences.

You have no control over your mentee's actions and you can't take things personally. You can only do the best that you can during the time that you get to work with him or her. If your mentee misbehaves or runs away, understand that there are so many factors that they must deal with every day; issues they have struggled with all their lives. They won't change overnight regardless of how much they like and respect you.

If your mentee is sent back to The Halls or to another penal institution, you might feel as if you have "failed" him or her. It's impossible for *anyone* to enter these troubled kids' lives and make a big impact without their being some setbacks along the way. All you can do is to be patient and understanding.

Let your mentee know that no matter what happens, they can always keep in touch with you through email, letters and phone. You may be the one person they reach out to who can provide them with the support they need.

You could have incredible influence on a youth and never even know about it.

Before I founded my organization **Create Now**, I taught a Screenwriting workshop to a group of coed teens at a detention center called Pride House. One of the girls, "Lawanda," had been sent there because she was always in trouble and couldn't get along with her parents. She bragged about her knowledge of different weapons and that she wasn't afraid to kill an enemy.

Lawanda had written some poems. She joined my Screenwriting workshop with excitement and was active in the program. She enjoyed improvising the roles of the gangsters and had a good ear for dialect. Her main strength, however, was her terrific sense of humor. Lawanda could make everyone laugh.

She began developing a comedy feature screenplay based on her life. When she was released from the detention facility, Lawanda continued writing her script while working part-time at the local mall. I gave her a computer and she was on her way to fulfilling her dreams.

Suddenly, Lawanda disappeared. Her parents said that she'd gotten into trouble with the law again and had even stolen some money from them. Nobody knew where to find her. I felt terrible, as if I had somehow failed her.

Six years later, Lawanda called me to say that she had never forgotten me. She'd just needed some time to mature and settle down. Instead of being a wild 17-year-old "gangsta," she was now a mature 23-year-old woman. Lawanda worked full-time at a group home for mentally-challenged adults. She received great joy out of helping the people there. She had written five wonderful comedy screenplays and was developing her sixth. Lawanda attributed her success to my assistance as her mentor.

Remember that even if your mentee has gone AWOL, gets arrested or worse, they will remember you and what you have taught them. They may be too young and immature to use that information right now, but it will stay with them forever.

CHAPTER EIGHT

Things to Do

It's important to expose your mentee(s) to different opportunities. At-risk kids have probably not experienced the same things that you did when you were growing up. Knowledge about the greater world around them can assist them in maturing and finding their special place in life.

A simple experience such as riding a bicycle seems like something that every child should know how to do, but perhaps your mentee's family was so poor, they could never afford a bike. Even if your mentee has a bicycle, it's very different for him to ride it in his own neighborhood as opposed to down at the beach, or up in the mountains.

Your family probably took you to the circus at least once in your lifetime. However, many at-risk youth have never seen anything like it. Imagine what such an extravaganza would be like from a child's perspective, no matter how old they are, if they have never been to the circus before.

There's another wonderful benefit when you introduce your mentee to the many incredible things that exist in our world. You get to experience them again through the eyes of a child. Using the above example, going to the circus is fun, but seeing it with a youth who has never been to the circus before makes it even more exciting for you.

It's delightful to know that she's enjoying a theater performance that she will never forget, and whenever she remembers this precious time, she'll be thinking about her mentor and how you introduced her to so many wonderful things. Later in life, she can share these experiences with more children. You are all "paying it forward."

Here's another benefit that you'll reap: remembering your own childhood and reliving the terrific experiences you had back then as you share them with your mentees. When you take in all the sights, smells and sounds, this will trigger precious memories of your own youth for you to enjoy all over again.

There are many diverse things that you can do with your mentees. You don't have to spend a lot of money, or any at all, and you can still provide them with thrilling activities so that the time you share has an even deeper impact.

Rhett mentored a youth named Andrew in Wichita, Kansas, through a program called *Youth Horizons.* "I started mentoring Andrew as a way of practicing unselfishness and learning how to reach out and reach into another person's life," Rhett said.

"Mentoring is not always the easiest endeavor in the world, but it is good to know you mean something to somebody else. Andrew is a good kid and I'm glad to be able to do things with him. We do sports together. We go out to eat. I take him home with me on the weekends to meet my family and see what it's like living on a farm."

It's important to remember, however, that it's not where you go or what you do with your mentee that counts. It's the relationship that you build through the activity that makes mentoring so powerful. Whether you're playing basketball, painting a mural or just hanging out and watching TV together, the time and care that you give to your mentee is what will make the biggest impact.

GAMES AND ICEBREAKERS

It can be awkward the first time or so that you meet with your mentee(s). You probably don't know much about him or her, and vice versa. You're checking each other out and deciding if you can trust one another. Games may help to "break the ice." They could assist you to relax, break down social barriers and motivate you to "think outside of the box."

There are many books and websites devoted to warm-up exercises that can be used for groups or individuals. They're also referred to as "energizers," and "De-inhibitizers." Do some research, play around with them and try those that are most appropriate. Also, use your creativity to come up with your own ideas.

Toilet Paper Game

Bring a roll of toilet paper to your first meeting. Tell your mentee(s) to unroll it and tear off the amount they would normally take when they use the bathroom. This is sure to bring some laughter and teasing, especially when done with a group.

After your mentee(s) have torn off some toilet paper and you have also taken your share, tell them that they now must tell you (or the group) something that isn't known about them — once for each sheet of toilet paper in their hands. If they took just a small amount, there might be four or five small sections of paper. If they took a lot, they could have ten or more pieces of toilet paper.

Start off the game to let your mentee(s) know how it's played. If you took six pieces of paper, you might hold up the first one and say, "I have a granddaughter who is five." For the second piece, you could share, "I am a total chocoholic. I can eat chocolate all day and night," and so on.

Word Associations

Call out a word. Your mentee(s) should say the first word or words that come to mind. Try it with a few simple words, like "Cat," "Salt," "Cold," etc.

Next you can focus on a particular topic. Have them take out a scrap of paper to write down their first responses to the words that you'll present. You could say the word out loud or write it on a sheet of paper. Tell them to take about thirty seconds to jot down all of the word associations that they have with the topic. Afterwards, go around and discuss what they wrote.

Questions to ask could include: Why do you think you have that association? What's positive about the topic? What seems to draw people toward it? What seems to repel people from it?

This activity is an especially useful process for getting at preconceived notions, myths and fears right up front. It can be used to introduce and begin discussion on any topic, like sex, drugs and violence. Just be careful not to focus on any subjects that might be sensitive to your mentee.

Points-of-View

Identify different points-of-view in a specific situation and create "roles" for each point of view. For example, if you are discussing cigarette smoking, possible points-of-view could include:

From a tobacco farmer, advertising company executive, doctor, store owner, employee of the American Lung Association, patient with lung cancer, smoker, nonsmoker, parent of a 12-year-old child, an unborn fetus, and an ex-smoker.

Have group members participate in a discussion about the issue, taking on different points-of-view. You could also use improvisational theater, where youth act out their parts. For an interesting experience, switch roles after about five minutes, but have the same conversation continue. You might even have participants switch roles more than once if the conversation is lively.

This activity can be done with many different issues. One example is same-sex marriage. The roles could be: a minority youth, landlord, employer, person with AIDS, gay man or lesbian, minister, straight man/woman, etc.

Another idea is the war in Afghanistan. Various roles include a soldier, military officer, Afghani child, Afghani woman, and the U.S. President.

This process is a very useful "Empathy Builder" that helps participants break out of often limited points-of-view that create obstacles to harmony.

Jingles

This is a fun icebreaker that I learned in South Africa, which is perfect for a group of kids. It gives them a chance to be in the spotlight, and also helps you to learn their names.

All of the youth should stand with you in a circle. One person is selected to go first. They move to the center and recite: "Hi Jingles." Everyone in the group repeats, "Hi Jingles." The chosen one then says, "My name is…" and everyone in the group repeats, "My name is…" Then the child says his name, "My name is Ryan," and everyone repeats, "My name is Ryan."

Then Ryan says, "And this is how I jingle." He then creates a fun movement, such as a dance, broad gesture or a silly wiggle. All of the kids imitate him by saying, "And this is how I jingle," and they copy his movement.

Ryan then calls out the name of someone else in the circle and they take his place in the center. The game continues until everyone has had a chance to go.

The Situation Game

This is another great icebreaker for a group of kids. On a sheet of paper, everyone writes down these words at the top of the page: "You are." Then they add the name of a famous person or character. As an example, they could write "You are Spiderman." Urge them to be creative. When they are done, they should fold the paper to hide the words.

Have everyone pass the paper to the person on their right, who then writes "You are" again, but this time they add a location in the space below. For instance, "You are under the table," or "You are in the tub." When they are done, they should fold the paper to hide the words.

All the kids pass their papers to the person on their right again. This time, they jot "You are wearing _____," which they fill in with a funny response. In the next pass, they write, "You are doing _____" and they write an activity.

After the last paper is passed around, each youth unfolds one and tells the group who s/he is, where s/he is, what s/he is wearing and what s/he is doing. This can create some great laughs. For example, "You are Justin Timberlake sitting on a boat wearing a tutu while fleecing a sheep." For more laughs, ask each person to act out the scenario that they have selected.

PLACES TO VISIT

Before you take your mentee(s) on any outings, be sure that it's okay with their parents, guardians or staff. They may not want you to take your mentee hiking because of his allergies, or to see a particular play because they consider it inappropriate.

If they give you permission to go, then start researching in your own community and see what type of unique places there are to visit. Every town has some attractions, even if you have to travel a little while to get there. If so, then it's even more likely that your mentee has never visited it before. The time you spend together while going to the location will give you more time to bond.

Don't feel obligated to take them to expensive places. There are lots of free activities that you can share with your mentee(s). Even small towns have bowling alleys, football fields, public swimming pools, libraries, parks, or a lake for swimming that freezes over in winter for ice-skating.

Your community probably has at least one theater where concerts or plays are performed, as well as a local movie theater. There's most likely an arena for sporting events and other activities nearby.

Be sure to customize your activities according to your mentee's interests and needs. If she's curious about going to college, spend time visiting university campuses. Take her to the library so that she can research scholarship opportunities.

Amy is a CPA who works on a variety of consulting projects in Detroit at one of the nation's largest certified public accounting firms, Plante & Moran. She became a mentor through *Faces of the Future*.

Part of the Oak Park Business and Education Alliance in Michigan, *Faces of the Future* recruits adult mentors from businesses in the Detroit Metropolitan area. Mentors are asked to participate in a one-year small group-mentoring program working with Oak Park eighth grade students who are transitioning through their first semester of ninth grade.

Amy said, "Through this program, young teens are able to interact with working professionals that can provide advice and guidance. It starts students thinking about their future at a young age, whereas many may not even begin to think about their future until their senior year, when it is too late. Through the field trips that this program takes, students are offered the chance to go see university and college environments."

Destini, one of the students, said, "Being in this program helped me a lot and I wish every school would do this because it helps kids think more about planning their future."

If your mentee loves car racing, find activities that are related to that. Visit a local go-cart racetrack. Explore an automobile museum. Research NASCAR on the Internet. Make a toy model car together or share auto-racing magazines. Find out about career opportunities for car racing, like mechanics or car designers.

If you are working with high-risk youth who are gang members or they are incarcerated for a violent crime, you might think about visiting your local morgue. While this seems creepy, the coroner might be willing to give a special tour to your mentee(s) to show them what happens to their bodies after they have been killed. Many gang members are numb to the consequences of violence. It can be a shocking "wake-up call" for youth who think that gang life is cool.

Another option would be to visit a funeral home and let them find out how morticians prepare bodies for burial. This also exposes youth to potential careers.

I recommend that you check the Internet and local listings in your community to see what interesting places are around that you might not have ever heard about before. You will probably be surprised by what's in your area once you scratch the surface of typical places to visit (the mall, movie theaters, parks, etc.).

Another idea for finding unique places to take your mentee(s) is to buy a travel guide. *Frommer's* puts out a series of guidebooks for most cities and they give many suggestions of unusual tourist sites. Other great travel guides are the *Fodors* books and the *Lonely Planet* series.

You can generally get this information for free by contacting your local Convention and Visitors Bureau and asking for their literature, and also researching online.

Below are some more ideas of places to visit. Make a list or check off those that are of interest to you and ask your mentees which locations are exciting to them. Then go have fun!

MUSEUMS

Museums are great places to take kids, especially children from poor families who may have never been to one before. Many museums offer free admission for one day or evening a week. Some also provide students with special membership cards.

The Los Angeles County Museum of Art (LACMA) gives all K-12 students cards so they can attend any time for free, including admission for one adult. Learn more at www.lacma.org.

There are a variety of museums:

❖   *Children's Museums* - Most cities have one. They include fun exhibits and projects that are geared to kids of all ages, with interactive games and opportunities for children to stimulate their curiosity and enhance their education.

❖   *Art Museums* – There are different types and sizes of art museums depending on where you live. Big cities usually enjoy the benefits of large cultural institutions with extensive collections of artwork and rotating exhibitions. An example would be the *Metropolitan Museum of Art* in New York, which is also home to the *Museum of Modern Art*, the *Solomon R. Guggenheim Museum* and the *Whitney Museum of American Art*. New York City also has dozens of smaller museums, including the *American Folk Art Museum*, the *American Craft Museum*, the *Children's Museum of the Arts* (in addition to the *Children's Museum of Manhattan*), the *Museum for African Art*, the *National Design Museum*, the *New Museum of Contemporary Art* and others too numerous to list.

❖   *Transportation Museums* – Many communities are proud of their museums that focus on different types of transportation. All around the U.S., there are museums dedicated to classic trains, automobiles, ships, airplanes, trolleys, buses and even bicycles. In Los Angeles, we have the famous *Petersen Automobile Museum* with four floors that are packed with cars that trace the history of the automobile. You can learn more at www.petersen.org.

❖   *Science Museums* – These museums often call themselves "Discovery Centers." They include exhibits on natural history, paleontology, geology and industrial machinery. Many cities also have an astronomical observatory with telescopes and planetariums.

❖   *Music Museums* – These museums might celebrate the lives of certain musicians, such as the *Rock and Roll Hall of Fame* in

Cleveland, OH; or the history of music, like the *Grammy Museum* in Los Angeles and the *National Music Museum* in Vermillion, SD.

❖ *Oddity Museums* – Many of you have heard of *Madame Tussauds*, where famous celebrities are replicated in wax. They have museums all over the world, including Hollywood, Washington, DC, Las Vegas and New York. You are probably also familiar with *Ripley's Believe It Or Not Museums*, which are located in 35 cities around the world, including ten different states, such as Missouri, Tennessee and Wisconsin. Their vast collections are packed with all kinds of weird objects and curiosities. There are many unusual types of museums around our country. Examples are the *Trash Museum* in Hartford, CN; the *Toy Museum* in Branson, MO and the *Kansas Underground Salt Museum*. I've included more fun museums in the Appendix.

COLLEGE AND UNIVERSITY CAMPUSES

Going to college is something that at-risk and high-risk youth may have no clue about. Their family members have likely never gone to college, and may not have even graduated from high school. They might never dream about university since they assume that they couldn't afford it.

If your mentee is an average or poor student, they may hate the idea of continuing their education.

When I graduated from high school, I didn't want to go to college. I was always an average student and I was bored in most of my classes, so the idea of going to school for another four years wasn't something that I wanted to pursue. My parents had to convince me to try it out.

Once I went to college, I realized that it was vastly different from high school. I loved the freedom to take the classes that I was interested in and also the higher level of education. College wasn't boring at all and I soared in my education!

Introduce your mentees to college life. Take them on an outing to the local campuses in your area and let them hang out for a while. They can soak in the ambience, visit the library, gym, student union and peek into classrooms.

Explore the postings on the college message boards around the campus so they can see the types of notices people leave (looking for roommates, study buddies, band members, shared rides, etc.).

Be sure to get them catalogues from the universities. Try to assist them to identify the subjects that they want to study and what classes are available.

If your mentee wants to apply to college, give him or her support with filling out the applications and researching financial aid. There are many scholarship opportunities out there, and community colleges are also inexpensive.

ZOOS AND AQUARIUMS

Many at-risk kids have never been to the zoo. This might be surprising to you, but consider the high cost of admission and the fact that many zoos are located in areas that are difficult to reach without a vehicle and you can see why your mentees might not have been to the zoo before. It can be a thrilling experience for a child or youth to see wild animals up close for the first time in their lives.

Paul became a mentor when he was a freshman at the College of Allied Health Sciences. He joined *Zoo-Mates*, which pairs students from the University of Cincinnati in Ohio with children from *Project Connect* for year-long mentoring relationships.

Project Connect, part of Cincinnati City Schools, is the only program in Greater Cincinnati exclusively serving children experiencing homelessness. They provide advocacy with specialized educational services and lifestyle enrichment opportunities for children who have neither a voice, nor a choice in being homeless.

Zoo-Mates meets once a week at the Cincinnati Zoo. Mentors and mentees explore the animals, flowers and plants there.

Paul said, "This is my first year being part of the *Zoo-Mates* program and I've enjoyed every minute of it. The best thing about *Zoo-Mates* is the bond that I have developed with my mentee. He has become like a little brother to me. Being a mentor has helped me learn more about myself while making a difference in a child's life. Spending time with all the children exploring the zoo makes me feel like a little kid again. *Zoo-Mates* has definitely enhanced my experience at the University of Cincinnati."

There are also specialty zoos, like *Gatorland* in Orlando and *Reptile Gardens* in Rapid City, South Dakota. Check out the Seattle *Bug Safari* in Washington. In Sevierville, Tennessee, visit the *Smoky Mountain Deer Farm and Exotic Petting Zoo* where your mentee can pet zebras, camels, reindeer, kangaroos, miniature goats and other rare animals.

Most kids don't have a clue about what goes on underneath the ocean waves. They may even think that "SpongeBob SquarePants" is realistic. Think of what they will experience at an aquarium, where they can watch sharks swimming with exotic tropical fish.

Audubon Aquarium of the Americas is located in New Orleans and it includes a scavenger hunt and a seahorse-breeding program. The *Shedd Aquarium* in Chicago includes exhibits on the Caribbean coral reefs, the Amazon, and the Pacific rocky coasts. The *National Aquarium* in Baltimore has a 265,000-gallon stingray pool.

FAMILY FARMS AND DUDE RANCHES

If you live in a community where there are horse ranches and farms in the vicinity, try to arrange a visit with your mentee. Some of these ranches will allow children to help groom the horses and feed the livestock.

Imagine the excitement of riding a pony or a horse for the first time in your life, or milking a cow. That's something your mentee will never forget.

The Gentle Barn is a ranch located just north of Los Angeles in Santa Clarita, CA. This unique wildlife sanctuary is home to 130 horses, donkeys, cows, pigs, sheep, goats, turkeys, chickens, llamas, dogs, and cats that have been rescued from horrible abuse. They invite at-risk youth and special needs children to visit and nurture their animals, which is very healing for the kids and the animals. Learn more at: www.gentlebarn.org.

THEME PARKS

If you live in a large city or town, there is probably at least one theme park in your vicinity. Southern California has *Disneyland, Universal Studios, Six Flags Magic Mountain, Knott's Berry Farm, Raging Waters, Medieval Times, Legoland* and *SeaWorld.*

New York has a variety of theme parks with *Playland, Adventureland, Enchanted Forest/Water Safari, Darien Lake Theme Park, Seabreeze* and *Coney Island.*

Florida has *Disneyworld, Epcot, Busch Gardens, SeaWorld, Universal Orlando, Wet 'n Wild* and *Lion Country Safari.* Arkansas has *Funland, Wild River Country* and *Willow Springs Water Park.*

NATURE HIKES AND PARKS

Most communities have local parks, which include hiking trails. Take your mentees on a stroll in nature where they can smell fresh air and experience wild plants and animals.

It could be their first time seeing tall, beautiful trees, as well as the birds, squirrels and deer that you come across. Explore an ant hill, collect berries or pine cones.

OCEAN

Even if you live near a port or the beach, chances are that your mentee(s) might never have been to the shore and experienced the ocean. This could be because of transportation challenges or fear of leaving their territory.

Think of how inspirational it can be to breathe in the salty air of the sea and realize how vast the world is, and the many exciting opportunities that exist. Stroll along the sand, take a swim and let your mentee relish the ocean setting.

Fantasize about what it would be like to own a beautiful, big house right on the beach, facing the water. If possible, go boating, water skiing, surfing, fishing, snorkeling or scuba diving.

LIBRARIES

Every town generally has one and it's the greatest resource available to at-risk youth, yet most kids haven't got a clue about all the riches their local library has to offer.

Prepare them ahead of time about how the system works and then take them on a visit to one or two libraries so they can experience it first-hand.

Help them to get a membership card, while stressing their responsibility to care for the books, DVDs and other materials that they can borrow. Show them how to use the computers there, if your library has them available.

COMMUNITY AND RECREATION CENTERS

Most towns have a place for kids to hang out where they provide sports equipment, games and different activities for youth. These could be community-oriented, privately funded, government or faith-based groups.

As an example, in your area there might be a *Boys & Girls* Club, or a youth project run by a church. Public parks usually have a recreation center, or the school has a special after-hours program. Explore these resources with your mentee so they can meet new friends and learn about interesting things as they expand their horizons.

LOCAL LANDMARKS

You might live in a city that has famous attractions, such as the *Statue of Liberty*, *Carlsbad Caverns* or the *Liberty Bell*. Experiencing these landmarks could be something that your mentee could only dream about, since the admission costs can be very expensive. Lack of transportation can also prevent them from going.

Take your mentee(s) on a tour of your community and you might be surprised by their positive responses. I have included more special attractions broken down by States in the Appendix.

USING RITUALS AND CEREMONIES

Many at-risk and high-risk youth need ritual in their lives. If you analyze gangs, then you understand that the reason many kids are attracted to join them is because of their desire to belong to a group, and also the necessity for initiation.

Since ancient times, young men and women have "come of age" through rituals, which can be bloody and violent. Kids are "jumped in" to gangs by withstanding brutal beatings from gang members. That's also the only way they can get out of gang life, to be beaten, but not broken.

Native Americans have used ancient rituals as a rite-of-passage for hundreds of years. These same techniques can influence modern-day youth. Sweat lodges are a powerful way for youth (male and female) to participate in a cleansing ceremony that brings them spiritual guidance with a positive message to be natural and respect our Mother Earth.

Award-winning novelist Luis Rodriguez is considered one of the leading Chicano writers. He's mostly known for his fascinating memoirs on gang life in East L.A. You can learn more about Luis and his work on his website: www.luisrodriguez.com.

Luis had a mentor who helped him to change his life. "At age 16, I was a high school dropout and a drug user. I met a youth worker at the community center that served my East L.A.-area neighborhood. He offered me a deal - if I returned to school, he'd help me get training and work as a muralist. After two years, I finally agreed. My mentor never gave up on me. I painted murals at the youth center, a local library branch and several businesses, the latter with 13 other gang members."

Luis now runs the thriving "Tia Chucha's Centro Cultural & Bookstore" in Sylmar, CA (www.tiachucha.com). He helps gang members in the Northeast San Fernando Valley by holding sweat lodges. He uses other indigenous ceremonies to provide a spiritual component to helping our youth to mature.

The San Francisco Children's System of Care (CSOC) is a federally-funded initiative located within the Community Behavioral

Health Services office in the Department of Public Health. They focus on the use of cultural rituals to increase a positive sense of identity and self-esteem amongst diverse youth. You can visit their website at www.sanfrancisco.networkofcare.org.

One of their ceremonies is based on "healing circles," a common ritual within many Native American communities. Typically, individuals sit within a circle and meditate, perhaps sharing a story, with the intent of receiving healing.

"The youth gather and have spiritual healing in a communal way," said Esperanza Echavarri, the integration coordinator. These events often involve other traditional practices and are linked with natural healers in the community.

Another one of their programs, "Rites of Passage" involves mentors from the African-American community leading young males in a 12-week course of study, activities and community service. The last day ends with a ritual ceremony, "Rites of Passage," which recognizes a young man's entry into adult life and his responsibility to his community.

The African-American youth also conduct Rites of Passage during Kwanza, a seven-day celebration of African heritage, held annually in December. "These activities connect them to their past and provide cultural affirmation of who they are, which is just so powerful," Echavarri said. "The kids just gravitate towards it."

There are other types of rituals and ceremonies that you might want to explore with your mentee(s), as long as they are not cultish or negative in any way. You certainly wouldn't want to explore black magic rituals like Voodoo, or any sacrificial ceremonies.

However, remember that if you have a preference for a particular religion, you cannot impose that on your mentee. Your religious practice may include certain rites or prayers, but you must not introduce these (or any other spiritual practices) to your mentee unless his or her family or guardian gives you permission. Otherwise, you could upset or offend them, especially if your beliefs are different.

MORE THAN 100 FUN ACTIVITIES

Always start by asking your mentee what she or he wants to do. They may have very specific goals, so find out what they would enjoy sharing with you, or if there is any particular activity that they want to experience.

There are hundreds of different things that you can do with your mentee. Just open up a local newspaper and see what's going on in your community. There will likely be an "Art and Entertainment" section, as well as sports, and one for the whole community with a calendar of special events.

Look at the world around you through a child's eyes and you will probably come up with many fresh ideas of fun things to do. Think about your own youth and what you enjoyed the most. Put yourself into your mentee's shoes and use your imagination to create entertaining activities.

FITNESS AND FUN

What better way to teach your mentees about staying healthy then by introducing them to fitness activities that can also be fun. Sports are great for kids to get in good shape while they burn off excess energy. Many youth are already interested in sports. They just need someone to share their passion with.

When Todd of Pawtucket, R.I. was 10-years-old, he met fellow sports fan and Big Brother Matt Lauer, the host of NBC-TV's "Today Show."

Todd's father passed away when he was seven. The boy longed for someone to share his passion for sports. While his mom and sister provided him with a loving, warm home, his mother realized that a strong male role model might make all the difference. She contacted the local chapter of *Big Brothers/Big Sisters* and soon her son was matched with a local TV celebrity, 23-year old Matt Lauer.

At the time, Matt co-hosted a daily TV show in Providence called "PM Magazine," but his true passion was sports. Matt took Todd out for ice cream during their first outing and they became fast friends. Weekly visits for the next three years included ballgames and trips to the "PM Magazine" set. Todd's most vivid memory was when, at the request of Todd's mother, Matt tried to teach him about "the birds and the bees."

"I think he was more uncomfortable than I was," Todd recalls.

Matt's career led him to Boston and beyond, and the two lost touch. When the "Today Show" held a special reunion program that brought together important people in the cast members' lives, Matt's surprise guest was Todd, whose 6'2," 240-pound body-builder's frame towered over Matt. Having last spoken on the phone six years earlier, the face-to-face reunion held special meaning for both Matt and Todd.

At-risk youth may not always do very well academically, but they can excel in sports. These are some terrific activities to build their self-esteem and confidence, as well as teamwork:

❋ *Gymnasium* – Some gyms have rules about allowing children near equipment, but many places like the *YMCA*, encourage at-risk youth to join their gym. They even have financial aid for those families that can't afford membership. While younger kids aren't allowed on the equipment, you can let them enjoy the indoor swimming pool, as well as specialty classes like martial arts and gymnastics. They also have arts and crafts and special projects for younger children. There are also programs for teens to get fit.

❋ *Swimming Pools* – Local parks and recreation centers often have indoor pools for year-round swimming. Classes are offered for all ages.

❋ *Bowling Alleys* – Not only is bowling fun, but it is great exercise. Youth build their strength, learn balance, discipline, coordination and persistence.

❋ *Baseball* – If your mentee is interested, you can sign him or her up to play Little League, or T-Ball for younger children.

❋ *Basketball* – Most parks, recreation centers and schools have a basketball court. This is a great sport for teens since they can let out a lot of their pent-up energy on the court, while building teamwork and working on their agility, speed and coordination. For younger kids, there are hoops that can be lowered to accommodate their size.

✿ *Tennis* – This is a great sport to teach kids. They learn to be fast on their toes and develop flexibility and strength. They also learn how to follow rules and good sportsmanship.

✿ *Soccer* – Since "football" (as it is known everywhere else in the world except the U.S.) is the most popular sport in most countries, it's natural that kids would like to play. They learn to be creative and to think on their feet (literally) as they play the game.

✿ *Football* is also popular with children and youth. Check the school and community message boards to see if there is a local team that your mentee can join. Football helps to enhance self-discipline, confidence, and sportsmanship.

✿ *Golf* – This is a great game for kids. You can start them off with "miniature golf," which is a fun game and good training. Older youth might enjoy playing golf on a nine or even an eighteen-hole course. Golf builds stamina and keeps children healthy.

✿ *Boxing* – This sport enables youth to learn defensive fighting skills, while also building up their muscles and self-esteem. Boxing is a fantastic way for kids to let out their aggression as they learn to take out their anger on a punching bag and to use special techniques.

✿ *Table Tennis (Ping Pong)* is a popular game with kids. Younger ones enjoy table tennis since the paddle and ball are light and the table is small enough that they can easily maneuver without having to run a lot. Competitive table tennis is popular in Asia and Europe and is gaining momentum in the United States.

✿ *Wrestling* – Even though the wrestling shown on television is fake, it's a great activity for teaching youth how to safely let out their aggression as they build muscles and mental toughness.

❀ *Pool or Pocket Billiards* has hundreds of different variations of the game. Be very careful that your mentee doesn't hurt someone with the cue stick. Teenagers will probably be able to manage the cues a lot better than younger children. While many people associate pool tables with bars, most recreation centers and youth clubs like the *Boys and Girls Clubs of America* and *Challenger Boys and Girls Clubs* often have pool tables available.

❀ *Trampolines and Batting Cages* – Many towns have these fun activities available year-round, located inside climate-controlled buildings.

❀ *Walking* – This is one of the best exercises in the world, yet many kids never walk anywhere. They ride skateboards, bikes, scooters and roller blades, or are driven by adults to their destination. Take a long walk somewhere nice. If it's cold, raining or snowing and you need to get some exercise, go to the local mall for your walk. Let your mentee know before you leave that you're just window-shopping. Walk around the different floors of the mall and check out the items on sale. Maybe your mentee will be inspired to save his money for something special that he sees in a store. He'll learn about putting money aside until it accumulates. After you return home from the mall, you will appreciate what a good workout you can get by simply walking.

ARTS AND CRAFTS WORKSHOPS

There are some franchised stores where you can make great items that are fun to decorate and keep as souvenirs or give away as presents:

❧ *Build-A-Bear Workshops* are located around the country. They provide materials and easy instructions on how to create unique teddy bears in an eight-step process.

❧ *Color Me Mine* is a pottery store franchise where you can select from dozens of ready-made ceramic objects like mugs, dishes, figurines vases and fountains. Once your item is chosen, you can paint it to make a unique gift.

ಏ Many communities have small shops where you can gather to make candles, soap, knit and crochet.

In all of these types of arts and crafts environments, you and your mentee will be mixing with other adults and children who are also making creative items. It's a great way to show your mentee how to socialize and possibly even make new friends. Best of all, they get to keep lasting souvenirs to remind them of the good times that you shared.

AMUSEMENT CENTERS

If your mentee is young, he or she would probably enjoy visiting fun places like:

✱ *Chuck E. Cheese's* - A pizza place often used for birthday parties since they have fun activities, like diving into colored plastic balls and playing arcade games that award prizes, as well as live performances.

✱ *Laser Tagging* - A popular game that uses infrared emitting "weapons" that shoot colored beams of light at the intended target, so a fun battle takes place.

✱ *Paint Ball* – This is similar to *Laser Tagging* but is more of a serious war-type game, better suited for teenagers than younger kids. The game can take place indoors or outside. Be careful since the thrust of the paint could leave a bruise or mark. Check with your mentee's parents before getting involved in this game and make sure they wear old clothes.

CLASSES AND WORKSHOPS

Depending on your mentee's interests, you might find a class or workshop that would be great for you to do together. As an example, if you both share an interest in computers, perhaps a class is offered on website design. You might take a dance or an art workshop. Cooking classes are also fun. Perhaps you can sign up for a class in alternative energy systems at your local community workshop in home repair.

COMMUNITY SERVICE

Many youth, especially high school and college students, must do community service as part of their educational requirements. Check into a homeless shelter or school in a poor area that might require some help. You can work together, assisting them to clean up the place or paint a room.

Rake the leaves at a senior center or spend time with some of the elderly people there who are lonely for company. They could also clean horse stalls at a ranch or cages at the local animal shelter. Even if your mentee is not required to do community service, this is a great opportunity to learn about the joy of giving back to others.

Here are 100 more fun things you can do with your mentee(s):

1. Help with homework and academics;

2. Assist your mentee to organize her schoolwork;

3. Teach your mentee how to keep his room in order;

4. Read a book together. Try a whole series of books;

5. Read newspapers and magazines together;

6. Go to a concert or the theater;

7. Write a journal together, or share your individual entries in your personal journals;

8. Learn new words from the dictionary each week;

9. Play Hangman and crossword games;

10. Work on a jigsaw puzzle together;

11. Play board games like Monopoly and Scrabble to help build their skills;

12. Play cards;

13. Draw mazes;

14. Use a globe and maps to explore the world;

15. Play math games using flashcards and computer games;

16. Write and send "snail mail" letters or cards to each other;

17. Teach your mentee how to create a thank you card to show appreciation to somebody. This is very important if they are looking for work and going on job interviews;

18. Attend school functions with your mentee: sports games, performances and special events;

19. Attend a festival or fair;

20. Don't forget to celebrate occasions like your mentee's birthday, Christmas or graduation;

21. Play with a Frisbee;

22. Join a sports team together, like ice hockey;

23. Stroll through the park;

24. Study bugs and worms;

25. Discover different flowers;

26. Go bird-watching;

27. Visit a pumpkin patch, select a pumpkin and carve it;

28. Make a Halloween costume together;

29. Take a long drive in the mountains or nature to see the autumn leaves changing colors;

30. Collect beautiful leaves and iron them between waxed paper to preserve them;

31. Build a scarecrow out of leaves, straw and old clothes. Give it a rake to hold;

32. Make caramel apples;

33. Cook soup or chili together;

34. In winter, take your mentee sledding down a hillside;

35. Go ice-skating on a frozen lake;

Jeffrey and Andrea from Denver took their mentee Lucas, age 12, on family trips, like white water rafting and skiing. These were activities that he would normally never get to experience, even though they go on all the time right in his own community.

Lucas also enjoyed simple things like sharing a family meal. He even liked to do chores. As the oldest of four children with a lot of responsibilities, Lucas loved to be a part of a family unit where he was celebrated for being special.

---

36. Go skiing. Start your mentee off on an easy slope;

37. Decorate a Christmas tree;

38. Create a wreath;

39. Build a snowman or a snow woman;

40. Have a snowball fight;

41. Build a snow fort or igloo;

42. Make birdfeeders and keep them stocked with seeds;

43. Decorate Easter eggs;

44. Bring some wild spring flowers to a nursing home;

45. Do some vegetable gardening;

46. Go roller-skating or rollerblading at a rink, on the street or in a park;

47. Try skateboarding;

48. Go to a playground and join in the fun;

49. Ride your bikes in the countryside, surrounded by nature;

50. Pick fruit at a local farm (with permission) and bring them to a homeless shelter;

51. Go camping, even in the backyard;

52. Roast marshmallows over a campfire;

53. Take your mentee water-skiing;

54. Go on a picnic at a park or the beach;

55. Rent a canoe, kayak or paddleboat;

56. Go inner-tubing on a lake or river;

57. Look for fossils;

58. Explore a local river or creek;

59. Go fishing;

60. Fly a kite;

61. Walk or train a dog together;

62. Rake leaves for an elderly neighbor;

63. Play in the mud;

64. Run through the sprinkler on a hot day;

65. Wash the car together (and give your mentee a reward);

66. Sell lemonade;

67. Have a garage (rummage) sale together;

68. Work on a spaceship model;

69. Build your own robot.
    Visit www.RollingRobots.com in Los Angeles;

70. Rent a fun trampoline and invite your mentee to play on it, along with his or her friends;

71. Arrange a tour of your local radio or TV station;

72. Go on special field trips with your mentee, arranged through schools or a community center;

73. Take them to a bank and show them how to use a check register;

74. Help create a list of goals they can reach;

75. Treat them to an ice cream, or make your own;

76. Give her a make-over: a new hairstyle, makeup session and/or piece of clothing;

77. Take photos of each other and put them into an album;

78. Collect Christmas toys for a shelter;

79. Organize a Treasure Hunt or a Scavenger Hunt;

80. Play kids games like Hopscotch and Hide-and-Seek;

81. Make fruit popsicles;

82. Bake bread;

83. Decorate a cake or cookies;

84. Cook dinner together;

85. Run a car wash to raise money for a local charity;

86. Learn ballroom or swing dancing;

87. Teach how to knit, sew or crochet;

88. Learn a language together;

89. Create a community newsletter or contribute an article to your local paper;

90. Make a scrapbook together.

91. Organize a group to sing at a nursing home or a shelter.

92. Go for a walk in the woods;

93. Draw designs on the sidewalk with chalk;

94. Take a ride on the merry-go-round;

95. Play a videogame together;

96. Arm wrestle and thumb wrestle;

97. Play charades;

98. Look for shapes in the clouds;

99. Show them deep breathing techniques;

100. Teach them how to relax and meditate.

There are hundreds of other fun activities to share with your mentee(s) that you can discover if you use your imagination. Do some research on your community and use the Internet and the library.

Don't forget to ask your mentee what she or he wants to do, and then take it from there. The most important thing to remember is to just have fun!

CHAPTER NINE

Creative Arts Mentoring

CREATIVE EXPRESSION

It can often be challenging for traumatized children to share what they have experienced. Deep emotions can be blocked and talking about sensitive issues can be very difficult for them.

Creativity is a very powerful tool that allows youth to express themselves with a constructive outlet. Music, dance, writing, painting, drawing and other creative arts can release pent-up feelings in a safe manner that can be used to stimulate discussion about painful topics.

Hilary Sloane is an experienced artist who wanted to help troubled youth to discover the joy of visual arts. Through **Create Now**, I helped her to set up an "Introduction to Art" workshop at Vista Del Mar, a large group home in Los Angeles for children ages 7-18 who have been severely abused, neglected, abandoned and orphaned.

Every week for almost two years, Hilary mentored a small group of 10 teenage foster girls in her class. One of the projects was a "Self-Portrait." The girls took photos of each other. Hilary printed the pictures and gave each girl a photo of herself. They were provided with art supplies and encouraged to design a picture based on their own self-image.

One young lady had missed the photo session, so Hilary told her to draw a picture of herself and then to decorate it. The girl drew a detailed face, coloring in her hair and facial features. After the self-portrait was completed, she used a thick black crayon to mark out her face.

This girl obviously suffered from low self-esteem, which is a common trait of youth who are abused and neglected. She might have been told all of her life that she was ugly and stupid. She could have been blamed for her family's problems or felt guilty even though nothing at all was her fault.

It was probably difficult for this girl to tell anyone, "I hate myself and I think that I'm worthless." Yet by providing her with some materials, guidance and encouragement to express how she felt about herself, she was able to demonstrate these deeply-rooted emotions in that simple act of creation.

This artwork also became a valuable tool that could be used by her therapist and other counselors to assist the girl in healing.

Another benefit of creative expression is that while high-risk and at-risk youth may struggle with academics and fall far behind their peers, many of them excel in the arts. They develop confidence and self-esteem while discovering creative expression to be uplifting and a positive release.

Kids involved in art, music, writing, dance, theater and other creativity are more motivated to stay in school. A 1999 study by the "Imagination Project" at *UCLA Graduate School of Education* found that youth involved in the arts dropped out in fewer numbers.

There is extensive research that proves the creative arts stimulate the brain and also impact and expand learning. For example, the *Dana Foundation's* "2008 Consortium Report on Art and Cognition" states that their research on the exposure to visual arts correlated with improvements in children's math calculation abilities. They also had a higher degree of phonological awareness.

Another study[13] found that students involved with music scored an average of 100 points higher on SAT tests than students who did not play music.

Following are different types of creative expression with a few ideas of ways to include them in your mentoring programs. Remember that creative arts activities are just a springboard for you to connect with your mentee(s). It's not the music performance or the painted canvas that's important. The arts are a catalyst for you to bond and to have something to share and focus on as you get to know each other better.

---

[13] College Board Survey Of Sat Test Takers, 2000

STORYTELLING AND WRITING

I have been writing stories, poems, essays and articles since I learned penmanship at the tender age of seven, and it's what has gotten me through life's toughest challenges. Whenever I have been in a funk or needed to express intense feelings, then creating fresh characters and story plots has been an outlet. My stories have always allowed me to fantasize about other worlds, lives and situations.

Storytelling hasn't been my only therapeutic form of expression. As a youth, I kept a daily journal. Creating poems also helped me to release feelings. Even writing letters to my family and friends has been a healing process throughout my life. Writing has given me the chance to integrate intense emotions and to discover creative solutions to challenges.

Encourage your mentees to express themselves through writing. Even if they don't have a great command of the language and can't spell, that doesn't matter. They can find comfort and joy through written expression. They can communicate things that might be difficult to share in other ways.

If your mentee doesn't want to write, then telling a story is a great way to start. Oral tales have been around since the time of cavemen. Because writing isn't involved, illiterate youth won't feel intimidated or embarrassed about participating. It's a fantastic tool for children who have been traumatized, because storytelling validates their experiences and allows them to express their feelings. It increases their self-awareness, knowledge and helps them to heal.

You could read a story to your mentee(s) and then ask them to make up their own. You can also make up your own story and encourage them to do the same.

I worked with a group of children ages 8-12 who were living at *Hollygrove*, a large group home in Hollywood for abused and neglected children. The facility had just held marathon games for all the kids. I gathered them in a circle around a table and told them we were going to make up stories.

At first, they were quiet and shy, so I invented a quick little yarn about a boy who raced in a contest and really wanted to get the first prize. He almost gave up, but he continued to race and he finally won. It was a very short and simple story and it just took me a minute to make it up, yet the kids really enjoyed hearing it. They reacted with delight and liked this game.

Once I broke the ice, those children who were initially timid about sharing were now shouting to have their stories told. All the youngsters then made up their own little tales. A few of the kids really got into it and created elaborate stories that seemed very personal.

Here is another game for kids of all ages that will help get storytelling going:

Round Robin

Everyone sits in a circle. The leader of the group starts off a story with a sentence. For example, "Once upon a time, a girl named Vicki wanted to get together with her best friend." The person to the right continues the story with another sentence like, "She decided to take the bus." Each child continues adding a sentence to the story until it comes to a conclusion.

The same technique can be used where each child adds just one word to make up the story, instead of a whole sentence. The first player might say, "A…" and the second player adds, "girl…" and the third player replies, "wanted…" and so on until everyone gets a turn and the improvised story comes to a good conclusion. The ending always seems to naturally evolve, and the kids feel wonderful that they worked as a team to create a story.

There are many different types of writing: short stories, poems, essays, articles, journals, song lyrics, novels, autobiographies, nonfiction books, blogs, copywriting and more. Your mentee can choose whichever style of writing is most comfortable for them.

Ron Osborn is a screenwriter who wrote "Meet Joe Black" with Brad Pitt and was nominated for Emmy awards for his work on "West Wing" and "E.R." He taught a wonderful Screenwriting workshop at a boys' detention camp. At first, the kids were excited about learning how to write a movie. We gave them copies of scripts that they could relate to: "Antwone Fisher," "My Family/Mi Familia" and "Mask." They read them with interest.

However, after a few weeks, the boys expressed different goals. While one gang member worked on a script about gang life, another boy wrote an autobiography. A third was interested in writing poems and a fourth wanted to write song lyrics.

The workshop was customized to meet the youths' needs. Ron was able to give each of the boys individual attention so they could develop their own writing projects, while they also shared their work with the whole group. Nothing was forced on them, so they enjoyed it even more.

Don't raise your mentee's expectations about getting paid to have their writing published in the traditional way. Many writers are now self-publishing through print-on-demand (myself included). Start-up costs are free or inexpensive and they can benefit from the royalties.

New media is very promising: blogs, forums, chats and social networking sites like Facebook, My Space and Twitter are the rage. These sites encourage youth to write, even if they are in tiny bite-size chunks and spelling is often twisted. Think about "tweets" as haikus – you have to use every character very carefully and make each word count, yet the significance of the writing can be profound.

Perhaps you can help your mentee to set up her or his own website and they can include a blog. Encourage them to share their thoughts on different social sites and to submit their writing, in whatever format, to some of the many websites that help writers to get their work out.

There are hundreds of sites where youth can publish their writing online for free. Even if it's their own website with little traffic, kids are thrilled that there is the potential for many people around the world to read what they have to express. This small feat is a huge boost to their self-esteem.

Screenwriting is very popular with youth. Most kids are into movies, but they don't realize how important a screenplay is in order to create their favorite TV shows and feature films. I have had youth tell me that whatever they see on TV is real. I did a poll once and around 50% of 100 youngsters thought that actors make up all of their dialogue. One kid showed me his bullet wound and said, "That (bleep) hurt! It don't look that way when I see gunshots on TV."

Many kids are surprised that writers actually create this content and the actors aren't just making it up as they go along. Reality TV doesn't help to change these misconceptions (even though many of these shows are actually written). By learning this art form, they realize that they also have the power to express their unique stories, which could possibly be made into movies or TV shows.

One of our mentors was matched with a girl in a detention center who was illiterate. When the girl learned that her mentor was a screenwriter, she was instantly motivated to learn how to read and write so that she could write her own life story as a movie script.

As I mentioned in my Introduction, I was amazed by the transformations of the incarcerated youth who participated in my two Screenwriting workshops. Many of these kids were illiterate with perhaps a third-grade reading level. They would never pick up a book to read, but when I offered them the chance to study some of the scripts of their favorite movies, they jumped at the opportunity.

When I taught the Screenwriting Workshop at Optimist Youth Homes, around 30 boys had signed up for the class. Most of these juvenile delinquents were African-American and Latino. I started with a basic premise: two rival gang members (Latino and African-American) end up at the same detention camp. They learn to resolve their differences and end their war. My idea was that the script would have a typical happy "Hollywood" ending with both gang leaders settling their problems when they returned to the streets.

One of the participants was "Roberto," a powerful 17-year-old who was the leader of the Latino residents. He was incarcerated because of a gang attack. Roberto argued about my ending of the story. He stated that there was no way these rival gang leaders would *ever* stop their war. They would fight till death. The script had to have a tragic ending. I tried my best to convince him otherwise.

When we broke for dinner, Wanda Patterson, my contact at the detention center, reminded me that this was the youths' story. She was absolutely right! As a mentor, I had to listen to what they had to say. I couldn't impose my own values in hopes of inspiring them to change their lives.

After dinner, we returned to our meeting room for the rest of the Screenwriting Workshop. I was excited to share my realization with Roberto and the other boys. The script would end just as they wanted it. But it was too late!

During dinner, Roberto had decided to boycott my workshop. He convinced all the other Latino youth that my class was bogus and they were all wimps if they attended. I'm paraphrasing since his language was much spicier than that!

Participation in my workshop suddenly dropped, with only the African-American teens and one or two Latinos who were new to the camp in attendance. After some time, Roberto and his friends realized that I had incorporated their ideas into the script, so they finally returned to my workshop.

Once the basic plot and characters were created, I developed a simple technique. I suggested one of the scenes in the story. The boys immediately shouted out their ideas. I tried to get them to raise their hands, but it wasn't always possible to keep them quiet when their imaginations were active. I repeated the best of their suggestions and everyone voted on the final decision: "How many want his street name to be 2Crazy? How many for Sniper? What's his dream career?"

Then I invited the youth to act out the scenes. "Okay, we're going to do the part where Sniper meets 2Crazy for the first time at school. Who wants to be in it?" The selected players went to the front of the room and improvised the scene by pretending to be those characters. They spoke and acted as if they were living the story.

I tape-recorded everything. After the workshop, I transcribed the scenes that the kids had improvised, writing down every word they had said just as they'd said it. I typed it into screenplay format (which is very specific) and made copies of the scene for all the kids.

In the next class, we sat in a circle and they took turns reading the scene, line by line. Each youth read one character's line or else the descriptive text. For those kids who couldn't read, they simply indicated that they didn't want to read out loud, so the youth sitting next to them recited instead. However, the illiterate boys followed along with everyone else and heard the words being pronounced, so they learned how to read through this technique, without having to suffer any embarrassment.

Sometimes I misunderstood a word (usually slang) and when we got to it, they would all groan and say, "We would never say it *that* way. We would say this." I polished the script so that it was written exactly as they wanted it.

When the script was completed, we all sat at a big table and I brought pizzas and drinks. Roles were assigned, so those who could read either pretended to be a character or they read the narrative portions. We went through the entire screenplay.

The story came to life and it was an incredibly powerful experience. It flowed so that you could see the characters and plot progress naturally. Everyone became caught up in the emotions of the story. It was indeed a tragic ending when both gang leaders were killed. However, there was also a sense of hope, because their 6-year-old brothers played together.

At our final read-through, when we got to the end of the script, there were sniffles and tears as the boys experienced the impact of their words. Several of the kids told me that they personally related to the loss of their own family members and friends, as portrayed through the characters they had created.

Several boys told me that they wanted to do well in school and even attend college. The biggest surprise came from Roberto. The same young man who had put up such resistance in the beginning of the workshop subsequently had several gang tattoos removed from his neck and hand. As his self-esteem increased, Roberto changed the image that he projected to the world.

While screenwriting is a relatively young art form, it's an important part of modern storytelling, which is what attracts many youth. We can't force them to always read classic literature that is totally foreign to their world and expect them to be interested. I personally think this is why our dropout rates are so high. Many youth are just plain bored.

I believe that if we can engage our kids by using media that is popular and fun, then their desire to grow and learn will be stimulated. They are our future generation and we need to respect what they have to say and how they want to say it.

You can help your mentee(s) to create a short screenplay. One page equals roughly one minute of screen time. They can work on individual scripts, a group project, or both. You can give them weekly assignments and everyone can share their work at your meetings. Of course, if they want to jump into writing a feature film or TV shows, that's great, too.

There are a number of websites where you can download and print scripts of popular movies and TV shows for your Screenwriting Workshop for free. Drew's Script-O-Rama is at: www.script-o-rama.com.

Also try Simply Scripts at www.simplyscripts.com/movie.html. A search on the Internet will reveal additional resources.

It's important that your mentees learn screenplay format, since any deviations are a red flag that the writer is an amateur. There are many books and websites dedicated to proper script format, which is different for television and movies. There are also a number of software programs specifically for screenwriting. Currently Final Draft and Movie Magic Screenwriter are the most popular programs in the entertainment industry.

Here's a fun way to study the importance of screenwriting. Find a movie that your mentee(s) like. Have them read a draft of the screenplay for that film. You might find a "First Draft," which is very different than a "Shooting Script" (what was produced). Even this last draft will differ a lot from the completed film, since during production, the director and actors continue to revise the screenplay as the movie is being shot.

Your mentees can read the script and then watch the movie to see how it has changed. They will discover that scenes might have been deleted or moved, with new ones added. Dialogue will be different and characters will seem unlike the way they might have imagined them.

Storytelling and writing are powerful tools for self-expression. Encourage your mentee(s) to practice often. Buy them a notebook that they can decorate so they can keep a diary, or splurge on a more-fitting journal. You can also use a three-ring binder with lots of paper. Another idea is to make a special box or decorate a large envelope where they can store their stories, essays and poems.

Most importantly, always, always *always* be ready and enthusiastic to read whatever they have written. If your mentee hands you a poem, story or chapter of a book that they have written, drop everything to read it. They want to know what you think and to also please you, so give them very positive feedback and encourage them to keep writing. Your words will be like gold.

VIDEO PRODUCTION

Another popular media for today's youth is video. We live in a visual world. Anyone can use their cell phone camera or inexpensive digital equipment to instantly share their own video productions with millions of people via You Tube, social sites, cable news and other outlets.

You can help your mentee(s) to become filmmakers by organizing the equipment and guiding them on what kind of video they might like to create.

For instance, this could be a good follow-up project to your Screenwriting Workshop. If your mentee has written a short script, imagine how fun it would be to film it and create a short movie that could be submitted to You Tube and shared with the rest of the world.

The same holds true for plays. If you've worked with your mentees on putting together a theatrical performance, why not capture it on video and edit it for a lasting arts project that everyone can have as a souvenir, or to use for building a portfolio.

Documentaries also make excellent video projects. Let your mentee find a topic that's of interest, and then use a video camera to showcase the issue, shoot interviews with people who are knowledgeable and present it to the public.

You don't need professional equipment. As mentioned, video cameras are pretty inexpensive. You can also rent them cheaply. I recommend asking your friends and associates if they have any video cameras and if they want to help you with this project.

Sometimes people have equipment that sits in a closet or a garage that just gathers dust. You'll be providing them with the chance to make use of their camera for a good cause — education. They might even be inspired to help out and run the camera for you, or mentor youth in how to use the equipment.

If you let people know that you are mentoring an at-risk youth, it might surprise you to discover that other people also want to mentor, but they don't want to commit to a long-term relationship. However, if you invite them to help out, they would probably enjoy the chance to support a child and to give back to their community. Giving is one of the greatest joys of life.

In this same way, you could possibly find a professional videographer to volunteer. Someone who shoots videos at weddings and special events, or who operates the camera at your local TV station might love to teach his or her craft to a youth. These people would be able to bring professional equipment plus their expertise, and you yourself could also learn a lot.

If you can, try to edit the video on your computer. There is plenty of software out there to help with this. Otherwise, reach out to professional editors in your town. Every TV station has one. There are probably some local production companies that make commercials and TV shows. Hobbyists who are creating their own home videos might be inclined to help. Also, college and high school students could want the experience.

Your mentee(s) should be involved in the video production process as much as possible. It's much more rewarding if he or she can see the editor cutting the video then if it's just done for them. That way, they can learn how to do it themselves.

Videos can be complex or simple. You might want to do a fancy production with wardrobe and props. The kids can work together to make a slick video. Or else, it can be as simple as your mentee talking directly to the camera.

I worked with a group of high-risk teenage girls to make a video project. They lived in a group home for youth with mental health challenges. Most of the six girls in my workshop came from wealthy families in Malibu and Beverly Hills, but they all had severe emotional and behavioral problems.

One girl got into raging fights with her mother. Another was a "cutter" (self-injury). One of the girls was on strong medication and she usually fell asleep during our meetings.

I met weekly with the girls and tape-recorded our writing sessions. The script was based on characters, plot and dialogue that they had invented, and they were also the stars. I assigned them the tasks of picking out their wardrobe and selecting the music.

Through **Create Now**, I recruited volunteers who brought equipment and did all of the technical work. I gave the girls things to do that they could easily accomplish. This helped to develop their confidence and self-esteems. They also learned how to operate the cameras and went to an editing session at a professional studio where they learned how to edit.

They had a lot of fun and the video came out great. The girls were so proud of their work and each of them now has a lasting souvenir of the project, which they can share with their families and friends.

Once your video is completed, teach your mentee how to load it on You Tube and other video sharing sites like Yahoo! and Vimeo. They will gain a lot of pride when others see their videos, and it could possibly lead to more opportunities for them.

THEATER

Theater is fun and includes a number of different arts, such as wardrobe, set design and direction. Many kids are interested in acting. They assume that it's easy, until they learn all that goes into being a good actor. They have to discover how a character thinks, feels and behaves. They must memorize lines and learn to say them with emotion while responding on cue to other actors. Blocking is essential. Using tools like props are important. Giving a performance in front of an audience can be intimidating.

A good way to get youth prepared for acting, and to get them to open up in so many other ways, is with improvisation. There are lots of different exercises that are entertaining, challenging and the kids love doing them. Here is a popular one:

Freeze Tag

Freeze Tag is a game where everyone stands in a circle. Two youth are selected. Other players call out the names of locations. Let's say you select this one: "You're in the jungle." Also ask for their ideas of an activity. Encourage them to be creative. "You're climbing a tree to pick bananas."

Once the location and action are decided upon, then the two selected youth (#1 and #2) stand inside the circle and act out that scenario. Tell them to use broad physical gestures as they improvise the scene. In the above example, they would pretend to climb a tree in the jungle to pick bananas. They should ad-lib dialogue and try to make it funny (while not being crude).

At any point, another youth (#3) can shout out "Freeze!" and both of the original kids (#1 and #2) must stay frozen in their last positions. The new youth (#3) taps the shoulder of one of the original kids (we'll say #1 for this example), and takes his or her place. The original kid (#1) joins the others in the circle.

The new youth (#3) must start off copying the exact physical position of the previous youth. If #1 was just reaching up to grab a banana, then #3 must put his hands up in the same way.

However, #3 must then take the scene into a totally new direction. Instead of being in the jungle, maybe he decides that he and youth #2 are playing basketball. Instead of reaching for a banana, he could indicate through his physical actions and words that he's trying to score points on the court.

Maybe #3 pretends that instead of grabbing bananas, he's getting deodorant off a high shelf for a customer in a store, or anything else that his wild imagination can come up with.

Youth #2 should play along and agree with whatever #3 is saying, so if he says "Do you prefer this stick deodorant or the spray-on kind?" then #2 has to pretend to be in the store and respond accordingly. They continue with that scenario until another youth in the circle calls out "Freeze!" and taps #1 or #3 to take their place, and change the scene into a new direction.

Many kids enjoy the creative challenge that this game provides, and the chance to be in the spotlight. You'll find that shy youth will often come out of their shells when they become involved in these types of fun exercises. There are books and websites devoted to improvisational games. However, don't force anyone to play if they don't want to.

To teach dramatic acting, ideally your mentee(s) will write their own play and develop great scenes so they can show off their skills. You can also download monologues for actors from the Internet, or buy books with monologues at bookstores. Coach them in audition techniques and plan a session where they can actually do a mock audition or give a cold reading. Try videotaping it, since they can learn a lot when they see themselves on the screen.

If you're working with younger children, you can read a popular book aimed at kids. Then find props and costumes that the children can wear and read the story again. This time, the kids can dress up as the characters and act out the plot as you read it aloud.

As an example, a fairytale about a King and Queen can be easily enhanced with handmade crowns and capes. Props like sticks for wands can be added as needed.

A theatrical production is more fun when a number of kids participate. That way some can help behind the scenes with set construction, costumes and running the lights, while other youth focus on the acting, directing, promotion and marketing the performance. After all, what kind of theatrical performance would it be if there wasn't an audience to see it. You should also create a program to hand out, and make sure that everyone who participated in the project is given a credit. Then go put on a show and have a great time!

<u>MUSIC</u>

Learning how to play music can have a profound impact on a child. They develop many skills like discipline, persistence, as well as knowledge about rhythm, tempo, melody, harmony and other important musical elements.

Children often want the opportunity to learn a musical instrument, but they lack the resources to own one. If you're a musician, check with your friends and associates to see if they will donate an instrument to your mentee. Perhaps they have an old guitar laying in the attic, or a piano that's just taking up space.

Look through the "For Sale" ads in your local paper. Search Craig's List at www.craigslist.com and other websites like eBay for bargains on musical instruments. There may be some treasure at garage sales. Also, visit any shops in your community that sell or repair instruments and ask if they can make a contribution or give a great discount.

Many cities around the world also have access to a website called www.Freecycle.com where you can post notices requesting musical instruments. Someone may already be offering one for free.

Percussion instruments are relatively cheap and easy to obtain. A nonprofit organization called SERRV International at www.serrv.org sells musical instruments made by artisans from all over the world, like drums from Africa, panpipe whistles from South America and gourd maracas from Indonesia. These instruments are very inexpensive. It's also a wonderful way to show children how to create music from natural materials.

Percussion instruments may also be created from found objects, like plastic cups tapped onto the sidewalk or banged against each other. "Tic Tacs" candy containers make excellent shakers. Pots and pans with wooden spoons and buckets with sticks can create music.

Maracas could be easily produced from plastic bottles. Fill them partly with rice, beans, sand or pebbles. Screw the cap on tightly. Depending on the size of the bottles, plus the type and amount of filling, then you'll get different sounds when they're shaken. Experimenting is fun. You can glue the top closed to make sure there are no spills. Kids can then decorate their handmade maracas.

Regardless of the type of musical instrument that you use, be sure to give your mentee(s) help with learning it. They might get frustrated in the process and want to give up. Guitar playing looks easy, until their fingers get sore from the strings. Piano seems like fun, but now it's boring. Whatever you do, don't force your love of playing music onto your mentee if he or she doesn't want to follow through, but be encouraging and give guidance if they do.

Music can also include simple appreciation. Bring samples of different types of music, such as jazz, rock 'n roll, classical and country to expose your mentee to something other than hip hop and rap music, which is popular with most at-risk kids.

Create Now Board member Mark Schulman is a world-class drummer who has spent years touring the world with P!nk, Cher, Destiny's Child, Foreigner, Billy Idol, Stevie Nicks and many other famous performers.

In addition, he teaches a powerful motivational drumming program called "Find Your Rhythm." Mark shares stories of his survival of testicular cancer fused with wisdom from life on the road. He talks about how positive attitudes change our lives and the need for us to set goals. His presentations are popular with top corporations like IBM and Mattel, and universities like M.I.T..

Whenever Mark has free time, he presents his seminar to hundreds of incarcerated youth at detention centers and juvenile halls. Mark said. "If I can change one kid's attitude, then he can change his life. If he has changed his life, then he has changed the world forever."

Many of the kids that **Create Now** serves aren't into rock music, but they learn to really appreciate it after Mark's amazing drum performance. Some of the youth are inspired to play the drums themselves. Mark gives them the chance to use his drum kit so they can show off for their peers and the staff. He invites all of them for a free drum lesson or a chance to record at his studio. However, very few actually take him up on his generous offer.

Mark has a phenomenal impact on the youth. Many of them hang out after the program to learn more from him. These are kids who usually don't care about anything. It's rare that they take such an interest, especially in a type of music that they normally wouldn't listen to.

Demond was in and out of detention camps starting when he was 12-years old. He saw Mark when he was incarcerated at Camp Holton in L.A.. That same afternoon, he wrote **Create Now** a three-page letter, telling Mark how much he had impacted him. Demond has stayed out of trouble ever since. He partners with Mark at his presentations to share his story about how he has overcome his challenges through the support of his mentor.

Beatboxing is vocal percussion, the art of producing drum beats, rhythm, and musical sounds with just the mouth, voice, lips and tongue. As mentioned, street kids have to be very innovative to express themselves, since they don't have money. They've created this amazing art form that's the backbone of hip hop. Beatboxing is often showcased during hip hop contests, and there's even a world championship competition.

Music can be taught in many different ways. **Create Now** mentor Anastasia Nikiforova taught a wonderful Percussion Workshop to a group of homeless children. She used this popular exercise:

Rhythm

All of the kids choose different percussion instruments, which they rotate and share. One youth is selected to be the Conductor. They initiate a rhythm with their musical instrument. Perhaps they are playing the conga drums, or the maracas.

The other kids follow the Conductor's rhythm with their different percussion instruments and they come together as a band. If the Conductor plays faster, so does the rest of the band. This builds a lot of self-esteem, as the Conductor realizes that they are setting a beat and others are following. Every child gets to be the Conductor at some point, so they all benefit tremendously.

A variation of this game is when the youth who is the Conductor raises their hand up high when they want the band to play their instruments very loudly. They lower their hand when they want the other kids to play softly.

In both exercises, the whole group of youth benefits since they bond with their mentor and each other while they collaborate. This builds confidence and teamwork.

DANCE

Many at-risk youth are very much into dance, particularly hip hop style. Hip hop is a cultural movement that began amongst urban youth in New York thirty years ago and has since spread around the world. It's the most popular music and dance for kids today.

The four main elements of hip-hop are MCing ("rapping" or singing), DJing (spinning and scratching records), graffiti art (spray painting) and breakdancing (aka "b-boying"). Some consider beatboxing the fifth element of hip hop.

The moves in breakdancing can be extraordinary. Some of these kids perform amazing feats through this dance, spinning on their heads and twisting in unbelievable poses.

If your mentee is into breakdancing or hip hop, encourage them to expand their skills. Find out about local hangouts where breakdancing takes place. You can even organize a dance competition to give more kids the chance to show off their moves.

You can also introduce your mentee to different types of dance. Take her to the ballet. Teach him how to Foxtrot or Cha Cha.

Introduce them to Swing Dance or Country Two-Step. Popular TV shows like *Dancing With the Stars* and *So You Think You Can Dance* will expose your mentees to new types of dance. It could be entertaining for you to watch these programs together.

Create Now mentor Lindsay Bogan is a Marriage and Family Therapist at a large group home for foster boys in Los Angeles. Her job is to help them "age out of the system" when they turn 18, so they can adjust to society and become independent.

Lindsay grew up taking ballet lessons, and that became a passion throughout her life. She wanted to share this love of dance with foster youth at another group home. Through **Create Now**, I arranged for her to teach a Ballet Workshop at Hillsides, a large foster group home in Pasadena.

I went to the class to take photos and to get some quotes from the kids for our newsletter. It was wonderful to see how excited the children were when Lindsay arrived for the workshop. There were around a dozen girls with a couple of boys from ages 7 to 14.

Lindsay had taken their shoe sizes the week before and brought the kids a treat: canvas dance bags that they could decorate, and ballet slippers. The children tried on the shoes with tremendous delight.

On this Sunday, many new kids had just joined the workshop, so Lindsay didn't have enough shoes. One girl, "Valerie," was very upset that there were no shoes left in her size. Even though she was around 13- years-old, she cried like a little girl.

Lindsay knew exactly how to react, based on her years of experience as a therapist. She apologized to Valerie several times and told her that it was a mistake. She didn't intentionally give away her shoes. The girl refused to believe her. Lindsay tried to soothe her feelings by asking Valerie to be her assistant in the workshop. The girl just cried and her staff finally had to take her out from the room.

Valerie came back a few times, but was still very upset and crying. Lindsay again offered her the chance to assist with the class, but the girl kept crying and the staff forced her to leave.

After about 15 minutes, Valerie calmed down. As Lindsay was giving the kids instructions on how to dance and jump across the floor, Valerie quietly moved next to her mentor and just stood there.

Lindsay immediately turned to her and asked the girl to assist with the counting of the steps, and then to dance with her as she showed the others how to do the movements. Valerie quickly got into place and helped out. By the end of the session, she was having a great time and the ballet slippers were forgotten.

ART

Visual art can be a powerful tool to help at-risk and high-risk youth to open up. A child doesn't have to be a talented artist in order to benefit therapeutically from creating art. It's very subjective and everyone is an artist no matter what others may think.

Teaching art appreciation is also a great opportunity for your mentee(s) to learn about the history of art and what makes an artist. Each week, you can highlight a particular artist, like Van Gogh or Picasso. Show copies of that artist's work and give some background information. Even younger children are fascinated by fine art. It's very inspirational for them to want to create their own artwork.

Create Now mentors sometimes bring simple crayons and coloring books to their arts workshops. They find that even the older youth and adult staff have a blast. Just by selecting colors, using pressure on the crayons to get dark or light strokes and staying within the lines of a picture, a youth can feel good about creating art, while relaxing and having fun.

A popular project is making a collage. Have your mentee cut out different images from old magazines and glue them onto a large piece of poster board or cardboard. Be aware, however, that this project is only for youth who are able to safely deal with scissors and glue, and it must be cleared by staff beforehand. Some detention facilities or prisons won't allow these materials inside.

The collage can have a theme, like self-respect or true love. My suggestion is to encourage your mentee(s) to make a "Vision Board," which includes pictures that represent all of their dreams; what they want in terms of a house, car, ideal partner, career, vacation spot, clothes, etc. Encourage your mentee to study the board and to fantasize about having all of the images that he or she has selected for their Vision Board. They can enhance it with ribbons, beads, paint, and natural objects, like flowers and leaves.

A variation of the collage is to make a CD cover and an inside jacket for their favorite music. They can bring the plastic case and decorate it, or embellish the cardboard sleeve.

Scrapbooking is also fun and easy to do. There are stores that specialize in materials for scrapbooks, or just adapt an old photo album and decorate it to make something new and special. You can make scrapbooks to commemorate an event that you attended together, a birthday, graduation, etc..

Designing a mural is a fabulous project for a group of kids, or even just for you and your mentee to do. Find a good wall. Decide on a theme. Draw the image on large paper like butcher block or pieces of paper taped together to replicate the dimensions of the wall. You can also make a collage with images from magazines that you like. Create your design the exact way that you want your mural to appear. Now it's time to transfer your design onto the wall using chalk.

There are three techniques to do this: (1) Freehand, which can be difficult unless you have a sharp eye and a steady hand; (2) Transfer your design onto a transparency. Project it onto the wall and trace your outlines. This can be challenging if the space isn't big enough to allow the distance; (3) Use a ruler to draw a grid on top of your design, measuring one-inch squares across the paper. You can use a marker, pen, pencil or any other implement that will show up clearly. Then use chalk to draw a larger grid with one-foot squares across the wall. Copy the design in each square of paper onto the wall squares. You'll be amazed how well it comes together.

When painting on brick or cinderblock, you can count and measure the blocks and draw them to scale over the original. Regardless of which technique you utilize, once your design is transferred to the wall, then it's time to paint it. Start with the background colors first and fill in the rest. Before you know it, your mural will be completed. The impact on your mentees and everyone who sees it can be very powerful.

Katherine O'Connor works in the education department at the Getty Museum. While she had studied art history and theory at college, she had never created a mural before. That all changed when she volunteered through **Create Now**.

We matched Katherine with *Star View Adolescent Center*, a residential psychiatric health facility in Torrance that is home to 56 severely emotionally-disturbed youngsters, ages 12-17, who had been abused, neglected, abandoned and orphaned. Dale Young, the Director of Group Services, asked Katherine to help ten of their girls to create a mural in their group therapy room.

I introduced Katherine to another mentor, Roger Dolin, a talented muralist. He gave her some pointers and **Create Now** supplied her with paints, brushes and other supplies.

The girls decided on a jungle theme. Katherine said, "One of the challenges set out in the beginning was to get the girls to work together, but that was never a problem. The enthusiasm engendered by the girls for this project was amazing and I am so proud to have worked with them."

Dale said, "Some of the girls were very self-critical and wanted to give up easily, but Katherine encouraged them to let go and experiment and to trust that it would all come together, and it did!"

Camille, 16-years-old said, "Working on the mural was exciting. It was magical and now the Day Room looks like a forest with a waterfall."

Dale remarked, "The mural is beautiful and vibrant and reflects the many different personalities that created it. Thank you for such a wonderful and therapeutic experience!"

A variation of the mural is Graffiti Art (aka "Graff"), which is hugely popular with youth. Find an old wall that can be painted (with permission by the owner). This might be a shop that wants graffiti-style letters or a unique design created for marketing, a private house or a decrepit, abandoned building. You could also prop up a gigantic slab of wood. With different colored cans of spray paint, kids can create graffiti art, which is a highly respected art form in many parts of the world. They can paint their names, the school's mascot, promote special events or just "freestyle," where they produce their own unique designs and share it with the public. Be sure that they spray the paint in a well-ventilated area.

Clay is very versatile, and it's also inexpensive. There are some clays that you need to bake. Others can harden naturally. You can sculpt figures, design a mug or cup and create a vase. Let your mentee's imagination run wild.

Contour drawing is a popular exercise, although it can be challenging. Give your mentee a sheet of paper and a pencil. Put some fruit or flowers on the table and have them draw the outline of the objects onto their paper, but without looking down at the page.

Our mentor Corinne Mazzola taught groups of incarcerated girls a fun painting project, which is to glue a favorite magazine image onto a piece of cardboard, like the top of a shoebox. Heavy card stock paper will also do. Give your mentee some paints and a brush, with a paper plate to use as a palette. Let them paint on top of the image by mixing the colors to match the picture. This is a great way to teach about primary colors and blending.

Thanks to our mentor Melissa Hogan for sharing this idea. A fun drawing game is to give a group of mentees a sheet of paper and have them fold it into thirds. On the top third, each child should draw a funny-looking head of a creature. Then fold all of the papers backwards so the image is hidden. Distribute the papers so that the kids have someone else's sheet. In the center part, they should now draw a weird torso. Fold the center portion backwards so the only visible piece of paper is the lower third. Pass the sheets around to other youth again. This time they draw goofy feet. One more pass, and then have them unfold the papers. They will find a silly creature made from different parts of their drawings, which will provide lots of laughs.

Arts and crafts are very popular with kids. For example, cigar boxes are excellent to turn into "treasure chests." Some cigar shops will donate a variety of sturdy wooden boxes in different shapes and sizes. You can also use cardboard boxes. Kids love them, especially those who are living in shelters and temporary places. They have something to store their precious possessions. Decorate the boxes using paint, markers, rhinestones, mylar paper, feathers, beads, ribbons and stickers with fun images. You might want to get a few cigar boxes so that your mentee can also make gifts for their family and friends.

Thanks to Victoria Jensen for this one: cute animal critters can be made from empty toilet paper rolls, which serve as the torso. Colorful construction paper can be cut and glued to cover the paper roll torso. Then use more paper to cut out arms, legs and heads of animals, like a frog, dog, cat or bunny. The paper limbs can be glued onto the sides and the bottom of the roll. The head sticks to the top and googly eyes can be attached. A tail can be added in back. I always encourage children to give a name to their creations, so they become more personal and "alive" in their vivid imaginations.

Painting T-shirts is always delightful. Get the right size for your mentee. There are special fabric paints and also markers. Draw the design on paper first and then transfer it to the shirt with pencil if possible before painting or coloring it. You can use the grid technique previously mentioned.

There are thousands of arts and crafts ideas on the Internet and in books and magazines. Kids love them since they're fun to make and create great souvenirs.

TALENT SHOWS

Starting when I was ten-years-old, I organized Talent Shows in my neighborhood. While hanging out with my friends, I would suggest that we put on an event to show off our talents and then charge our parents a dollar. Everyone came together as a team. Some of my friends wanted to dance, others sing, tell jokes, share their different talents and have fun while earning some money.

I would ask my friends to volunteer for tasks based on their interests. Some helped with costumes, getting the chairs, making flyers and baking cookies to sell. I usually directed the performances: singing, dancing, comedy, magic tricks and acrobats.

These talent shows were always a huge success. All of us had a blast. We learned business skills, received applause for our efforts and split the proceeds equally so everyone earned some money. Our parents really enjoyed seeing our shows and were very proud of us.

Most at-risk and high-risk youth rarely have the chance to show off their talents. Their parents may be working at several jobs or absent for other reasons. They might not even know that they have special gifts unless someone notices and points it out to them.

You can easily organize a Talent Show that provides these kids with the chance to shine in the spotlight, while giving their parents the opportunity to see their child in a new way.

I organized a Talent Show at *L.A. Family Housing*, a large homeless shelter in North Hollywood, CA with 60 families and 120 children. **Create Now** sponsored a Singing Workshop, a Hip-Hop Dance Workshop and a Comedy Workshop. All three of our mentors met once a week for a month or two with the children who had signed up.

The Talent Show enabled us to culminate the workshops while bringing 25 of these children (ages 4-10) together, so they could work as a team. Someone had donated "Transformers" T-shirts so that became our costume and theme: Youth transforming the world through their creativity. The kids loved it!

The Singing Workshop, taught by talented young singer Shalayna Janelle, focused on learning two popular songs. The girls in the class had to memorize the lyrics, which helped build their literacy skills, and then sing in harmony, backing up one girl who had a beautiful voice and was the soloist.

The Hip-Hop Dance Workshop was taught by Mandi, Mettler a dancer with the L.A. Clippers. This workshop was very popular. Around 15 boys and girls practiced hard as a team to learn two fun dances. Mandi choreographed a special dance to the theme song for "The Transformers."

Comedy was taught by our mentor Daniel Rothenberg, a stand-up comedian. Daniel had the kids do improv comedy exercises, where they practiced silly walks and put together a funny scene called "Get to Your Chairs."

We selected the date for "The Transformers Talent Show" and everyone worked hard, including some of the kids' parents. It was amazing to see how these parents became so involved and passionate about helping their children to make this a great experience. They were also living vicariously through them.

I brought in volunteers to help the kids make a giant colorful banner: "Transformers." Even the littlest children participated. Some local high school students who needed to do community service helped with arranging the tables and chairs, hanging the banner and balloons, and videotaping the show.

The kids were so energized that some of them couldn't sleep the night before. These are children who have never had the chance to perform for an audience before. Feeling butterflies was a wonderful new experience for them.

Create Now invited special guests to attend our event, including Dame Barbara Hay, the British Consul-General whom I had met before embarking on the Global xChange program, and some musicians, DJs and rappers from Egypt and Morocco who were visiting through the U.S. State Department. The children were very excited to have some important strangers in the audience, especially since they were from other countries far away.

The Talent Show was a huge success. The joy and sheer delight that the kids experienced was evident. Some of our guests were brought to tears. The best part was when I handed out small gift bags with some toys, candy and Certificates of Completion to each child. The children were delighted. One of the mothers was so proud of her three children that each time one of them got the gift bag, she shouted loudly "That's my baby!" Those are beautiful emotions and words that will live with these kids forever.

We gave everyone a party after the show, with lots of refreshments. The mentors loved the experience as much as the kids did and they intend to keep coming back to teach them each week. One of our volunteers noted, "The kids were so proud of themselves. I think it gave them the confidence that they can do anything." Our "Transformers Talent Show" is now offered to other youth agencies that we serve and it has become a regular event.

If you're working with a large group of youth, have the kids help you to coordinate the show. They can learn business skills by putting together a budget and balancing the books. Marketing and PR is fun when they form a "Street Team" to post flyers and promote the event through social media. Let them take turns performing, directing and assisting with the decorating.

You could organize a Youth Marketplace at the event, where the kids can set up tables to sell their handicrafts, artwork in an exhibition, music and baked goods.

I think it's great to get the parents involved because it helps them to bond with their children. However, be careful that they don't interfere or try to take over.

We had that situation with our Talent Show at *L.A. Family Housing* when one of the mothers was trying to coach the kids, which conflicted with what our mentor was teaching them. This was understandably upsetting to our mentor. As a result, the Volunteer Coordinator at the shelter asked the parents to leave the room. They were allowed to help the children to fix their hair instead. If you create boundaries from the start, then everyone will know what they are expected to do, and what is not allowed.

After the Talent Show is over, celebrate the success by giving the kids a party. This is another area where the parents can help, by putting together a potluck meal. Make sure that you provide the children with lasting souvenirs.

It's also important to document the event with video and photos. We used an inexpensive camcorder to record the show, and had a photographer take photos. Each child will receive a DVD of their performance and a CD with all the pictures. These will be precious mementos of their experience that they can share with their own children and grandchildren one day. The impact on kids, and their families, from Talent Shows is tremendous.

CHAPTER TEN

Ending Your Mentoring Relationship

It's been proven that the longer you mentor, then the bigger the impact. Ideally, you will become a lifelong mentor to your mentee. A great goal is to be like a family member to them; someone who will always be around for support. It's very gratifying for you to see your mentee mature and to realize the effect that your guidance has had on him or her.

Many foster kids, or children with little or no family, need someone they can turn to for advice or help. In those situations, mentors can sometimes become like surrogate parents.

You might be asked to serve an important role at their wedding, or to be a Godfather or Godmother to their children.

Don't take your relationship with your mentee(s) lightly. Even if they don't show much (if any) emotion when you're together, that doesn't mean they are not deeply impacted by your guidance.

If you're mentoring through a school or special program, your commitment as a mentor might naturally come to an end after a pre-determined period of time, such as one year. You might also be forced to stop mentoring due to unforeseen circumstances.

Regardless of the reason, if you absolutely *must* end your mentoring relationship, then it's essential for your mentee to have a sense of closure. It's important to let her or him know that it's not an ending, but rather a transition. Hopefully you will still be an essential part of your mentee's life.

WHAT IF MY MENTEE DROPS OUT?

Your mentee might suddenly decide not to meet with you anymore. This could happen for any number of reasons. Maybe her family has moved to another city. Perhaps his involvement in a local gang is so tense that he has to leave town. She could have a new boyfriend and want to spend all of her free time with him. He could be bored and prefer to hang out with his friends.

If your mentee wants to drop out of the mentoring relationship, chances are that he or she will not tell you this in person. They may be embarrassed, not know what to say, or not want to hurt your feelings.

You'll probably sense if there's a problem before it becomes "official." They'll miss several meetings. They'll always come very late. They might have a negative attitude. They could be rude, or tell you directly (no holds barred) exactly what they don't like about your relationship.

Whatever the reason and however you learn about it, don't take it to heart. Kids often have their own agenda. Most of them, especially teenagers, would rather hang out with their peers than be forced to stay with an adult who is like a parent-figure.

They might worry that their friends think it's nerdy to have a mentor. Perhaps they're missing out when all of their buddies are at the local basketball games.

Also, the chemistry between two people just may not click. Your mentee could sense how much you hate that he smokes cigarettes, yet he's addicted and can't stop. She could know that you disapprove of the way she dresses, so she feels uncomfortable around you.

If you find that your mentee is skipping your meetings and losing interest, try to have an intimate talk about the situation. Ask them to be honest with you, so you can resolve the issues. This could be all that you need to set your relationship back on track.

Ask the Volunteer Coordinator to mediate and find out the problem. Very often, kids will talk to someone else about their feelings so they don't say something offensive. Staff at the school or mentoring program can find out what the situation is and possibly resolve it.

The important thing is not to take it personally. As a mentor, you can't control how your mentee thinks or feels. You shouldn't take credit for their successes, nor blame yourself for their failures.

Tim is the owner of a leadership consulting business in Salt Lake City, Utah. He once struggled as a youth, but through his mentors in the Job Corps, he was encouraged to go to college and to improve his life.

Now Tim is paying it forward through mentoring at-risk youth at the Job Corps, as well as incarcerated boys at Farmington Bay Youth Correction Facility.

Tim said he has seen many youth succeed, but he's also been devastated by some failures -- such as one student's death. It took him a while to learn that he couldn't take the results of his work as a mentor so personally.

Tim said, "I'm not responsible if students don't turn their lives around. Instead, I just enjoy helping them become empowered. Being a part of their successes is fun, but taking credit for it is not recommended.

If your mentee has not made any progress and you feel like they didn't get anything from your mentoring relationship, then don't despair. As I've mentioned before, you may never see the impact that you've had on your mentee(s), but it doesn't mean that you didn't have an effect.

Even if you didn't make one iota of difference in your mentee's life, the important thing is what *you* got out of it. What did you learn from the experience? How will that knowledge allow you to improve yourself and help others?

HOW DO I END MY MENTORING PROGRAM?

It's important that your mentee(s) know in advance that your relationship is coming to a close, so they should have plenty of time to digest the change that will be coming. Try to give them a date in the future so they know what to expect.

They may feel a sense of abandonment at the end of the mentoring experience. Finish on a high note. Don't be critical, defensive or cold. You should be warm and understanding. Let them know that you're sorry the relationship didn't work out. Express the positive things that you have accomplished together. Share what you have learned.

You can say something like, "I'm sorry that you don't want to meet anymore, William. I've really enjoyed knowing you. And thanks for teaching me about reggae music. I bought that CD you recommended and I love it."

By finding the positive things to emphasize, it will show your mentee that you respect them and that you don't consider the time you have spent together to be a waste.

Also, share with the mentee the things you liked about them personally. You don't want them to feel that they are unlovable or flawed in some way.

You could say, "Alison, I love your passion for trying new things and the way you persist with your goals. I really hope you'll stay in touch with me."

Encourage your mentee to express him or herself freely. Even if there were bitter moments between you, be sure to give them a hug, handshake or a warm pat on their shoulder to end the relationship on a positive note.

When mentoring through a school, religious center or a community-based organization, talk with the Volunteer Coordinator. Explain your situation and ask this person if they have a special process for ending mentoring relationships. Find out what they recommend.

The Volunteer Coordinator may suggest that she or he be the one to inform your mentee of the situation, or else they might ask you to break the news, but to do so in their company. Every mentoring program will probably have their own system and protocols for dealing with this, and it's important for you to follow their regulations and best practices if they exist.

Whether you're alone or with a Volunteer Coordinator, teacher or other staff member, it's important to have a heart-to-heart talk with your mentee. Assure them that you care about them and that your relationship must end, but that it's nothing personal. If they said or did something to upset you, then be honest and tell them exactly why your relationship is ending.

Doing this on your own has the advantage of allowing you both to speak freely without your mentee feeling embarrassed about sharing his or her true feelings with someone else present.

However, at the same time, trained staff can help smooth over any bumps and communicate more effectively since they have some experience in ending mentoring relationships. You can ideally do a combination: have a Mentor Coordinator initiate the conversation, and then follow up with an intimate discussion with your mentee so that you can both openly express yourselves in private.

Make sure that your mentee feels a great sense of accomplishment and knows that they're headed in the right direction toward achieving their goals. Encourage them to keep up the good work.

Tell them that you are proud of their achievements. You can mention that since they have grown such a great deal, it's now time for them to pursue their goals in a different way.

Stress how much you have enjoyed mentoring them. Emphasize that you've gotten as much from the experience as you hope they have.

Let them know in every possible way that you care about them. Assure them that your mentoring relationship is coming to an end only because of circumstances. It's not due to their personality or anything that they said or did. However, if that's not the case, then be honest with them.

WHATEVER YOU DO,
DON'T END YOUR MENTORING RELATIONSHIP
WITHOUT GIVING YOUR MENTEE(S) CLOSURE!

Just think how it would feel if you really looked forward to seeing someone who was your mentor; someone you considered to be a close friend. All week you were excited to visit with them, perhaps to share your progress in school or on a special project. But then the time comes and your mentor flakes out and doesn't turn up. There's no phone call or any reason given. You just never see them again. This is after you finally started to trust them and confide things about yourself.

You think that maybe you drove your mentor away and they just don't like you. Whatever the mentor's reason for dropping out, you will never know and you'll carry that feeling of rejection with you for the rest of your life. Since you already suffer from low self-esteem, you feel even more worthless. You think that no one in the world cares about you and you can't trust anyone.

This may sound farfetched and you might think that I'm exaggerating about how at-risk and high-risk youth might react to their mentor just disappearing without any warning. However, it happened a few times through **Create Now**. I've placed mentors with youth and they have simply vanished, ditching the kids without a word of apology or explanation.

A mentor I'll call "Cathy" was going to college and she wanted to mentor a group of teenage foster girls living in a group home. Since she was only five years older than these girls, they really looked up to her as a role model. They asked her questions about college, her boyfriend and her personal life.

Cathy had a family emergency and she had to suddenly go out of town for a while. When she called to tell me that she couldn't return to the group home to mentor, I begged her to take a moment to call these girls to let them know why she couldn't be there. I also asked her to send them a card or write them a letter. She didn't do anything. Even though I passed her message along to the staff at the group home, it wasn't the same as the mentor directly notifying her mentees about the situation.

Around a year later, Cathy called to let me know that she was back in town. She was excited to meet with her mentees again, but they had all moved on, since they had "aged out" of the foster system (been emancipated). There was no way to track them down. These girls were out there feeling that their mentor whom they had looked up to had abandoned them without even the courtesy of a phone call or a letter. Cathy felt guilty and was very disappointed that she wouldn't get to see these girls again.

Don't do more damage than good by abandoning your mentee(s) without giving proper closure to your mentoring relationship.

You may ask, "What exactly is proper closure?" To me, it means reviewing with your mentee what you gained from the experience. It's a time to reinforce how much they have accomplished and to share with them the benefits that you have also gained as their mentor.

This is also the perfect opportunity for you to discuss where the relationship will go from here. Do you plan to end it permanently?

Do you want to stay in touch with your mentee, even if it's not on a regular basis? Having closure is the chance to talk with your mentee(s) about your goals for the future, which will hopefully include the chance for you both to keep in touch.

The most important part of having closure with your mentee is to assure them that your relationship is changing or ending because of circumstances, not because of something they said or did.

Many kids take the blame for things going wrong, especially foster youth. Their parents might have verbally abused them, saying things like, "You're so stupid! Can't you do anything right?" or "Your father left us because you're so ugly," or other mean and hateful things.

Even those kids who grow up in a loving home with two wonderful parents might have a lack of confidence and not much self-worth. This is especially common with teenagers, when they're maturing and trying to figure out whom they really are deep inside. When they discover that their mentor is not going to meet with them anymore, they could feel like they're being dumped because of their personality, the way they look or something they said.

Let them know the exact reason why you have to stop mentoring them or to change your relationship. Convince them that it's not their fault; you are sincere and really mean what you say.

At your last session, you can "soften the blow" of separation by having a party or perhaps bringing a special dessert. Maybe you can each create gifts to exchange as souvenirs. Pick something special that will remind your mentee(s) of the positive experiences you've shared.

Have your picture taken together and get it framed, then give it to your mentee. You might also prepare a scrapbook or photo album, or write poems for each other.

If you're part of a larger mentoring program, then the entire group of mentors and mentees should have a final banquet, picnic, or awards ceremony for the last meeting. This will help your mentee(s) to realize that they are not the only ones losing a dear friend. All of the kids in the mentoring program must go through the same weaning process.

If you and your mentee(s) have signed agreements that have committed you to be in the mentoring relationship for a specific period of time, this is a great chance to celebrate that milestone.

Your mentee will be proud of "graduating" from needing a mentor and for finishing their commitment to be mentored by you. Providing them with a "Certificate of Completion" (a sample is available in the Appendix) can boost their self-esteem tremendously.

Attitude is important. The way that you present the end of your mentoring relationship could flavor the way that your mentee reacts. When you meet for the last time, you might be:

(1) Sad and guilty that you are ending the mentoring relationship;

(2) Happy that you can celebrate all of your accomplishments with your mentee.

Your mentee will pick up on your outlook and react accordingly. If you're wearing a long, sad face and saying over and over again how sorry you are that you have to end your mentoring relationship, then she might get depressed. She could also feel angry with you, even though you haven't done anything wrong (assuming that you have given her enough warning that the relationship would come to an end).

That's not to say that you should be bubbling over with joy when you say a final good-bye to your mentee. You need to strike a balance. Let him know that you really care about him and while you're sad that your regular meetings have ended, you're thrilled to have known him. Tell him how happy you are that he's grown so much, and how proud you feel about his accomplishments.

End your relationship with smiles and hugs. Most importantly, leave the door open for your mentees to stay in touch with you.

MAINTAINING CONTACT

When changing or ending your mentoring relationship, you should assure your mentee of your intent to stay in touch. If you are mentoring through a school or special program, they might have rules about sharing your contact information with your mentee. This may be forbidden. If that's the case, then ask if the school or organization can serve as an intermediary to relay messages or forward mail.

For instance, if your mentee wants to reach you, maybe she can write you a letter and give it to her teacher or the Volunteer Coordinator at the local Boys and Girls Club where you met. That individual would forward the letter to you (hopefully unopened). You can then write back and send it to the Volunteer Coordinator to give to your mentee. This system is a safe way to stay in touch. It also helps kids to develop their literacy skills.

If you're permitted to communicate directly with your mentee, then try to call them regularly. At least every couple of weeks would be great! Even phoning them monthly or periodically can make an impact, but the more frequently you connect, the better. It only takes five minutes for you to make a call, yet it will mean so much to your mentee.

Holidays and birthdays are an important time to reach out. For many of these kids, especially those with no families, these special occasions are when they feel the most depressed. Getting a phone call, birthday gift and Christmas card from you could change their attitude and get them out of a deep depression.

At-risk youth often move from place to place, leaving no forwarding address. Their families may be so poor that they can't afford the rent and are frequently evicted, forced to live on the streets. They might be fleeing drug dealers, gang violence or the police. Since they may suddenly move, you could lose touch forever. It's important that you give him or her your contact information.

Marle, age 7, lived with her family in a homeless shelter in Phoenix, AZ. That's when volunteer mentor Deborah entered her life and began showing her mentee different options.

Nine years later, they're still matched and have weathered a lot; one year the girl's family moved 14 times, each meaning a different school. Her mentor was a consistent force in her life.

Marle is now in high school and takes classes for college credit. With Deb's encouragement, she has had a number of unique educational opportunities, including a wilderness adventure, international travel, and sharing the stage with Retired Supreme Court Justice Sandra Day O'Connor.

If you are allowed to share your contact information with your mentee(s), then do so with caution. Unless you know your mentee very well, then I wouldn't recommend giving out your home phone number or address.

I mentored a foster girl we'll call "Taminika" for over ten years. I met her when she was 13-years-old and living at a large institution for foster youth. Taminika was sitting on a bench writing a poem. I told her about Create Now and gave her my business card. I learned that she had been in the foster care system since she was 8-years-old. The girl came from a violent family involved in drugs and murder.

Over the years, Taminika would contact me from time to time. I gave her encouragement and introduced her to "Poetry Slams." I provided her with books on writing and gave her a computer. I supported her with all kinds of mentoring guidance.

As she matured into a young woman, I continued to help her. Unfortunately, she suddenly latched onto me as a mother figure. Taminika began to call me "Mama Jill" and phoned me at least ten times daily, including at 2:00 or 3:00 in the morning! No matter how many times I told her to stop calling, she wouldn't listen.

I wrote her letters explaining that she was disturbing my life and while I cared about her, she needed to stop calling. I repeated this many times on the phone. She would get hurt and promise not to call and then the next day, she would ring me up again. Finally, I had to block her number. I was so grateful that she didn't know where I lived!

Chances are that you won't run into a similar problem. Your mentee will probably have enough common sense to limit their calls to you and to only reach out during normal hours. You can use your instincts and trust your mentee accordingly, but it's always better to be safe than sorry.

The following information is to help you be extra cautious, *just in case.*

If you want to give your mentee a phone number, set down the rules of when they can call. Some youth have little adult supervision at home, so they keep late hours. Calling their friends after midnight could be part of their lifestyle, but they need to respect your time. Let them know how late they can call.

Also, I would recommend giving them a cell phone number rather than your home phone. This could save your family from having to take their calls. If you were to run into a situation where you had to change the phone number, it could be easier to do that with a cell phone.

Don't give out your home address unless you know that your mentee is trustworthy. If this is the case and you believe that your mentee is mature and respectful, then feel free to give them your address. However, remember my situation. If I had given my address to Taminika, she would have turned up on my doorstep asking me for help.

If you want to communicate with your mentee(s) by writing letters and you don't want to reveal where you live, then rent a postal box to protect your address.

If your mentee knows where your business is located, make sure they also know the best time to visit you there. When you end your mentoring relationship, you might say, "I hope to see you again soon. Stop by the store sometime." However, without parameters, that could infringe on your work.

For instance, during a busy sale when you have lots of customers waiting for help, your mentee might show up and be disappointed that you can't give him your attention. To avoid this situation, you can be more specific. "Stop by the store between 2:00 and 5:00 when I'm usually free."

Perhaps there's a local café, library, recreation center or another place that you frequented with your mentee. Ask the owner or clerk if they would serve as an intermediary.

Facebook is popular with kids. "Friend" them and you can keep up with each other. Email is another possibility for communication. Most at-risk youth don't own computers, so they may not get online frequently. However, they could go to the library to use the Internet, or borrow a friend's computer.

Your best bet for staying in touch is probably texting. This is the way most kids communicate these days. Texting is like emailing on your cell phone and almost everyone (including at-risk youth) has a cell phone. Be aware that some people buy cheap phones with limited minutes, so it's hard for them to maintain the same phone number. However, if your mentee has your cell phone number, then you can text each other to stay in touch.

Ask your mentee what the best way is for them to keep in contact with you. They'll really appreciate knowing that you want to continue your mentoring relationship, even if you can't always be in physical contact.

EVALUATING YOURSELF AS A MENTOR

It's important in life to take stock of what we have accomplished, and to determine if our efforts were successful or not. This helps us to grow as individuals, and also highlights our weaknesses and strengths. Rather than being negative and judgmental, a self-evaluation can teach us how to channel our energy more productively and can shine a light on where improvements can be made.

Evaluating yourself as a mentor can also assist the school or mentoring program that matched you with your mentee(s). This youth agency will need your feedback in order to enhance their mentor training and resources. Other mentors can also learn from your mistakes, as well as your successes, and the variety of experiences you've had as a mentor.

You can create your own Mentor Evaluation Form. Here are some examples of questions:

Was I dependable as a mentor?
___ Always ___ Most of the Time ___ Sometimes ___ Never

Did I make myself consistently available to my mentee?
___ Always ___ Most of the Time ___ Sometimes ___ Never

I feel like I made an impact on my mentee(s):
___ To a Great Extent ___ Somewhat ___ Not At All

This information will help you to dig a little deeper into your heart and to discover what you have gotten from being a mentor.

Think carefully about the questions you pose to yourself, and also how you respond to them. Try to be as objective as you can in this process, since you are the one who will benefit the most from learning about your true motivations and feelings. What you find out will not only impact you, but also your family, friends, associates, community, and especially the youth that you have mentored -- and will mentor in the future.

You can also ask your mentee(s) to evaluate you as a mentor. Here are some questions that you might ask:

My mentor listened to me carefully.
___ Always ___ Most of the Time ___ Sometimes ___ Never

I trusted my mentor and could confide things.
___ Always ___ Most of the Time ___ Sometimes ___ Never

The things that I enjoyed doing the most with my mentor were:
_____

The things that I disliked the most when I spent with my mentor were:
_____

I'm sure that you can come up with a number of questions for your mentee in order to learn his or her opinions on your role as a mentor.

To be really fair, ask someone at the school or youth agency to give your mentee(s) the evaluation form with your questions when you are not present. If your mentees know that you're going to read it directly, they might not be totally up front with their answers. Another option for evaluating groups of youth is that mentees can also leave their names off the survey to remain anonymous.

Don't be afraid to learn the truth from your mentees. You might be pleasantly surprised at their responses. You might discover that things you said and did actually made a deeper impact than you could have imagined. A youth who was quiet and seemed to be in another world may have been holding on to your every word.

Continue to build your skills as a mentor. When one mentoring relationship ends, another can begin. Each mentee will be unique and your bond with them will be distinct.

While your influence as a mentor might not be evident for years to come and you may never find out about the actual impact of your mentoring, just know that you can transform young lives as a mentor, and if you have been mentoring for awhile, then you probably already did.

More importantly, what have YOU gotten from mentoring?

Have you learned about another person; someone who comes from a different culture than you and has unique views on life?

Did you share any interesting conversations or activities that are memorable?

Did you have fun?

These are the elements that make mentoring successful. It's an ongoing process that will teach you many things as it enriches your life, as well as the lives of your mentees and their families, friends and neighbors.

As the tremendous benefits of mentoring ripple out into your community, and then stretch across the country and the rest of the world, then we can develop new generations of healthy and happy children who also receive incredible joy by giving back to others, as we all work together to **Create Now**.

APPENDIX

In this section, I've included some sample templates that you can use as is, or adapt for your specific needs. The Mentor/Mentee Agreement is an option for you to have a written commitment with your mentee that you should both sign and adhere to in order to make your mentoring relationship official. It will help your mentee to understand that they are signing a contract with guidelines that they need to follow.

MENTOR/MENTEE AGREEMENT

As a participant in this Mentoring Relationship, I agree to:

Commit to mentoring for ____ (length of time) ____ ;

Meet every____ (day of the week) ____ ;

Meet from ____ (time) ____ to ____ (time) ____ ;

Be together for at least _____ hour(s) per session;

Meet at a ____ (previously agreed upon location) ____ ;

Be on time for scheduled meetings;

Notify my mentor/mentee right away if I am unable to make it to our mentoring session;

Notify my mentor/mentee right away if I will be late for our mentoring session;

Engage in the relationship with an open mind;

Respect the wishes and requirements of the mentee's parents/guardians;

Keep our discussions confidential, unless someone's safety or well-being is at risk;

Always tell my mentor/mentee the truth.

Signed and Agreed to by:

_____   _____
Mentor Signature   *Date*

_____   _____
Mentee Signature   *Date*

<u>MENTEE SURVEY</u>

Name:

Family members:

Age:

Birthday:

Favorite colors:

Check all the things that you like:

Arts and Crafts ___ Bicycle Riding ___ Bowling ___

Camping ___ Computers ___ Dancing ___ Fashion ___

Hiking ___ Internet ___ Movies ___ Reading ___ Skating ___

Swimming ___ TV ___ Videogames ___

Other_____

What are your favorites:

Animals:

Books:

Clothes:

Foods:

Games:

Movies:

Places to visit:

Songs:

Sports:

TV shows:

Videogames:

Other:

✣ ✣ ✣

This certifies that

Mentee's Name

Having successfully completed a

Mentoring Relationship

with mentor

Your Name

is hereby awarded this

Certificate of Completion

on this ___day of Month, Year

Jill Gurr

LIST OF RECOMMENDED MOVIES

Here are suggestions of some feature films that highlight mentoring relationships, or give a realistic depiction of life on the streets of America's inner cities:

American Me
Antwone Fisher
Billy Elliott
Dead Poets Society
Finding Forrester
Freedom Writers
Gang Tapes
Girl, Interrupted
Good Will Hunting
Karate Kid
Menace II Society
My Family/Mi Familia
Pay It Forward
Precious
Role Models
Rudy
School of Rock
Short Cuts
Stand and Deliver
Star Wars
The Blindside
The Pursuit of Happyness
Thirteen

MORE FUN PLACES TO VISIT BY STATE

Alabama Battleship Memorial Park Birmingham Museum of Art DeSoto Caverns Park Talladega Superspeedway U.S. Space and Rocket Center	**Alaska** The Imaginarium Pioneer Park H2Oasis Elmendorf State Hatchery Mount Robert Tramway
Arizona Old Tucson Studios Grand Canyon Drive the Apache Trail Rawhide Wild West Town Lake Havasu (London Bridge)	**Arkansas** Go cave spelunking Hike in the Ozark Mountains Visit the Hot Springs Hunt for quartz crystals Magic Springs Theme Park
California La Brea Tar Pits Queen Mary Yosemite National Park Monterey Bay Aquarium Hearst Castle	**Colorado** Wildwater Rafting Horseback riding Pick fresh fruit from trees Go dogsledding Tour the U.S. Mint
Connecticut Lake Compounce Family Park Dinosaur State Park The Children's Museum Mystic Whaler Cruise The Garbage Museum	**Delaware** Midway Speedway Skate at Pond Ice Arena Viking Golf Theme Park Delaware History Museum Treasures of the Sea Exhibit
District of Columbia International Spy Museum Earth Treks Rock Climbing Mule-Drawn Canal Boat Ride Discovery Creek Children's Museum Planet Fun	**Florida** Monkey Jungle Daytona Beach Fun Zone Canoe on "River of Turtles" Gatorland Jacksonville Landing
Georgia Atlanta Botanical Gardens Marietta History Museum Atlanta Cyclorama	**Hawaii** Hike in Waimea Canyon Snorkle at the beach Visit gorgeous waterfalls

Mary Miller Doll Museum The Elachee Nature Science Center	Swim with dolphins Bike down the volcano
Idaho Experience Lava Hot Springs Moon National Monument North Idaho Fair and Rodeo Ski at a resort Pocatello Zoo	**Illinois** John Hancock Observatory Wrigley Field Tour Visit Children's Museum Wheels O' Time Museum Chicagoland Speedway
Indiana Visit the Haunted Castle Buffalo Run Farm Grill Take a balloon ride Go to Indianapolis Speedway NCAA Hall of Champions	**Iowa** Hitchcock Nature Center The Effigy Mounds National Monument Kaleidoscope Factory Tour Phelps Youth Pavilion Take a River Steamboat Ride
Kansas Mid-America Air Museum Visit Science City Kemper Museum of Art Oceans of Fun Toy & Miniature Museum	**Kentucky** Kentucky Down Under Shaker Village Los River Cave Race World American Cave Museum
Louisiana Dixie Landin' Theme Park USS Kidd Blue Bayou Water Park Global Wildlife Center Lil' Cajun Swamp Tour	**Maine** Arcadia National Park Visit lighthouses Maine Solar System Model Fairfield Antiques Mall Maine Art Museum Trail
Maryland Cecil County Dragway Clark's Elioak Farm Discovery Center Geppi's Entertainment Museum Medieval Times Dinner	**Massachusetts** New England Aquarium Skywalk Observatory The Children's Museum Plymouth Wax Museum Salem Witch Museum
Michigan Curious Kids' Museum	**Minnesota** Science Museum of

Olde World Canterbury Village Mackinac Butterfly House Huckleberry Railroad A-Maze-N Mirrors	Minnesota Historic Murphy's Landing Underwater Adventures Jeffers Petroglyphs Spam Museum
Mississippi Rainwater Planetarium Cruise the Mississippi River Lynn Meadows Discovery Center Visit the State Capitol Elvis Presley Center	**Missouri** Gateway Arch Ride the ducks (boats) City Museum The Magic House Six Flags
Montana Garnet Ghost Town Exploration Works Museum Hockaday Museum of Art Glacier National Park Little Bighorn Monument	**Nebraska** Wyobraska Wildlife Museum Carhenge Howard County Village Fremont Dinner Train FunPlex
Nevada Wild Island Family Park Flyaway Indoor Skydiving Lied Discovery Museum Nevada Northern Railway Heavenly Aerial Tram	**New Hampshire** Fly fish at Profile Lake Watch the Northern Lights Ride a gondola at Loon Mountain See bears at Clark's Trading Camp in the White Mountains
New Jersey Grounds for Sculpture Pontoon Boat Ride Camden's Children's Garden Land of Make Believe Lakota Wolf Preserve	**New Mexico** Lodestar Astronomy Center Pueblo Cultural Center Cliff's Amusement Park Sandia Peak Tramway The Beach Waterpark
New York Ride a horse-drawn carriage Take the Staten Island Ferry Climb rock wall on	**North Carolina** SciWorks Emerald Pointe Water Park Chinqua-Penn Plantation

Broadway Go sledding in Central Park Visit the Statue of Liberty	Mint Museum of Art Greensboro Children's Museum
North Dakota Lewis & Clark Riverboat Dakota Dinosaur Museum Bonanzaville USA International Peace Garden Thunder Road racing	**Ohio** US Air Force Museum Canton Classic Car Museum Cedar Point Bicycle Museum of America The Santa Maria

Oklahoma
National Wresting Museum
Leonardo's Discovery
    Warehouse
Sun 'n Fun Family Waterpark
Frontier City
Fred Jones, Jr. Museum of Art
	Oregon
	Portland Saturday Market
	Columbia River Gorge
	Ski on Mount Hood or
	    Bachelor
	Oregon Coast Aquarium
	Ride a bike down the coast

Pennsylvania Knoebels Hershey Museum Sandcastle Waterpark Houdini Tour and Museum Game Preserve	**Rhode Island** Great Road Historic District Take the Block Island Ferry Providence Place Mall Roger Williams Park Zoo Visit Fort Adams
South Carolina Magnolia Plantation Go to Dock Street Theater Charleston IMAX Theater Carolina Ice Palace Audobon Swamp Garden	**South Dakota** Bear Country USA Experience Mt. Rushmore Sitting Bull Crystal Caverns Wild Water West Thunder Road Family Fun Park
Tennessee Rock City Gardens Fire Museum Elvis Presley's Graceland Ruby Falls Nashville Toy Museum	**Texas** Volente Beach Visit the USS Lexington Enchanted Rock See NASA Experience the Alamo
Utah Zion National Park Dinosaur National Museum	**Vermont** Vermont Teddy Bear Corn Maze and Science

Canyonlands National Park Trolley Square FastKart Indoor Speedway	Center Ben & Jerry's Factory Tour Smugglers' Notch Bromley Adventure Zone
Virginia Wolf Creek Indian Village Beagle Rich Herb Farm Shenandoah Caverns Natural Bridge of Virginia Virginia Quilt Museum	**Washington** World Kite Museum Imagine Children's Museum Whale Watching in Westport Pike Place Market Museum of Flight
West Virginia Kruger Street Toy & Train Museum Palace of Gold West Virginia Penitentiary Women's History Museum Beckley Exhibition Coal Mine	**Wisconsin** Marion Amazement Park Grand Opera House Crystal Cave Noah's Ark Waterpark Circus World Museum
Wyoming Dancing Bear Folk Center Casper Planetarium Cowboy Carousel Theme Park Cheyenne Civic Center Museum of the Mountain Man	

THE STATE OF AMERICA'S YOUTH

The purpose of this report is to alert as many people as possible to the urgent need to support our youth. It is to be used in any way that you see fit, as it will help you to understand the scope of the problems that many of our kids face. Fasten your seat belt, because this will be a bumpy ride (or at least one filled with some staggering numbers).

SUBSTANCE ABUSERS

There are approximately fourteen million people in the United States who are addicted to alcohol and millions more who display symptoms of alcohol abuse, including binge drinking. Sadly, a reported 2.6 million binge drinkers in 2002 were between the ages of twelve and seventeen.

In the U.S., the average age that kids begin to drink is twelve-years-old.[14] Youth who report heavy alcohol use are the most likely to participate in delinquent behavior.

Children of alcohol and drug-addicted parents are up to four times more likely to develop substance abuse and mental health problems than other children.[15] 23 million people in the United States are addicted to drugs. 203,000 kids were arrested in the U.S. on drug charges in 2002.[16] This is just the arrest rate. Substance abuse treatment admission rates for marijuana as their primary substance of abuse increased nationally by 162 percent. Another 13 percent of our youth population reported cocaine as their primary substance of abuse.[17]

Again, all of these statistics are for reported cases, but how many millions of kids in our country use drugs that go unreported? With

---

[14] Narconon 2002
[15] National Association for Children of Alcoholics (NOACA) 1998
[16] Office of Juvenile Justice and Delinquency Prevention (OJJDP) 2002
[17] Substance Abuse & Mental Health Services Administration (SAMHSA) 2009

law enforcement in most communities stretched to the limits, we can only assume these numbers are just a fraction of the reality.

Joe Perry, the lead guitarist of *Aerosmith*, was drunk, broke, and hooked on smack. Both his first marriage and his band had broken up and his life had become a string of drug-induced seizures. Today, he's nearing his 20th year of sobriety and remarriage. Joe sold more than 100 million records with a reborn Aerosmith.

Joe said, "There were times when we were on our knees, literally, trying to find blow. There were times when we would drink just to see how much we could consume. Really ridiculous stuff. It was like, if we feel good, maybe the audience will feel good."

He wanted to help kids going through the struggles of addiction and mentored at *Road Recovery*. This program in New York brings together at-risk kids and young adults with professionals in the music industry, such as artists, tour managers, sound engineers, lawyers and others who work in this field. All of the mentors in the program are now sober, but they have been personally affected by alcohol and drug addiction in the past.

Joe told all of the youth there, "Together, through music and creativity with *Road Recovery*, you're gonna find your path.

"By talking with *Road Recovery*'s kids today, I'm reminded that it's one-day-at-a-time. You've gotta give it back. You gotta stay connected. That's how it works, it's 'tried & true' -- and hey, I'm living proof."

Through interactive discussions, educational seminars and live concerts, the kids at *Road Recovery* learn first-hand about the positive aspects of living a substance-free life. Some of the topics covered include the dangers and consequences of abuse and addiction, what happens when you hit bottom, plus different alternatives and solutions.

Mentoring makes a difference. When kids are tempted to try alcohol or drugs, they need a mature adult who can encourage them to stay straight. But what happens when your parents are abusers themselves? What if they are never around to give you guidance because they're working, at school, in prison or just negligent? That's when good role models are essential.

More than 1,000 different household and commercial products called "inhalants" can be intentionally abused by sniffing or "huffing" (inhaling through one's mouth) for an intoxicating effect. The chemical substances commonly found in adhesives, lighter fluids, cleaning solutions, gasoline, paint, glue and paint products have become popular with kids who are looking for a cheap and easy way to get high. 718,000 children at the tender age of twelve or thirteen have used an inhalant in their lifetime. These same kids were more than twice as likely to have been in a serious fight at school than youth their age who had never used inhalants.[18]

Crack cocaine usage is prevalent in the inner cities of the United States. Luckily, many of the kids who live in these communities are smart enough not to smoke crack, but they are the ones generally dealing the drug to the older generation. Since their parents, guardians, other family members and neighbors are often addicted to this lethal drug, the kids in urban communities are frequently neglected and left to fend for themselves.

Some inner-city kids like to get high on "Sherm," This is a marijuana joint or a cigarette dipped in embalming fluid (formaldehyde). Some speculate that the chemical used for dipping is actually PCP, or "Angel Dust." The Sherm user, like PCP-addicts, goes into a trance and can become extremely violent and unpredictable. While these drugs declined in the 1980's, there seems to be a resurgence of its use.

Other popular drugs amongst kids today are Ketamine, which is an anesthetic used for animals. Like PCP, it also gives the user a feeling of great power and it's sometimes used at "rave" parties.

Rave parties differ largely from clubs. A rave is "underground." Generally, every rave is held in a different location. It's unadvertised and the location isn't revealed until the day of the event. The party has no time constraints -- most raves last until dawn.

Teens and young adults who attend raves like to get high on Ecstasy and dance all night to rhythmic techno music that puts them into a trance. Ecstasy, or MDMA, is a synthetic, psychoactive drug that's chemically similar to methamphetamine and the hallucinogen mescaline. It gives users the feeling of euphoria and intense love. In 2003, an estimated 470,000 people in the U.S. age 12 and older used

---

[18] Substance Abuse & Mental Health Services Administration (SAMHSA) 2002-2003

MDMA in the past 30 days.[19] This drug can cause danger to health, including death on some occasions, especially when mixed with alcohol and other drugs.

Oxycodone ("Oxycontin"), an opium derivative that's prescribed for moderate to severe pain, can be very habit-forming. An estimated 11 million Americans aged twelve and older have used oxycodone non-medically at least once in their lifetime. About 42 percent of the persons who used oxycodone reported family incomes in the past year of $50,000 or more.

1.9 million Americans have used heroin in their lifetime, and 1.7 million have used both oxycodone and heroin in their lifetime.[20]

Methamphetamines, which go under slang names like "crystal," "ice" or "crank," are highly addictive. This drug is more addictive than cocaine, harder to kick than heroin and it's cheap and easy to make. 12.3 million Americans in the U.S. reported lifetime use of methamphetamines in 2003.[21]

Hawaii has one of the worst crystal methamphetamine problems in the country and it's destroying local families and communities there. 905 of the 2,300 confirmed child-abuse cases in the state each year were caused by crystal meth. Children are forced to raise their younger siblings, if they don't succumb to the drug themselves. In one town on the Big Island, 50 percent of the teenagers are addicted to this drug. Crime is rampant in the state.

The Pulama Project mentoring program in Hilo, Hawaii links caring adults in direct mentoring activities with at-risk youth of East Hawaii. Participants engage in fun projects, such as painting buildings, enjoying a "Healthy Drug-Free Camp-Over" at the local gym and dressing up for a Halloween Dance. The mentors have assisted these kids in dealing with their future goals, with the focus on preventing and reducing substance use among Pulama youth.

A detailed evaluation[22] of the *Pulama Project* found that kids who participated in the program had increased positive results in drug knowledge. There were also significant reductions in injection

---

[19] Substance Abuse and Mental Health Services Administration, April 2005

[20] National Survey on Drug Use and Health (NSDUH) January 2005

[21] Substance Abuse & Mental Health Services Administration (SAMHSA) 2003

[22] Conducted by The Catalyst Group, August 2004

drug use and positive trends for discontinuing the use of inhalants, "ice," heroin, LSD, Ecstasy and other illegal drugs. The kids learned that drugs aren't good for them and there are alternatives. One young man stated, "They keep telling us that there are other things we can do with our lives, and it's true."[23]

ABUSED, NEGLECTED AND ABANDONED

Many kids use alcohol and drugs to escape from abusive lives. Child protective services agencies received reports on 3 million children that were allegedly mistreated in the United States in 2004. While many of these cases were not validated, 900,000 children were confirmed as being maltreated.[24] Considering that hundreds of thousands of occurrences of child abuse are not ever reported to the authorities, the numbers are probably a great deal higher. Studies in Colorado and North Carolina have estimated that as many as 50 to 60 percent of childhood deaths resulting from abuse or neglect are not even recorded.[25]

Four types of maltreatment are generally recognized, including physical abuse, sexual abuse, neglect and emotional maltreatment. Reported rates of neglect are higher than other types of child maltreatment.[26] More than six million school-age children are left alone after school each day without supervision.[27]

More than 2 million children and youth in the United States have at least one parent in a Federal or State correctional facility. Over 75 percent of the female prisoners in the United States are mothers. Aside from suffering disruption in the relationship with their parent, these kids struggle with economic, social, and emotional burdens due to the incarceration of their parent.[28]

An estimated 2,000 children in the United States die of child abuse and neglect each year. Approximately 40 percent of them are younger than one year old, while children younger than four years

---

[23] www.pulamaproject.org/
[24] The State of America's Children 2004
[25] Crume, DiGuiseppi, Byers, Sirotnak, Garrett, 2002; Herman-Giddens, Brown, Verbiest, Carlson, Hooten, et al., 1999
[26] National Child Abuse and Neglect Data System (NCANDS) April 2005
[27] The State of America's Children 2004
[28] U.S. Dept. of Health and Human Services, Administration for Children & Families, 2005

accounted for 76 percent of fatalities. This population of children is the most vulnerable for many reasons, including their dependency, small size, and inability to defend themselves.[29]

When a child experiences abuse and/or neglect, they are usually scarred for the rest of their life.

I visited a facility in Los Angeles called *Bienvenidos Children's Center*, which provided a number of services to foster children and families. They once ran an emergency shelter where children from birth to age eight were taken immediately after being removed from their homes due to abuse, neglect and abandonment.

The Director of Residential Care at this facility told me a story that is typical of many abused and neglected children. *Bienvenidos Children's Center* had a little boy aged two that had been sent to their shelter at birth. They placed this toddler with more than a dozen different foster homes. Sadly, nobody wanted to keep him because he was so violent and destructive. This child will be seriously impaired for the rest of his life.

Why would a 2-year-old child be such a nightmare, so that 12 different families couldn't handle him? Perhaps he was a crack baby who cried constantly. When foster parents couldn't deal with his continual screaming, he was brought back to the foster agency, just like returning merchandise at a store. The infant was already traumatized from being abandoned by his birth mother. Then the foster parents rejected him, which might have upset him more. Each time he was forced to change homes, his anger grew. As he got older and mobile, he could have lashed out at other children or the family's pets. I'm told that this child eventually found a loving home with a family that could deal with his problems, but how many other kids like him aren't as lucky?

Who are the people behind child abuse, neglect and abandonment? Certain characteristics reappear in many studies. One or both parents are involved in 80 percent of child abuse or neglect fatalities. Frequently the perpetrator is a young adult in his or her mid-20s without a high school diploma, living at or below the poverty level, depressed, and who may have difficulty coping with

---

[29] The National Child Abuse and Neglect Data System (NCANDS) 2002

stressful situations. In many instances, the perpetrator has experienced violence first-hand. Most fatalities from physical abuse are caused by fathers and other male caretakers. Mothers are most often held responsible for deaths resulting from child neglect.[30]

Nearly one-half of substantiated cases of child neglect and abuse are associated with parental alcohol or drug abuse.[31] The cycle of abuse and neglect continues through many generations. Men and women serving time in our nation's prisons and jails report a higher incidence of abuse when they were children than the general population.[32]

Since its inception in 1977, the goal of *Family Outreach Corpus Christi (FOCC)*[33] in Texas has been to strengthen families and prevent child abuse by providing free services to families with child-related problems. Positive child-rearing strategies are taught to primarily low-income Hispanic families and at-risk youth in their community.

Under the direction of a Casework Manager, *FOCC* trains volunteers to mentor, teach and support families in need through home visitations and one-on-one counseling. Additional programs include "M.O.M.S." (Mothers Offering Mutual Support), "Young Parents," as well as a telephone resource and referral service.

In addition to witnessing the growth and positive change in client families, the mentors enjoy the time they spend working with the parents and youths. *FOCC* is one of 34 Family Outreach centers under the leadership umbrella of *Family Outreach of America.* They have a proven success rate of 91.9 percent of preventing mentored families from entering the Child Protective Services System.

Sexual abuse is very indicative of how the cycle of abuse affects victims. While I've been citing a number of government statistics about at-risk and high-risk youth, please be aware that most abused and neglected children never come to the attention of government authorities.

---

[30] U.S. Advisory Board on Child Abuse and Neglect, 1995
[31] Child Welfare League of America, 1998
[32] U.S. Department of Justice Bureau of Justice Statistics, 1995-1997
[33] www.socservices.com/best-practices-pdf/focc.pdf

This is particularly true for sexually-abused children, who may not show any physical signs of harm. In the case of sexual abuse, secrecy and intense feelings of shame may prevent children, and adults aware of the abuse, from seeking help. Official government statistics don't indicate actual rates of child abuse and are only the "tip of the iceberg."[34]

While 15 percent of all reported cases of abuse are sexual violations,[35] frequently the person who sexually molests a child is also a child. One of every seven victims of sexual assault reported to law enforcement agencies in 2000 were under age six. 40 percent of the offenders who sexually assaulted children under age six were themselves juveniles (under the age of eighteen).[36]

GEMS (Girls Educational & Mentoring Services)[37] in Manhattan, NY empowers young women who have experienced sexual exploitation and violence to exit unsafe and abusive lifestyles and to develop their full potential. They offer a variety of programs, including crisis counseling, group therapy and peer mentoring.

Dominique was once their client and through GEMS, she received extensive mentoring. She's now the GEMS Assistant Outreach Coordinator. "I first came here when I was 16 years old, scared with no place to call home. Through their support, I have my own apartment, attend school and I'm employed here as an outreach worker. There are an estimated 400,000 children just like me who are sexually exploited each year in the U.S. Unlike many of my peers however, I was able to escape, thanks to my mentors at GEMS."

TEEN PARENTS

Date rape is a growing problem. One in five female high school students reports being physically or sexually abused by a dating partner.[38] Many of these girls become pregnant. 34 percent of young

---

[34] Child Abuse: Statistics, Research and Resources by Jim Hopper, Ph.D., April 2005
[35] United States Department of Health and Human Services, 1993
[36] U.S. Department of Justice Bureau of Justice Statistics, 2000
[37] www.gems-girls.org/
[38] Massachusetts Youth Risk Behavior Survey (YRBS), August 2001

women become pregnant at least once before they reach the age of 20 -- about 820,000 a year. Eight in ten of these pregnancies are unintended and 79 percent are to unmarried teens. Teen pregnancy costs the United States at least $7 billion annually.[39]

Teen mothers are less likely to complete high school (only one-third receives a high school diploma) and only 1.5 percent has a college degree by age thirty. Teen mothers are also more likely to end up on welfare (nearly 80 percent of unmarried teen mothers end up on welfare).

The children of teenage mothers have lower birth weights, are more likely to perform poorly in school, and are at greater risk of abuse and neglect. The sons of teen mothers are 13 percent more likely to end up in prison while teen daughters are 22 percent more likely to become teen mothers themselves.[40]

The good news is that teen pregnancy is on the decline. This is due to less sexual activity and more contraceptive use. However, the U.S. rates are double, triple, even ten times those of other western countries. And since a new crop of kids becomes teenagers each year, prevention efforts must be constantly renewed and reinvented.

Only one in two teens says they trust their parents most for reliable and complete information about birth control. Teens from intact, two-parent families are less likely to give birth in their teens than girls from other family backgrounds,[41] but what about kids who are at-risk or high-risk? They often don't have the benefit of two or even one parent who can guide them.

There are many programs around the country that help to prevent teen pregnancy and that work with teenage mothers to provide support.

One such ' project is *StartRight/Teen MOMs Mentoring Program*,[42] located at the clinic of Truman Medical Center in Kansas City, MO. They help teen mothers delay second pregnancies to beyond the teen years, teach life skills, and encourage them to develop and pursue education and career goals. Mentors meet One-

---

[39] Teenpregnancy.org, March 2005
[40] Teenpregnancy.org, March 2005
[41] Teenpregnancy.org, March 2005
[42] www.etr.org/recapp/theories/mentoring/caseStudies.htm

on-One with pregnant or parenting teens on a regular basis. During the meetings, they provide guidance and support with the goal of establishing a trusting relationship between the pregnant or parenting teen and the caring adult mentor.

Like most successful mentoring relationships, mentors consistently go beyond program requirements to support their teens. Many mentors actively help to make community referrals for housing, childcare, transportation, etc. They help teens re-enter school and/or develop future goals regarding career plans. Because of their mentors, several teens remain committed to the program after they graduate and become peer role models to other teens.

RUNAWAY YOUTH

Many teenagers who become pregnant often run away from home. The National Runaway Switchboard states that between 1.3 and 2.8 million runaway and homeless youth live on the streets of America. One out of every seven kids will run away sometime before the age of 18. According to the Children's Defense Fund, 1,234 youth run away from home every day of the year. Approximately 5,000 runaway and homeless kids die from assault, illness and suicide each year.

A youth may run away from home when situations become unbearable to them. Their problems may involve family conflict, school pressures, substance abuse, sexual identity pressures, abuse and neglect or pressure from peers. It's important to understand that a youth's reason for leaving is unique to that individual. There is no such thing as a typical runaway. These kids come from every kind of neighborhood: rich or poor, suburban, rural or urban. There's also no differentiation between race and religion

Many runaways leave home more than once. The first time they run, they typically stay within 300 miles of their homes, usually with friends or relatives. As the length of time away from home increases, these kids often flee to urban areas where they can blend in with other kids and are less likely to be noticed by authority figures. They tend to hang out at fast-food restaurants, shopping malls and video arcades. They live in abandoned buildings or underneath highway bridges. In warmer climates, they may spend their days and nights on the beach.

As bad as things may have been at home, runaways soon find life on the street can be even worse. Most leave home without understanding the troubles they will encounter once they've run away. The most basic problem faced by runaways is getting money for food and shelter.

The longer a runaway is on the streets, the greater the struggle for survival. Youth under the age of sixteen have difficulty finding and keeping jobs. They may start by panhandling for change, but eventually a runaway will most likely turn to illegal means to survive. Many will become involved in prostitution, pornography, drugs, stealing, and other crimes.[43]

Los Angeles is a hot spot for runaways. There are around 13,000 kids living here on our streets. Many youth come to L.A. in hopes of making it in the entertainment industry. They look forward to warm beaches and an easy life. What they find is quite the opposite. Yes, some of them do make it into movies – porno films, since the San Fernando Valley in our community is the center for the pornography industry. Many runaways are lured by drug dealers and abused by treacherous pimps.

THROWAWAY YOUTH

Besides runaways, there are kids who are living on the streets because they have been kicked out of their homes or abandoned by their parents. This could be for a number of reasons, including the youth's sexual preferences, a parent's jealous lover, lack of funds for food, poor behavior of the youth, a bad argument, or for no logical reason whatsoever.

I met one of these throwaway youth in Hollywood, at one of the shelters in the community. There are around 8,000 kids living on the streets of Hollywood. Mike was one of the lucky ones. Most of the resources for homeless youth are just a few drop-in centers, where they can get a hot meal and a shower during the day. But then they have to sleep on the streets at night.

---

[43] National Runaway Switchboard: www.nrscrisisline.org

Mike was given a bed at a temporary residential shelter called *L.A. Youth Network* for 30 days, until the staff could find a better home for him. He was a handsome 16-year-old, with the dream of becoming an actor some day. He told me how he had been born and raised by his father in Maine. His mother had abandoned him at an early age. When he was much younger, his father moved with him to Los Angeles.

On Christmas Eve, when Mike was just 9-years-old, his father told him, "You're on your own now." He locked the front door, leaving his young child to fend for himself. Mike was placed in a number of institutions and foster homes. Now he just survives day-to-day, grateful to have a warm bed and hot meals for at least a month.

LGBTQ KIDS

There's a whole group of kids that are frequently thrown out of their homes -- those with different sexual preferences. It's estimated that up to 10 percent of the U.S. population is lesbian or gay.[44] That means there are more than 3 million kids in our society who are homosexual or transsexual. Lesbian, gay, bisexual, transgender and queer (LGBTQ) youth are often rejected by their families. When placed in public institutions, they're frequently harassed and beaten by other kids, and even the staff.

Homosexual kids suffer from increased risks in several different areas compared to heterosexual adolescents, including mental health problems, high-risk sexual behaviors, poorer school outcomes, homelessness and substance abuse. GLBTQ youth are subjected to higher rates of violence and victimization than heterosexual youth.

It's estimated that 40 percent of all the homeless youth in major U.S. cities are gay or lesbian, with many resorting to "survival sex" for food, clothing and shelter. Suicide is the leading cause of death amongst lesbian and gay adolescents.

---

[44] Mentoring Sexual Minority Youth; Public/Private Ventures, December 2000

TEENAGE PROSTITUTES

Child prostitution is a national tragedy. It's estimated that about 293,000 American youth are currently at risk of becoming victims of commercial sexual exploitation. The majority of these kids tend to be runaway youth who live on the streets. These children generally come from homes where they have been abused, or from families that have abandoned them. Child prostitutes are typically victims of incest at an early age. They run to the street during adolescence to escape the terrifying sexual exploitation by a trusted caretaker. They often get involved in prostitution as a way to get the things they want or need. Other children are recruited into prostitution through pressure from their parents.

I produced a Video Workshop with a group of around ten children ages 7-12 at *Hollygrove* in Hollywood, which used to have a residential treatment center for children who were removed from their homes due to abuse and neglect.

The kids came up with their unique video "Nerds to the Rescue." I took them to the circus and Griffith Park so they could have a variety of scenery for their movie. I noticed that the girls who were 10-12 years old were constantly pruning themselves and were very conscientious about their appearances.

I thought this was a little strange. It's natural for girls in that age range to want to look older and prettier and we were videotaping them for our project. However, these children seemed mature way beyond their years. I later found out that they were removed from their families because their parents were pimping them to get their drug money.

According to the U.S. Department of Justice report[45], of the street girls engaged in formal prostitution, about 75% worked for a pimp. Pimp-controlled commercial sexual exploitation of children is also linked to escort and massage services, private dancing, drinking and photographic clubs, major sporting and recreational events, major cultural events, conventions, and tourist destinations.

---

[45] Estes Report, 2003

About one-fifth of these children become entangled in nationally organized crime networks and are trafficked nationally. This same report states that the average age at which girls first become victims of prostitution is 12-14. It's not only the girls on the streets that are affected -- for boys and transgender youth, the average age of entry into prostitution is 11-13.

Pimps find kids in arcades, malls, entertainment centers, at tourist attractions and concerts. The pimp seduces a new recruit with the lure of wealth, fancy cars and designer clothes. They travel from city-to-city looking for children who are easy prey: alone, desperate and alienated. Their faces often end up on milk cartons as missing.

Pimps drug the youth, kidnap them and then move them around from state-to-state by a variety of means – cars, buses, vans, or trucks. Once he moves a child from their hometown into a strange city, he can easily force them to work as a prostitute. The lifestyle of these children revolves around violence, forced drug use and constant threats against their lives.

Hundreds of thousands of children are victimized every year. Child prostitution is an immense and devastating problem that nobody wants to recognize, nobody wants to talk about, and everyone wants to cover up. Child prostitutes are not only abandoned by their parents, but unfortunately by the social services system as well.[46]

SUICIDE

About one in eleven of all high-school students say they made a suicide attempt in 2002.[47] Suicide is actually the third leading cause of death amongst all kids ages ten to twenty-four. There are between eight to twenty-five attempted suicides for every suicide death.[48]

American Indians and Alaskan Natives are at the highest risk for suicide. In North Dakota, which has a large Native American population, suicide is the second leading cause of death among 10 to

---

[46] U.S. Department of Justice, Criminal Division ° Child Exploitation and Obscenity Section (CEOS)

[47] Centers for Disease Control and Prevention. (2002).

[48] National Institute of Mental Health; 2003

14-year-olds. In 2004, seven percent of all the kids in North Dakota made a suicide attempt.

Big Brother Big Sister (BBBS) of Fargo, North Dakota tries to combat the problem of suicide amongst youth by recruiting students from North Dakota State University to serve as mentors.

College senior Cassie shares her mentoring experience. "It's really neat to have someone who looks forward to seeing you every week -- even if all you two do together is talk."

Noah, a junior at the college, is a mechanical engineering major. "When I first became involved in the program, I wasn't sure what to expect. The more I met with my Little Brother, the more I liked the program."

Suicide often results from depression. As many as one in eight adolescents may be clinically depressed.[49] 10 percent to 15 percent of these kids eventually develop Bipolar Disorder (Manic Depression). Suicide is actually completed by 10 to 15 percent of those with Bipolar Disorder.

MENTAL HEALTH DISORDERS

Kids who have depression or Bipolar Disorder may also show signs of other emotional or behavioral problems, such as anxiety and panic attacks, self-esteem difficulties, Post-Traumatic Stress Disorder and oppositional and defiant behavior.

One in five children has a diagnosable mental, emotional or behavioral disorder. Attention Deficit Hyperactivity Disorder (ADD and ADHD) is probably the most common mental disorder in children, affecting three to five percent of all school-age kids. One in ten youth may suffer from a serious emotional disturbance, like Schizophrenia and other psychological diseases.[50]

Self-injury ("SI") is pretty serious. It's when a person tries to change the way they feel by causing physical harm that's drastic enough to damage their own body. This self-inflicted violence includes head banging, eyeball pressing, hair pulling or arm biting.

---

[49] Center for Mental Health Services, 1998
[50] National Institute of Mental Health, 1999

The most common form consists of cutting, burning, carving and stabbing the body with very sharp objects.

Here's a shocking statistic: It's estimated that 4% of the U.S. population report self-injury cases annually in the United States.[51] This works out to over 12 million people. The majority of those inflicting self-injury are pre-teens and teens. They're equally male and female.

Eating disorders such as Anorexia Nervosa, Bulimia Nervosa and Binge-Eating Disorder affect around 11 percent of all high school students. 10 to 25 percent of those battling Anorexia will die as a direct result of the eating disorder. Anorexia is the number one cause of death amongst young women.[52]

While 85 to 90 percent of those with eating disorders are teens and young women, around one million males also have an eating disorder.[53] Bulimia often occurs in athletes, such as gymnasts, wrestlers, dancers, horse jockeys, football players, and runners.

Binge-Eating Disorder is experienced by two to five percent of the American population.[54] Men constitute as many as 40 percent of those with this disease.[55] The onset of Binge-Eating Disorder usually occurs during late adolescence or in the early twenties.[56]

While much of the blame for these eating disorders can be placed on the media and cultural pressures to be thin, the fact that so many kids lack a father also adds to the problem. Not having a paternal role model can make a youth experience low self-esteem.

SINGLE-PARENT FAMILIES

In fact, the absence of a mother or father can be a contributing factor in various serious problems experienced by children. An estimated 24.7 million children live only with their mother, apart from their biological father.[57] The number of single fathers is approximately 2 million.[58]

---

[51] T. Aldeman, "The Scarred Soul," 1997
[52] ANAD
[53] Crowther, et al. 1995
[54] National Institute of Mental Health, 2000
[55] DSM IV, 1994
[56] DSM IV, 1994
[57] National Fatherhood Initiative, Father Facts, (3rd Edition
[58] U.S. Census Bureau, 2000

Only about 50 percent of kids today will spend their entire childhood in an intact family.[59] As a result, three out of four teenage suicides occur in households where a parent has been absent.[60] Children in single-parent families are two to three times as likely as youth in two-parent families to have emotional and behavioral problems.[61]

Fatherless children are at a dramatically greater risk of drug and alcohol abuse.[62] In studies involving over 25,000 children, it was discovered that kids who lived with only one parent had lower grade-point averages, lower college aspirations, poor attendance records, and higher drop-out rates than students who lived with both of their parents.[63]

Children in single-parent families are more likely to be in trouble with the law than their peers who grow up with two parents.[64] Adolescent females between the ages of 15 and 19 years old that are raised in homes without fathers are significantly more likely to engage in premarital sex than adolescent females reared in homes with both a mother and a father.[65]

DOMESTIC VIOLENCE

Nearly one-third of all women in the United States have reported being physically or sexually abused by a husband or boyfriend at some point in their lives.[66] 22,254.037, women are physically assaulted each year.[67]

Just so you don't think that it's only poor women that are battered, 26 percent of women with incomes above $50,000 reported domestic abuse in her lifetime by a spouse or boyfriend, as did 37 percent of women with incomes of $16,000 or less. These rates

[59] David Poponoe, American Family Decline, 1960-1990:

[60] The Christian Century (July 1993

[61] National Center for Health Statistics 1988

[62] National Center for Health Statistics. Survey on Child Health. Washington, DC, 1993

[63] McLanahan, Sara and Gary Sandefur; Harvard University Press, 1994

[64] National Center for Health Statistics. National Health Interview Survey; 1988

[65] Journal of Marriage and Family 56(1994)

[66] Commonwealth Fund survey, 1998

[67] Tjaden and Thoennes (1998) National Violence Against Women Survey, U.S. Department of Justice

hardly varied for women when comparing by race/ethnicity, educational level, or geographic location.

Kids might witness the terrible acts of violence against their parents or guardians. Some children may never actually see the violence, but they could feel the tension, hear the fighting, and see the injuries left behind.

They may be asked to call the police or to keep a family secret. These youngsters could even be physically injured themselves if they try to stop the violence.

A child's exposure to the father abusing the mother is the strongest risk factor for transmitting violent behavior from one generation to the next.[68]

I witnessed the effects of domestic violence when I mentored that group of children in the Video Production workshop at *Hollygrove*,[69] a facility for abused, neglected and abandoned children in Los Angeles. As mentioned, I took around ten of these kids to the Ringling Brothers Barnum and Bailey Circus. Most of them had never been to the circus before, so it was a great treat. We planned to videotape a scene with the kids afterwards near where the animals were kept.

The circus lasted longer than expected, so the male staff member who drove the van there insisted that the kids would have to wait to videotape until another time or they would miss dinner. One cute little eight-year-old boy, "Joshua," was furious with this decision. As we drove back towards *Hollygrove*, Joshua fought violently with the female staff member who was in the passenger seat. He screamed, kicked and bit her, until the male driver had to pull over and restrain the boy until he calmed down.

When we finally got to *Hollygrove* and the kids left to eat dinner, the female staff member told me that Joshua came from a home where he had witnessed his father beating up his mother. As a result, he attacked many of the female staff members. One time, he hit a woman over the head with a golf club, yet he never attacked any male staff.

---

[68] American Psychological Association Presidential Task Force on Violence and the Family, 1996

[69] www.hollygrove.org/

Many women and children who are victims of domestic violence flee to shelters or live on the streets. Every night, more than one million children in the United States face the dark and hunger with no place to call home. Forty percent of America's homeless are now women and their children.[70]

This was discovered during an extensive two-year research project, which also revealed that 92 percent of the homeless mothers studied had been sexually or violently abused. The study concluded that while living on the streets, homeless children endure such unsettling experiences that a full third of them have mental disorders by the time they are eight years old. Homeless children's rate of sexual abuse is three times as high as other children, and they endure twice the physical abuse.[71]

FOSTER YOUTH

We have explored the effects on children of living in a single-parent household. What about those kids who don't live with either of their birth parents? There are more than a half-million children in the United States who are in foster care. Around 50 percent of them live in non-relative foster homes, 24 percent in relative foster homes, 18 percent in group homes or institutions, four percent in pre-adoptive homes, and six percent in other placement types.[72]

Several studies have been done in this area. One found that between half and two-thirds of children entering foster care exhibited mental health impairments. The researchers concluded that foster children have difficulty developing an identity, achieving a sense of belonging, mastery of developmental tasks, and establishing meaningful relationships with people that stem both from foster care and from pre-care treatment.[73]

Another research project with 600 foster children discovered that 50 percent of them had more than one foster care placement; children who remained in care for at least four years averaged three or more foster care placements. In a follow-up study of 559 youth

---

[70] "The New Face of Homelessness is Youthful", *San Francisco Chronicle*, p A10, July 1, 1999
[71] Better Homes Fund, "Homeless Children: America's New Outcast," 1999
[72] National Clearinghouse on Child Abuse and Neglect Information (HHS). 2003
[73] www.trc.eku.edu/cwr/effects.htm

released from group homes or residential facilities, researchers found that 20 to 25 percent of these kids were imprisoned three to five years after exiting the system. The odds of them being imprisoned were double those of similar kids who returned to their homes.[74]

When foster youth become a certain age, which in many states like California is at 18-years-old, the government then "emancipates" them and they are suddenly thrown out of the child services system. These kids are then responsible for themselves. Generally, few resources exist to give them the basic life skills that are essential. Without any training or the slightest idea of how to get a job, balance a checkbook or even handle simple hygiene, many foster kids end up imprisoned or relying on government support like welfare for the rest of their lives.

Youth aging out of the foster care system are becoming homeless at disconcerting rates. Anywhere from 12 percent to 36 percent of foster youth transitioning out of the system experience homelessness.[75] The lucky ones get mentors to help them move into adulthood.

Orphan Foundation of America (OFA)[76] based in Sterling, VA helps orphans and foster youth to transition from foster care to young adulthood. The organization has a Virtual Mentoring program called vMentor.com. Using the Internet, foster youth ages 16-23 are matched with vMentors based on their needs. vMentors make a two-year commitment to email their mentees on a weekly basis, helping them with issues such as goal planning, career guidance and strategies for success in school and the workplace.

Here's what one of the mentees in this program wrote about her mentor: "My mentor has exceeded all expectations I could have ever had. We have become good friends and I feel as if I have somebody out there who cares about me. Someone whom I can share my A's with, someone to write to while my laundry is getting done; it feels like someone back home. Even though I know, I don't have a home. Without my mentor's support, I know that my first year at the university would not have been as fruitful as it has. Her emails

---

[74] www.trc.eku.edu/cwr/effects.htm
[75] Cook, 1991; Courtney & Pilivan, 1998; Reilly, 2003
[76] www.orphan.org/

cheered me up when I was down and gave me the support that other students are blessed with to receive from their parents."

ILLITERACY AND HIGH SCHOOL DROPOUTS

Many foster kids, as well as most of the youth that we have been describing, have a poor education and can barely read and write. 85 percent of the teenagers appearing in juvenile court in the United States are functionally illiterate.[77]

About a million students drop out of school annually.[78] 85 percent of high school dropouts are illiterate. It's estimated by the Department of Education that 35-40 percent of students in grades K-12 in the U.S. today are at risk of failing and not graduating from high school.[79] That's more than one-third of our youth population!

In the same report, it was revealed that almost half of the 191 million adults in the U.S. don't have the literacy skills necessary to write a business letter, complete a job application or read and comprehend a newspaper. 75 percent of the unemployed are non-readers. 65 percent of prisoners can't read. One out of three mothers on welfare can't read. An additional 2.3 million illiterates are added to the ranks of the illiterates annually, many of them our youth.

VIOLENCE AND CRIME

Considering all of these overwhelming statistics and information about the at-risk and high-risk youth in our society, is it any wonder that violence and crime is a serious problem in the United States?

In 2003, an estimated nine million kids aged twelve to seventeen had engaged in at least one delinquent behavior in the past year. Almost 6 million took part in a serious fight at school or work; 4.5 million took part in a group-against-group fight; 2.1 million youth attacked someone with the intent to seriously hurt them; 1.1 million stole or tried to steal something worth more than fifty dollars; over

---

[77] Youth Plus

[78] Departments of Labor, Health and Human Services, Education, and Related Agencies Appropriations

[79] U.S. Department of Education, September 1993

900,000 sold illegal drugs; and over 900,000 carried a handgun during the past year.[80]

While youth crime dropped in the 1990's, a report by the FBI released in September 2006 revealed that violent crime rose dramatically starting in 2004, including an 11 percent increase in robbery arrests and a 7 percent increase in weapon offenses.[81] Teens and young adults experience the highest rates of violent crime.[82]

In a single year, 3,012 children and teens were killed by gunfire in the United States, according to the latest national data released in 2002. That's one child every three hours; eight kids every day; and more than 50 children every week. And every year, at least four to five times as many youth suffer from non-fatal firearm injuries.[83]

In the U.S., homicide is the second leading cause of death among young people ages 10 to 24. It's the first cause of death among African-Americans. Homicide is also the only major cause of childhood deaths that has increased over the last three decades.[84] 79 percent of homicide victims ages 10 to 24 were killed with firearms.[85]

GANGS

More than one-fourth of all the homicides across the country are considered gang-related.[86] While the problem of gangs once only occupied major metropolitan areas, today gang violence occurs in rural areas as well as urban ones.[87] According to a 2004 report from the National Youth Gang Center, there are over 760,000 people in almost 24,000 gangs across the country. The Department of Justice estimates that approximately one-third of all gang members are under the age of 18.[88]

The impact of gang life doesn't just affect youth within the gangs, but it permeates through the entire community. Drive-by bullets kill

[80] Substance Abuse & Mental Health Services Administration (SAMHSA) 2003
[81] www.about.chapinhall.org/press/newsalerts/2006/CrimeRate06.html
[82] Bureau of Justice Statistics, 2007
[83] Children's Defense Fund and National Center for Health Statistics)
[84] Office of Juvenile Justice and Delinquency Prevention Bulletin, October 2001
[85] Centers fpr Disease Control and Prevention, 2005
[86] National Youth Gang Cemter/OJJDP; August 2006
[87] www.ncjrs.gov/pdffiles1/ojjdp/fs200601.pdf
[88] www.whitehouse.gov/news/releases/2005/02/20050202-15.html

innocent people, including young children. Families are torn apart and lives are destroyed. Crime by gang members is rampant. Millions of dollars are lost through vandalism and stolen property. But most importantly, these precious youth who are bright and talented and who should be contributing to society are instead perishing in record numbers.

Gang members commit a disproportionate number of offenses. They carry out serious and violent crimes at a higher rate than non-gang-members.[89] Gangs vary a great deal in language and other characteristics, depending on their culture, location and ethnicity. According to the 2004 National Youth Gang Survey, the ethnicity of gang members is 49 percent Hispanic/Latino, 37 percent African-American, 9 percent white and 5 percent Asian.[90]

Most fights break out over territory or else gangs retaliate for past attacks on fellow members. The hatred just keeps recycling generation after generation. Gangs have been around for centuries. The only thing that has changed from the past is the lethalness of their automatic weapons, which are easily obtained by these kids.

Most youth start hanging around with gangs at around 13-years-old, but that age is dropping quickly. Children as young as 7 or 8-years-old are initiated into gangs the traditional way -- getting jumped. New gang members usually have to experience a heavy beating by a group of gang members that kick and punch them repeatedly. If they can survive this without crying and running away, then they are invited to join.

Gangs are increasingly involved in hate crimes. The FBI reports that approximately 10,700 hate crimes were reported in the United States in 1996 -- approximately 29 such incidents per day. Since many hate crimes are never reported to police, it is likely that the actual number of hate crimes significantly exceeds this number. About 70 percent of all reported hate crimes were crimes against a person; about 30 percent were property crimes. Research indicates that a substantial number of these crimes were committed by males under age 20 and many were in gangs.[91]

---

[89] Howell, 1998
[90] Curry, 1996
[91] www.ed.gov/pubs/HateCrime/page2.html

Los Angeles has earned the title "Gang Capital of the World." It is estimated that there are 96,000 gang members in L.A.[92]

When I taught my first Screenwriting Workshop in 1993, with a group of teenage boys who were incarcerated at a detention facility, the kids told me that the African-American gangs fought other black gangs -- the Bloods vs. the Crips. And the Latino gang members told me that the Norteños battled with the Sureños (Northern Californians vs. Southern Californians). They kept emphasizing this to me as we developed our screenplay together.

Now that has totally changed. There are race riots in Los Angeles public schools and on the streets. Racial warfare is on between Black and Latino gangs. It started in the prison system. When gang leaders were sent to prison, the racial divisions there required former enemies to band together. Word trickled down to the streets and now racial hate-crimes are prevalent.

The racial tension has been greatly exacerbated by the Latino population surging into poor neighborhoods that used to be predominantly black. Differences in language and culture intensify the friction. Rival gangs of the same race continue their decades-old battles, compounded with racial attacks on other gangs. With the numbers already soaring for gang violence in Los Angeles, a 14 percent increase in gang crime last year has been attributed to this interracial conflict.[93]

This concludes my "State of America's Youth" report. Please feel free to share it, although I do hope that you will give me credit, since it has taken a lot of work to compile all this research.

Most importantly, write to your government Representatives, recruit mentors and spread the word that our at-risk youth urgently need help and MENTORING WORKS!

---

[92] www.streetgangs.com
[93] New York Times, January 16, 2007

AUTHOR BIO

Jill Gurr has mentored more than fifty at-risk and high-risk youth through **Create Now**, the non-profit organization that she founded in 1996. She has trained hundreds of volunteers to mentor thousands of the most troubled children in Los Angeles and Orlando.

She's a produced screenwriter, having adapted the book *Hit and Run* by James Hadley Chase into the screenplay *Rigged*, which stars George Kennedy. The film is distributed by Kodiak Films. Jill also wrote *Socrates*, a PBS pilot that stars Ed Asner. Several of her original scripts have been optioned by reputable producers.

Jill graduated with a B.S. degree in Broadcasting and Film from Boston University. She worked for 20 years all over the world as a Script Supervisor (continuity) on award-winning movies with famous actors and directors. She is fluent in Spanish, French and Italian.

She has been featured on *NBC Nightly News with Brian Williams*, CNN's *Anderson Cooper 360°*, ABC-TV, Fox11 News, NBC-TV and KTLA in their "Heroes at Home" segment, as well as in the *Los Angeles Times*.

Jill was one of eight people in the country selected by the Simon Wiesenthal Center to be featured in an exhibition at the Museum of Tolerance, "Everyday Heroes."

She was chosen as one of the first four Americans to ever participate in a multilateral *Global Xchange* program sponsored by the British Council and Volunteer Services Organization. In 2010, Jill spent six weeks in Durban, South Africa and Belfast, North Ireland with 26 other community leaders from six countries (Sierra Leone, Rwanda, South Africa, France, UK and US), sharing best practices in mentoring youth.

She has been giving acclaimed presentations to international arts leaders and diplomats through the International Visitors Council, an adjunct of the U.S. State Department. She was selected as one of "100 Making a Difference" by celebrity photographer John Russo and CNN Correspondent Elizabeth Chambers, published December 2012. Jill is available as a consultant, trainer and speaker. For more information, contact her by email at jill@mentoryouthnow.com.

Made in the USA
Charleston, SC
22 July 2013